TOP SECRET Intranet

How U.S. Intelligence Built Intelink—
The World's Largest, Most Secure
Network

ISBN 0-13-080898-9

9 780130 808981

90000

 # The Charles F. Goldfarb Series on Open Information Management

"Open Information Management" (OIM) means managing information so that it is open to processing by any program, not just the program that created it. That extends even to application programs not conceived of at the time the information was created.

OIM is based on the principle of data independence: data should be stored in computers in non-proprietary, genuinely standardized representations. And that applies even when the data is the content of a document. Its representation should distinguish the innate information from the proprietary codes of document processing programs and the artifacts of particular presentation styles.

Business databases—which rigorously separate the real data from the input forms and output reports—achieved data independence decades ago. But documents, unlike business data, have historically been created in the context of a particular output presentation style. So for document data, independence was largely unachievable until recently.

That is doubly unfortunate. It is unfortunate because documents are a far more significant repository of humanity's information. And documents can contain significantly richer information structures than databases.

It is also unfortunate because the need for OIM of documents is greater now than ever. The demands of "repurposing" require that information be deliverable in multiple formats: paper-based, online, multimedia, hypermedia. And information must now be delivered through multiple channels: traditional bookstores and libraries, the World Wide Web, and corporate intranets and extranets. In the latter modes, what starts as database data may become a document for browsing, but then may need to be reused by the reader as data.

Fortunately, in the past ten years a technology has emerged that extends to documents the database's capacity for data independence. And it does so without the database's restrictions on structural freedom. That technology is the "Standard Generalized Markup Language" (SGML), an official International Standard (ISO 8879) that has been adopted by the world's largest producers of documents and by the World Wide Web.

With SGML, organizations in government, aerospace, airlines, automotive, electronics, computers, and publishing (to name a few) have freed their documents from hostage relationships to processing software. SGML coexists with graphics, multimedia, and other data standards needed for OIM and acts as the framework that relates objects in the other formats to one another and to SGML documents.

The World Wide Web's HTML and XML are both based on SGML. HTML is a particular, though very general, application of SGML, like those for the above industries. There is a limited set of mark-up tags that can be used with

HTML. XML, in contrast, is a simplified subset of SGML facilities that, like full SGML, can be used with any set of tags. You can literally create your own markup language with XML.

As the principal enabler for OIM of documents, the SGML family of standards necessarily plays a leading role in this series. We provide tutorials on SGML, XML, and other key standards and the techniques for applying them. Our books vary in technical intensity from programming techniques for software developers to the business justification of OIM for enterprise executives. We share the practical experience of organizations and individuals who have applied the techniques of OIM in environments ranging from immense industrial publishing projects to Web sites of all sizes.

Our authors are expert practitioners in their subject matter, not writers hired to cover a "hot" topic. They bring insight and understanding that can only come from real-world experience. Moreover, they practice what they preach about standardization. Their books share a common standards-based vocabulary. In this way, knowledge gained from one book in the series is directly applicable when reading another, or the standards themselves. This is just one of the ways in which we strive for the utmost technical accuracy, and for consistency with the OIM standards.

And we also strive for a sense of excitement and fun. After all, the challenge of OIM—preserving information from the ravages of technology while exploiting its benefits—is one of the great intellectual adventures of our age. I'm sure you'll find this series to be a knowledgeable and reliable guide on that adventure.

About the Series Editor

Dr. Charles F. Goldfarb invented the SGML language in 1974 and later led the team that developed it into the International Standard on which both HTML and XML are based. He serves as editor of the Standard (ISO 8879) and as a consultant to developers of SGML and XML applications and products. He is based in Saratoga, CA.

About the Series Logo

The rebus is an ancient literary tradition, dating from 16th century Picardy, and is especially appropriate to a series involving fine distinctions between things and the words that describe them. For the logo, Andrew Goldfarb incorporated a rebus of the series name within a stylized SGML/XML comment declaration.

 # The Charles F. Goldfarb Series on Open Information Management

As XML is a subset of SGML, the Series List is categorized to show the degree to which a title applies to XML. "XML Titles" are those that discuss XML explicitly and may also cover full SGML. "SGML Titles" do not mention XML per se, but the principles covered may apply to XML.

XML Titles

Goldfarb, Pepper, and Ensign
- SGML Buyer's Guide™: Choosing the Right XML and SGML Products and Services

Megginson
- Structuring XML Documents

Leventhal, Lewis, and Fuchs
- Designing XML Internet Applications

McGrath
- XML by Example: Building E-commerce Applications

Goldfarb and Prescod
- The XML Handbook

Jelliffe
- The XML and SGML Cookbook: Recipes for Structured Information

SGML Titles

Turner, Douglass, and Turner
- ReadMe.1st: SGML for Writers and Editors

Donovan
- Industrial-Strength SGML: An Introduction to Enterprise Publishing

Ensign
- $GML: The Billion Dollar Secret

Rubinsky and Maloney
- SGML on the Web: Small Steps Beyond HTML

McGrath
- ParseMe.1st: SGML for Software Developers

DuCharme
- SGML CD

Other Titles

Martin
- TOP SECRET Intranet: How U.S. Intelligence Built Intelink—The World's Largest, Most Secure Network

TOP SECRET Intranet

How U.S. Intelligence Built
Intelink—The World's Largest,
Most Secure Network

Fredrick Thomas Martin

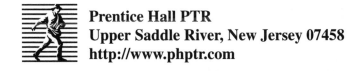

Prentice Hall PTR
Upper Saddle River, New Jersey 07458
http://www.phptr.com

Library of Congress Cataloging-in-Publication Data

Martin, Fredrick Thomas.
  Top secret intranet : How U.S. intelligence built Intelink--the world's
  largest, most secure network / Fredrick Thomas Martin.
    p.   cm.   -- (Charles F. Goldfarb series on open information management)
  Includes index.
  ISBN 0-13-080898-9 (alk. paper)
    1. Intelink (Computer network)   2. Intelligence service--Computer
  networks--Security measures--United States. 3. Intelligence
  service--United States--Data processing. 4. Intranets (Computer
  networks)--United States. I. Title.
  QA76.575.H36   1997
  025.04—dc21   96–47549
                                                              CIP

Editorial/Production Supervision: Craig Little
Acquisitions Editor: Mark Taub
Marketing Manager: Dan Rush
Manufacturing Manager: Alexis R. Heydt
Cover Design: Talar Agasyan
Cover Design Supervision: Jerry Votta

Published by Prentice Hall PTR
Prentice-Hall, Inc.
A Simon & Schuster Company
Upper Saddle River, NJ 07458

The publisher offers discounts on this book when ordered in bulk quantities. For more information, contact the
Corporate Sales Department, Phone: 800-382-3419, Fax: 201-236-7141, email: corpsales@prenhall.com or
write: Corporate Sales Department, Prentice Hall PTR, One Lake Street, Upper Saddle River, NJ 07458

Prentice Hall books are widely used by corporations and government agencies for training, marketing, and
resale.

Printed in the United States of America
10 9 8 7 6 5 4 3 2

ISBN 0-13-080898-9

Prentice-Hall International (UK) Limited, *London*
Prentice-Hall of Australia Pty. Limited, *Sydney*
Prentice-Hall of Canada, Inc., *Toronto*
Prentice-Hall Hispanoamericana S.A., *Mexico*
Prentice-Hall of India Private Limited, *New Delhi*
Prentice-Hall of Japan, Inc., *Tokyo*
Simon & Schuster Asia Pte. Ltd., *Singapore*
Editora Prentice-Hall do Brasil, Ltda., *Rio de Janeiro*

Contents

**This book is dedicated to the memory of my Mother
Charlotte June (Bowen) Martin**

Foreword

When your mission is protecting a nation's security, the term "mission-critical" takes on a whole new meaning!

In this extraordinary book, Fredrick Thomas Martin presents the never-before revealed secrets of Intelink, the world's largest and most secure information system—the intranet/extranet of U.S. Intelligence Service. Perhaps the most surprising of those secrets is that this totally closed system is built onopen system standards: industry recommendations and International Standards like TCP/IP, SGML, and XML.

Another secret is that Intelink is a cost-effective system, despite—or perhaps because of—its owners having an annual budget of 26 billion dollars. In one notable case, they achieved a cost savings of 90 percent in creating usable reports from raw intelligence, and reduced delivery time to one percent of what it had been.

Fredrick Martin is a superb guide to the present and future of highly secure information networks. As a NSA executive, he helped enhance Intelink, and is now helping the CIA move forward to the "Agile Intelligence

Enterprise" of the future. Throughout this book, he shares his expert knowledge, with a focus on applying it to the needs of business systems like yours.

So, whether you want to:

- Apply U.S. Intelligence security techniques to your own computer systems
- Profit from the present and future information management strategies of the world's largest network; or simply
- Enjoy inside information, like the Walt Disney–CIA connection or the secrets of steganography

you will want to read the first book ever to describe an on-going U.S. Intelligence operation—*Top Secret Intranet*.

Charles F. Goldfarb
Saratoga, CA
August, 1998

Prologue

The many independent agencies that make up the U.S. Intelligence Community are being drawn strongly toward the concepts of an "Agile Enterprise." These concepts were born in the private sector, as companies sought ways to address increasing pressures to speed up internal operations and derive competitive advantages from their widely distributed expertise and institutional knowledge. The business imperatives were to be first-to-market with new products, to be faster in responding to customer requests, and to create solutions more tailored to each customer's needs, or simply to reduce costs. The U.S. Intelligence Community is feeling similar pressures today. Tight budgets since the end of the Cold War have created pressures to reduce costs, and the needs of intelligence "customers" are pushing the Intelligence Community to achieve greater speed, capacity, and flexibility than traditional practices allow. Under these conditions, an Agile *Intelligence* Enterprise is essential.

Greater speed in intelligence is demanded by the pace of world events and global information services. The end of bipolar diplomacy created a complicated national security environment for the United States and its allies. Diplomacy today is highly collaborative, and shaped by many different foreign perspectives and goals. The absence of an overarching military threat has left economic, military, and political agendas competing for attention. As governments continually adjust to new developments among these competing goals and agendas, the conduct of foreign affairs can shift. Those who formulate and implement foreign policy must continually reevaluate situations as new information arrives. And new information is arriving faster today. Global news and information sources have expanded markedly, and continue to evolve rapidly. For intelligence to be useful in this environment, it must be able to add something of unique value to the stream of external information reaching U.S. officials. In business parlance, the Intelligence Community is facing a need to operate with a "shorter cycle time," to exploit the more frequent but fleeting opportunities to make a "sale." The Agile Enterprise, with its collaborative work processes and shared information access, offers exactly what the Intelligence Community needs.

Capacity is a serious constraint in the processing and use of intelligence data. Technology for collecting and generating information has far outpaced the development of tools for exploiting information. The growth of openly available information, and the proliferation of sources for this information, are now familiar trends. We should expect these trends to continue in coming years, with some new twists likely to be provided by emerging services on the Internet, interactive radio and TV, and commercial satellites that bring near-real-time overhead imagery to the nightly news. The responsibility of the Intelligence Community—to understand, integrate, and deconflict the disparate information coming to the U.S. Government—can only be fulfilled if the capacity exists to handle the volume of relevant data, from both classified and unclassified sources. Capacity is an urgent issue, therefore, and is being made more so by the pressure for greater speed, described above, which requires more data to be exploited in less time. Moreover, intelligence consumers themselves are struggling to keep up with the information explosion, and therefore require individual customization of intelligence support. So, more data needs to be exploited in more customized products in less time. These conditions are driving intelligence toward the same "mass customization" that businesses derive from the Agile Enterprise.

Flexibility is a major issue for intelligence today. Many security threats demand sustained attention, but there are also urgent issues that arise and fade, international military and humanitarian operations that put U.S. soldiers at risk for a time, and developments in unstable areas of the world that suddenly command high level attention. Intelligence has to adjust to these shifting priorities—without degrading its long-term efforts on the most serious threats to national security. The Intelligence Community is under pressure to reduce the cost of shifting priorities, and reduce the time it takes to ramp up to meet sudden customer needs. Readers will recognize in this intelligence challenge the same need for flexibility that led to concepts for an Agile Enterprise in the private sector.

The need for greater speed, capacity and flexibility is pulling each of the separate intelligence agencies toward greater use of on-line networks, more use of collaborative work processes, and more shared access to data—all core elements of an Agile Enterprise—even without any formal consensus to move in this direction together. In the pages that follow, Fredrick Thomas Martin provides a context and guidance for thinking about the additional breakthroughs that can be gained if the Intelligence Community pursues these concepts as a collective strategy.

Dr. Ruth A. David
Deputy Director for Science and Technology
Central Intelligence Agency
Langley, Virginia
August, 1998

Introduction

*I*t was a dark and stormy night.

I have always wanted to write a book that began with that sentence, and now I can, with a certain spin. Since shortly after the dawn of modern civilization, the leaders of civil and military organizations have always desired to have information that would reduce uncertainty and forewarn them of various dangers, preparing them for whatever future critical decisions they may face. What was *really* desired by these leaders was to know, *in advance*, whether or not it would be a "dark and stormy night" and whether the troops would arrive by sea, at a specified time, in a specified way. Money, national institutions, even lives would be at stake. Life as we know it may be at stake.

In the United States, the production of intelligence is a multibillion dollar effort that is vital to its security and prosperity, and arguably, of the free world. The various organizations that are collectively known as the U.S. Intelligence Community are in the process of tremendous cultural and technological change as we approach the Third Millennium. With technological changes, declining resources, an explosion of information, and a completely different set of geopolitical priorities, the U.S. Intelligence Community must find smarter ways to manage its most critical resource: *information*. This book addresses the future of open information management within the Intelligence Community and describes how they plan to become flexible, adaptive, and more "agile" as an enterprise. It describes their development and implementation of *"Intelink,"* an intranet that provides electronic publishing and dissemination of their finished intelligence as well as a multiple security level collaborative environment. A number of organizations with operational prototypes are described to demonstrate the progress that is being made to become more "agile." Lastly, the book describes the future of information management in the U.S. Intelligence Community, including its transition to an "Agile Intelligence Enterprise," where "virtual teams" collaborate on-line and all intelligence data becomes a shared asset as part of an enterprise-wide "information space."

WHY YOU SHOULD READ THIS BOOK

The practice of intelligence can be defined as the process required to obtain information about an adversary or potential adversary in order to guide the leaders and decision-makers of civil and military organizations. The practice of *intelligence* involves tedious collection, interpretation, analysis, and reporting of information; and like so many business processes today, it also must grapple simultaneously with removing or at least reducing the various problems and barriers encountered. Most people think of intelligence activities as occurring among foreign nations, powers, or other organizations (although "industrial espionage" involves the practice of intelligence among commercial, non-governmental entities) to determine various activities, plans, and even capabilities of those involved. But regardless of the "flavor" of intelligence, much of it comes down to the same set of activities that are so important to businesses today: making sense out of a deluge of information.

In today's world, the practice of intelligence is a key activity of the U.S. Government; indeed, it is vital to all governments, large and small, with an actual or perceived role on the international stage. Every single day, the various components of the U.S. Intelligence Community provide crucial information to those who manage our nation's strategic interests. Generally, the "requirements" of intelligence include:

- What are an adversary's intentions?
- What are his capabilities?
- What are his limitations?

- What are his vulnerabilities?

Collectively, the business of intelligence is really about *information*: the gathering, processing, analysis, reporting, and archiving for potential future analysis or reporting. The amount of information collected and processed is staggering and is measured in trillions of bytes.

Does this problem sound familiar? You are a business executive or person responsible for exploiting the information revolution for your company or concern. And while the area of espionage and intrigue perhaps has fascinated you, you really need to read this book because the folks who manage information for the U.S. intelligence apparatus are involved with arguably the largest data and information management area known to man. The lessons learned from an application of this magnitude have direct application to the activities of any person or company involved in information management today. This would include people interested in the World Wide Web, SGML and XML applications, intranets, and electronic publishing, including electronic publishing companies, information management and technology providers, including those involved in implementing intranets in organizations, and other companies and government agencies primarily here, in Europe, and in the Pacific Rim. You will also be interested in this book if you would like to learn more about specific "organizational right sizing" case studies that document government cost savings and improved performance achieved through the use of information management and the latest technology.

You should read this book because it addresses several areas of keen interest to you. It describes the U.S. Intelligence Community and provides insights into how it is significantly improving its own intelligence gathering and reporting operations by using technology and employing recent advancements in information management. These advancements include the development and implementation of international information standards such as the Standard Generalized Markup Language (SGML), SGML derivatives such as the Hypertext Markup Language (HTML), and the new eXtensible Markup Language (XML), as well as networking concepts such as intranets. This book takes you into the little known world of *Intelink*, the classified, worldwide intranet for the U.S. Intelligence Community. This network, experiencing exponential growth like the Internet, is used for electronic publishing and distribution of intelligence reports, analytical research, collaboration facilities, and training. The Intelink Community addresses perhaps the world's largest set of data management challenges—challenges that involve demanding requirements that are at the extreme of what normal enterprises require today. The book includes discussions on the special challenges that distinguish Intelink from the unclassified global Internet such as networking, encryption, and other security considerations.

The U.S. Government as a whole continues to lag behind the private sector in the application of *International Standards* to help solve our document management and interoperability challenges. By reading this book, you will learn about U.S. cooperation with the intelligence arms of the governments who are members of the North Atlantic Treaty Organization (NATO), addressing the use of standards and other World Wide Web-related applications. This cooperation has helped to begin to close the government-industry gap and is an important lesson learned.

The book also presents several case studies—actual U.S. Government user histories—that will provide you with detailed examinations of the unique experiences of specific SGML applications involving Intelink within several areas of the U.S. Intelligence Community. These case studies develop and present insights into the issues, problems, and solutions for organizations desiring to take advantage of information management and its related emerging technology. By understanding the case studies, you can gain insight into realizing tangible cost savings as well as significantly improving your capabilities.

You may also wish to read two books on related topics: a case study book on industry applications of SGML written by Chet Ensign and recently published in this series entitled, "$GML: The Billion Dollar Secret," and "*The 21ˢᵗ Century Intranet*," by Dr. Jennifer Stone Gonzales.

WHAT WE CAN TALK ABOUT—WHAT WE CAN'T

There is a unique story told here concerning the application and evolution of *open information management* within the top secret Intelligence Community of the U.S. Government. It is the story of how the government has vastly improved the way in which it manages its most crucial asset—*information*—through the use of intranets and standards such as SGML.

Although these open information management improvements have resulted in the savings of hundreds of millions of dollars, the most significant benefit is the improvement in operations, that is, the improvement of the intelligence product itself. This is also the story of some of the senior managers and visionaries across the U.S. Intelligence Community who have made these savings and improvements possible.

The goals, mission, and other details about the Intelligence Community recently have become more generally available to the public, particularly since the demise of the former Soviet Union. Most national-level intelligence agencies now have their own webpages on the global Internet. And large highway signs denote several agencies such as the National Security Agency, for example, where one will now find a handsome marble and stone sign at the entrance of its headquarters at Fort Meade, Maryland (approximately mid-way between Washington, D.C. and Baltimore, Maryland). Coming a long way since it was known as "No Such Agency," NSA has a "National Cryptologic Museum" that is open to the public, and approved a recently televised segment on the "Discovery" cable television channel. Permissions for the TV coverage and for publishing this book are clear signs of a more "open" Agency and Intelligence Community.

In this book, we will be able to discuss the background and reasoning that went into much of the past and present efforts to improve information management, including insights into the decisions that were behind the use of intranets, Web technology, and the use of standards such as SGML, HTML, and XML. We can describe the U.S. Intelligence Community, including its mission, and total overall budget (although we cannot divulge the budgets of individual agencies). We can describe the information management challenges of the Intelligence Community, and why an intranet—such as Intelink—is one of the solutions to these challenges. We can describe Intelink in great detail, its problems and successes, from its inception late in 1994 to the present. Finally, we can describe how the U.S. Intelligence Community is preparing for the future as it migrates to an electronically connected, agile environment with the capability to fully share data and manage its information across the entire enterprise.

Obviously, we *cannot* talk about sensitive intelligence techniques, i.e., what the Intelligence Community refers to as "sources and methods." Indeed, there are many areas in which we cannot discuss the fact that certain knowledge or information is known, maintained, or exploited. While we can discuss

Intelink itself, we cannot discuss specific on-going projects or the actual classified information that is "published" on Intelink. To ensure against accidental exposure, this book has gone through the very rigorous "pre-publication review process" of the Intelligence Community.

INTRODUCTION TO THE U.S. INTELLIGENCE COMMUNITY

The Ultimate Information Producers

The United States Intelligence Community is a coordinated network of thirteen primary agencies and a number of civilian and military organizations that work together to support efforts to ensure and maintain the security of the United States and its allies (Figure 1). This task is accomplished through the collection, analysis, and reporting of huge volumes of information that keep the President, Cabinet members, members of Congress, and other senior government decision-makers informed (Figure 2). Intelligence has become a vital element in every important activity of the U.S. Government. The thirteen primary agencies are

1) Central Intelligence Agency
2) National Security Agency
3) Defense Intelligence Agency
4) National Reconnaissance Office
5) National Imagery and Mapping Agency
6) Army Intelligence
7) Naval Intelligence
8) Marine Corps Intelligence
9) Air Force Intelligence
10) Department of State (Bureau of Intelligence and Research)
11) Department of Energy (Office of Energy Intelligence)

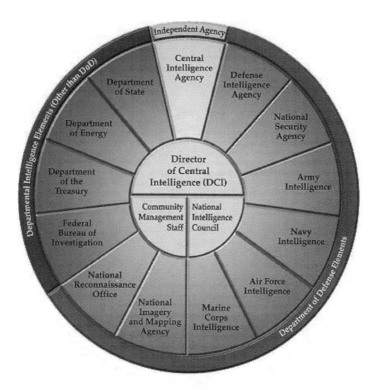

Figure 1 The U.S. Intelligence Community.

12) Department of the Treasury (Office of Intelligence Support)

13) Federal Bureau of Investigation

(See the appendix for additional details on each of the 13 primary agencies.)

The Mission of the U.S. Intelligence Community

In recent years, the lines among various intelligence activities have become less distinct, but the goal has remained unchanged: to support key government decision-makers with the best possible information. In his report to the National Performance Review in 1996, then Director of Central Intelligence John Deutch stated the following.

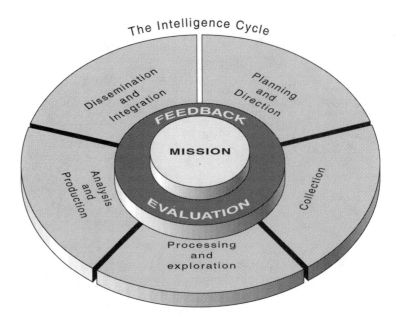

Figure 2 The Intelligence Cycle.

The United States intelligence effort shall provide the President and the National Security Council with the necessary information on which to base decisions concerning the conduct and development of foreign, defense, and economic policy and the protection of United States national interests from foreign security threats. Specifically, the missions of U.S. intelligence are to:

- *Provide intelligence support to national level policy makers,*
- *Provide intelligence support to military planning and operations,*
- *Provide intelligence support to law enforcement, and*
- *Counter foreign intelligence activities.*

For members of the Intelligence Community, these "missions" refer to ensuring that policy-makers and military leaders are provided with the information necessary to make decisions on matters, as shown on the next page.

1) Warning of impending crises, especially when national interests or the well being of citizens are threatened

2) Long-term dangers such as the manufacture of chemical or biological weapons

3) Helping to safeguard public security by countering threats from terrorists and drug traffickers

4) Economic security by uncovering foreign efforts to influence international trade

5) Increasing the effectiveness of U.S. military forces deployed for operations

The Cost of the U.S. Intelligence Community

Special "select" committees control congressional oversight for the U.S. intelligence efforts. In the U.S. Senate, this is accomplished by the *Senate Select Committee on Intelligence* (SSCI), chaired by Richard C. Shelby, from Alabama, and in the House of Representatives by the *House Permanent Select Committee on Intelligence* (HPSCI), chaired by Representative Porter J. Goss, a former CIA officer. The overall cost of intelligence production to the American public has remained secret as classified information since the inception of the Central Intelligence Agency over 50 years ago. However, the Intelligence Community of the U.S. Government confirmed in the summer of 1997 that its *total* budget for the previous year was $26.6 billion dollars. This total includes the budgets of the Central Intelligence Agency (Figure 3); the Pentagon-run agencies such as the National Reconnaissance Office, the National Security Agency, the National Imagery and Mapping Agency, and the Defense Intelligence Agency (DIA); and other operations and organizations at the Pentagon, State Department and the Federal Bureau of Investigation.

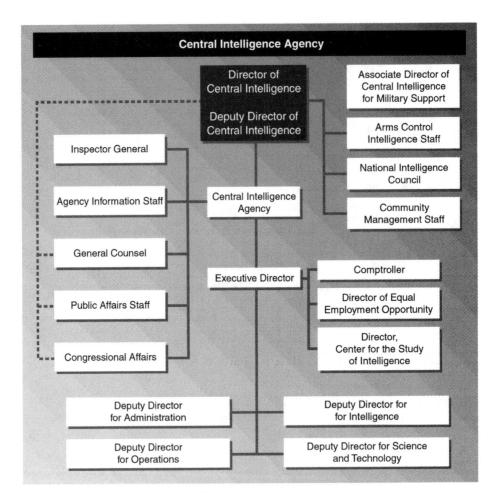

Figure 3 Organizational Chart—U.S. Central Intelligence Agency.

It is interesting to note that behind the primary missions of the National Security Agency, specifically the "signals intelligence" (*SIGINT* or "code breaking" mission) and the information systems security (*INFOSEC* or "code making" mission), is the fascinating story of the evolution of automation and information management. From the early code breaking days through the advent of the digital computer, the National Security Agency and the Intelligence Community played a critical role in shaping early automation, including mainframe and networking developments. For example, early cryptanalytical research was instrumental in the development of the first large-scale computer and the first solid state computer, leading to mainframe computers and today's modern systems (Figure 4).

As the ultimate information producers and users, the Intelligence Committee has always faced, and continues to face, enormous information management challenges. Like many large companies today, these challenges range from training and incentives for information management personnel, through security and security management policies and infrastructures, to technical challenges such as collaborative analytical and production tools to enable optimal information management services.

Also like many businesses, the Intelligence Community consists of a number of individual organizations that perform distinct missions, while supporting overlapping sets of customers. These separate organizations contain the individually distinct operations that collect, process, and exploit various types of intelligence data. The autonomous nature of these organizations has caused many people within the Intelligence Community to refer to them as "stovepipes," which connote the image of a large number of individual chimneys all heating the same building.

The "stovepipe" relationships among the 13 primary agencies of the Intelligence Community affect the technologies they choose and what they can do with them. Many studies have shown that—in order to make the Intelligence Community a more effective enterprise—they must begin to break down the barriers between institutions and improve their ability to manage information across the enterprise. Corporations do not face this challenge in quite the same way, since there is almost always someone at the top who can send orders down and allocate resources to back them up.

How This Book Is Organized

In short, this book accomplishes two things: First, it provides nuts and bolts, practitioner details of the issues, challenges, and implementation problems associated with building and using one of today's most important business tools: an inexpensive, secure, and reliable intranet/extranet. It is the story behind what is perhaps the largest intranet/extranet application in the world in

Figure 4 National Security Agency Supercomputers.

terms of both volume of information and number of users, how and why it came to be, details on how it works, its problems, its successes, and its future. Secondly, this book examines the role of intranets/extranets in the future, taking into account both the strategy and the economics of information. It will explain the actual plans that the United States Intelligence Community and the private sector, as exemplified by Walt Disney Imagineering, have for using and publishing on intranets/extranets, and how that future use differs from today.

To accomplish this, the book will demonstrate how the U.S. Intelligence Community is significantly improving its intelligence gathering and reporting operations through the development and implementation of an information management improvement model that takes advantage of advanced technology including networking concepts, intranets/extranets, and international information standards. The primary example used in the book will be *Intelink*, the classified, world-wide intranet for the Intelligence Community that addresses one of the world's largest data management problems, involving demanding requirements that are at the extreme of what normal enterprises require. Intelink is used for electronic publishing and distribution of intelligence reports, analytical research, collaboration facilities, and training, and has become the Information Management Improvement Model of the U.S. Intelligence Community. The book will describe how Intelink came to be, including what went smoothly and what didn't, and plans for the future, with discussions of the unique problems, concerns, challenges and special features that distinguish Intelink from other intranet applications. These issues include standards and architectural issues, analyst collaboration concerns, specific electronic publishing issues, and encryption and other special security considerations unique to this special environment. The Intelink story will include summaries of successes that will provide detailed examinations of the unique experiences of specific Intelink applications within the U.S. Intelligence Community.

Specifically, the book is divided into three parts. Part One provides the necessary background to better understand the evolution of Intelink, including the issues, goals, and methodologies/approaches that made this effort the successful prototype of the future for "Virtual Intelligence."

Chapter 1 sets the stage for our discussions and contains a brief introduction to the Intelink Community, providing some degree of insight into both the customers and producers of U.S. intelligence. It provides background on the evolution of the global Internet and explains the problem that Intelink addresses, and why an intranet solution was used.

Chapter 2 provides a high-level look at this tool, explaining the various Intelink instantiations, or "classes of service," which range from totally unclassified applications involving "open source" material or interfaces with the global Internet, to those afforded the very highest classification protection involving the highest level of U.S. Government policy and decision-makers. The chapter concludes with a discussion of the implementation philosophy of Intelink.

Part Two moves us to a detailed examination, the "nuts and bolts" of Intelink: the underlying carriage to all of the open information management improvements of the U.S. Intelligence Community and a harbinger of the real future of the world of Intelligence: The concept of "Virtual" or "Unlimited Intelligence." Each chapter contains lessons learned for the business enterprise.

Chapter 3 covers the use of standards. It explains their importance and provides details on the overarching architectural framework and the specific technical standards employed, including information on the new *Defense Message System.*

Chapters 4 and 5 address security. Chapter 4 defines security in the context of the Intelink environment, including a discussion on the psychology of network attackers. It also defines authentication techniques, including passwords, as well as encryption, digital signatures and certificates, access control and auditing. It concludes with a discussion on physical security and security policy. Chapter 5 then shows how the Intelligence Community is applying these security concepts to Intelink. It discusses the specific set of Intelink security building blocks and security services and how they are minimizing the costs associated with security. Chapter 5 also defines the official U.S. Government network security efforts under NSA's "Multilevel Information Systems Security Initiative" (MISSI), including the *Fortezza* and *Rosetta* cryptographic cards. It covers access control issues, including a discussion on the problems associated with the "instantiation" approach to security on Intelink. Chapter 5 concludes by emphasizing the importance of physical security and security policy and citing the lessons learned.

Chapter 6 examines the set of Intelink tools and services for the user. It divides these tools into three basic categories: search tools, collaboration tools, and reference aids. It also looks at the future and provides a glimpse into what the Intelligence Community is developing to meet its needs after the turn of the century.

Chapter 7 outlines the set of open information management concerns facing the U.S. Intelligence Community. Many of these concerns relate to their evolution towards perhaps the greatest paradigm shift in modern intelligence production: the transition to Web-centric, electronic publishing of finished intelligence. These concerns include the need for a "Joint Standards Board," the use of metadata (data about data), the use of Web publishing standards, push and pull technology, and training. Chapter 7 also includes how the Intelligence Community plans to improve their support infrastructure, relating these discussions to the business enterprise.

Case studies are documented in Chapter 8. In an environment like the U.S. Intelligence Community, as in any business scenario, taking advantage of what has been proven and done before you is always not only tempting, but downright smart. Although little known as one of our state secrets just a few years ago, collaboration on mutual projects of interest and other direct cooperation exists between our government and our allies and coalition partners such as the United Kingdom. The examples in this chapter involve that cooperation as it applies to document management and the use of SGML and intranets in the intelligence production process.

To accomplish this, Chapter 8 contains five case studies that document the experiences of the Intelligence Community in managing its most critical resource—information. Included are the U.S. Military Intelligence Production Center located in Hawaii and known as the "Joint Intelligence Center, Pacific" or JICPAC, the Office of Naval Intelligence, the National Security Agency, the Foreign Broadcast Information Service of the CIA, and the Intelligence Community's newest member: the National Imagery and Mapping Agency. These case studies, which provide you with an examination of their unique experiences, will develop and present insights into the issues, problems, and solutions for any business or other organizations desiring to take advantage of this technology. You will learn how they were able to realize tangible cost savings as well as to enjoy significantly improved capabilities.

The first case study, that of the Joint Intelligence Center, Pacific (JICPAC), represents a true prototype of the future intelligence production world. JICPAC is moving from a hardcopy environment to a true Web-centric environment using Intelink, standards including SGML, and the concept of an "information space." As such, they are the future, an embodiment of "virtual intelligence."

The second case study examines the process used by the Office of Naval Intelligence in the production and publishing of classified handbooks of the various characteristics of the world's Naval ships. It describes the SGML process that proved to be so successful, and documents the significant manpower savings coupled with real dollar cost savings. But most important of all, the end product was vastly improved.

The third case study will examine the reporting and publication of "end-product," or "finished intelligence," at the National Security Agency. It describes the difficult dissemination processes of the past, which used hand and computer-produced hard copy reports of text files, and cites the vast improvements that have been made.

The fourth case study will look at the U.S. *Foreign Broadcast Information Service* (FBIS). FBIS is the primary collector of foreign open source information for the U.S. Intelligence Community, offering the latest foreign

political, military, economic and technical information to the intelligence
analysis process. In order to enhance their publication of various products,
including softcopy delivery on CD-ROM, FBIS recently turned to SGML. As
in the other examples, significant manpower savings and other cost savings
were achieved in addition to enhanced capabilities and a vastly improved end
product.

The last case study looks at the National Imagery and Mapping Agency
(NIMA). Established in October 1996 as the consolidation of the former
Defense Mapping Agency, the Central Imagery Office, and the National Photo
Interpretation Center, NIMA provides access to the world's imagery, imagery
intelligence, and geospatial information. They are using SGML to publish
various intelligence reports over Intelink resulting in significant new
capabilities.

These case studies have direct application to the organization or business
today faced with the production and distribution of large volumes of
documents—virtually all businesses.

Finally, Part Three provides us with a glimpse of the future: how does the
U.S. Intelligence Community plan to implement all of the information
management improvements that it is working so hard on? What will the world
of "Virtual Intelligence" really look like?

To do this, Chapter 9 looks at the specific challenges facing the U.S.
Intelligence Community. It addresses what the Intelligence Community
believes will be the information revolution of the Third Millennium. This scope
of this revolution, it is believed, will have an impact similar to that experienced
in past millennia in both the agriculture and industrial revolutions. Also in this
chapter is an explanation of the possible role and impact that the Information
Technology Management Reform Act (ITMRA), passed by Congress in August
1996, will have on the future of information management in the government.
Chapter 9 also looks at the impact of technology and the global Internet,
including a discussion of their economic implications. How the private sector
views and copes with this revolution is important to the government and to you.
Therefore, Chapter 9 also looks at the direction being taken by an information
systems component (Walt Disney Imagineering) of one of the fastest growing
enterprises in the private sector today: Multibillion dollar Walt Disney
Enterprises.

Chapter 10 defines the future world of intelligence, explaining the concept
of a more "agile" intelligence enterprise, as envisioned by Dr. Ruth David,

current CIA Deputy Director for Science and Technology and author of the Prologue to this book. This chapter articulates her vision, and in doing so gives us an idea about how the U.S. Intelligence Community plans to achieve its goal of an electronically-networked environment for the production and exchange of intelligence, a goal essential to national security in the 21st Century. Chapter 10 also describes a new program for the Defense components of the U.S. Intelligence Community known as JIVA: Joint Intelligence Virtual Architecture. The concepts of an "Agile Intelligence Enterprise" and JIVA are being carefully coordinated within the Intelligence Community. The Chapter concludes with a brief summary of lessons learned for the business enterprise.

The book concludes with a comprehensive glossary of intelligence/security terms, and terms used in electronic publishing as they relate to the intelligence community.

ACKNOWLEDGMENTS

Writing a book was always something that I "was gonna" do, but over the years my responsibilities as a husband and father, my work within the U.S. Intelligence Community, and my adjunct faculty teaching at the American University always seemed to take up the time left for such a pursuit. But, as my favorite daughter always says, "was gonnas" don't count.

Therefore, I am extremely thankful for the opportunities that I have had these past several years that led to the publication of this book. First of all, I would like to thank Dr. Charles F. Goldfarb for his encouragement and support throughout this effort. Charles always took time for me, and fought for this project when we were sorting out our approach to Prentice Hall. He wrote the Foreword, and guided the project, literally defining many of the central themes. I would also like to express my gratitude to Mark L. Taub, the Executive Managing Editor at Prentice Hall who supported me, and worked with me as we shaped the best approach for this book. Mark always listened and responded immediately to all my questions and needs. His guidance and support throughout the project were greatly appreciated. Craig Little, my Production Editor, carefully and very professionally guided me through all of the intricacies of publishing. Scott Disanno, my Copy Editor, assembled the final text and worked long weekends to ensure that deadlines were met. Dr. Jennifer

Stone Gonzalez gave me much insight, encouragement, and concrete suggestions for improving the content of the book, always emphasizing the business side. I must also mention Dr. Eric van Herwijnen, a physicist from CERN who has written books on SGML and sparked my desire to write, and Chet Ensign, my friend and collaborator, who introduced me to Prentice Hall, and helped define the structure of the book. I cannot thank you all enough.

I owe much to my home agency within U.S. Intelligence. I first attended training for the National Security Agency as a teenager in 1960, and arrived at Fort Meade, Maryland, wide-eyed in 1963. By the time I retired in 1997, they had given me the privilege and honor to be involved in a number of exciting projects, working with the best and brightest people in this nation on intelligence activities that have had a profound impact on the security of this nation. In my last several years, I was indeed fortunate to be involved in a very special NSA program that took me literally around the world and gave me opportunities to be involved across the entire Intelligence Community. I am indebted to the program, as well as to its father, Mr. George R. Cotter. George, former NSA Deputy Director for Telecommunications and Computer Services and NSA Chief Scientist, has been a friend and mentor. Thank you, George.

Much has changed at the National Security Agency and across the Intelligence Community. When I began in the early 1960's, I remember signing a statement that promised that I would never write a book! Now greater openness is practiced, and even television documentaries are possible. Nevertheless, permission for me to write the first book describing on-going activities languished until Mr. William P. Crowell, then Deputy Director of the NSA, took a personal interest. His support made the book possible, and his encouragement was a great source of inspiration to me. I am most thankful, Bill.

This permission was subject to a rigorous "pre-publication review process" that NSA graciously performed on behalf of the entire Intelligence Community. Making that arduous process as painless as possible for me were Claudia Collins, Chief of Information Policy within NSA's Office of Public Affairs, and Linda Beall, their security classification expert. Claudia and Linda always found time in their busy schedules for me, returning draft material very quickly, allowing me to stay on schedule with Prentice Hall. In addition, Linda arranged permission for me to use many of the photographs and other figures in the book. I am most thankful to you both for your help.

I am deeply indebted to Dr. Ruth A. David, currently the Deputy Director for Science and Technology at the Central Intelligence Agency, for her support throughout this entire project, and especially for her willingness to write the prologue to this book. Her beliefs and vision for U.S. Intelligence, as articulated in her prologue, are clearly having a profound impact on the future of the U.S. Intelligence Community, and therefore helped to shape this book. An author as well as contributor to several books herself, her encouraging words were most helpful to me. One day, after lamenting about the number of hours this project was consuming, she explained to me that one's pay for such endeavors turns out to be "about 10 cents per hour." I now realize that, in my case, her estimate was very high. I am indeed grateful Ruth.

Of course, none of this would have been possible without the support of the Intelink Community. I am most indebted to Intelligence Community leader Admiral William O. Studeman (former Deputy Director of Central Intelligence, former Director of the National Security Agency, and former Director of Naval Intelligence) for his insightful "Afterword." Bill Studeman is a "giant" within the Intelligence Community and his efforts have significantly enhanced this book. I also owe thanks to Steven Schanzer, Ronald Elliott, and James Peak for their counsel, guidance, and support. The leadership team within the Intelink Management Office, specifically Bill Campbell, Bill Fleming, Randy Marks, and Jack Torok, spent considerable time guiding me through the maze, patiently providing me feedback and correcting my many mistakes and misconceptions. Bill Campbell and Randy Marks also provided much of the graphics material contained in the figures, including the Intelink photos and screen shots. For those areas of the book concerning Intelink that still need correction or polish, I accept full responsibility; and for those areas that appear concise and accurate, I give the credit to them. In addition, I must thank Intelink expert Mark Kelly. Even during challenging times in his personal and professional life, Mark helped in every way he could, always willing to go the extra length to make some aspect of the book better. Mark also spent many hours helping to develop and assembling the CD-ROM that accompanies this book.

I had the pleasure of spending time with Bran Ferren, Executive Vice President of *Walt Disney Imagineering*, at his West Coast office outside of Hollywood. Bran not only provided me with his perspective from the private sector, but he also took time from his hectic schedule to critique and provide feedback to what I had written. Thank you, Bran.

I believe that the case studies in this book tell a compelling story of the successes and challenges of the U.S. Intelligence Community. They could not have been told without the generosity of many people. My deepest thanks are extended to them all: Major Leland (Lee) R. Hopson, Joan Smith, Gail Picard, Peggy Fraga, Joe Fisher, Ed O'Conner, Katheryn Travers, Marian P. (Patti) Chandler, Michael Kiser, Calvin R. Wylie, and Ralph Steiniger. In addition to these people, many others shared their own ideas and insights, as well as reactions and critiques which significantly enhanced this book. Special thanks go to Andy Shepard, Avis Boutell, David Miller, and George L. Marling.

I also wish to express my appreciation for all of the encouragement and support that I received from my children, Fredrick Thomas Martin, Jr., his wife, Ruth Amber Martin, Robert Earl Martin, and Michelle Lynnette (Martin) Cohen, and her husband, Mark Lawrence Cohen. Many family plans had to be put on hold or cancelled for this project. Their love, patience, and understanding were an inspiration to me.

In particular, my son Robert (a computer engineer himself, assigned to the National Security Agency) gave up his social life and spent several months working with me on this book. Rob performed invaluable research literally around the clock and painstakingly edited and critiqued every chapter. He also directly contributed by providing an initial draft for the security aspects in Chapters 4 and 5. His insight and seemingly unending supply of fresh ideas nurtured this book from cover to cover. Rob, I cannot thank you enough.

Finally, there are no words to express my love and gratitude to my wife for her patience, prayers, support, and encouragement. Throughout our forty-one years together, my wife has always been my nurturing partner, best friend, and the most patient listener to all I would "dump" on her. At every career turning point or important moment, she has been there with her love and wise counsel. A precious gift from our Lord, she is truly the "wind beneath my wings" and no mere words on paper can express my heartfelt love, admiration, and appreciation.

Fredrick Thomas Martin
August, 1998

Afterword

Application of evolving Internet technologies to intelligence applications in the form of *Intelink* has been a transcendent and farsighted strategy. In theory, it addresses many of the current needs for access to intelligence databases, push/pull dissemination, a generally secure environment with multiple levels of security ranging from "codeword" through general service classifications, including support for U.S. allies, as well as unclassified access to "open source" data. Its user base is vast, so it can reach down to support lower levels of Department of Defense (DoD), intelligence and allied customers. Its future application requirements parallel those of the global Internet, so there is the expectation that, for continuing modest investment, intelligence can continue to ride the wave of Internet growth, with commensurate access to amazing and relevant commercial off-the-shelf (COTS) developments on tools, visualization, speed, search capabilities, increased capacities, improved data access, conferencing, segmentation, and many other areas where DoD intelligence and civilian Internet applications converge.

NEXT STEPS

So where do we go next in terms of satisfying user needs in peace and war? The use of *metadata* is a critical step. It could improve the ability of *Intelink* to allow users to ultimately cut across the various "web pages" produced by the disciplinary "stovepipes" at all levels of the Intelligence Community. These stovepipes relate to the intelligence disciplines such as *Imagery Intelligence* (IMINT), *Signals Intelligence* (SIGINT), *Human Intelligence* (HUMINT), *Measurement and Signature Intelligence* (MASINT), and *Open Source Intelligence* (OSINT). Second levels of stovepipes exist for operational/current intelligence correlation and analysis (usually done on an all-source basis) at the Service, "Commander-In-Chief" (CINC), Joint Task Force (JTF) and below levels, and finally, at the scientific and technical intelligence centers. The so-called stovepipes are both a blessing and a curse. They exist for the purpose of accountability, span of control and the ability to lead, manage and focus incredibly complex intelligence disciplines that are often multi-billion dollar a year enterprises such as the Central Intelligence Agency, the Defense Intelligence Agency, the National Reconnaissance Office, the National Security Agency, and the National Imagery and Mapping Agency. That said, their production of data files for *Intelink* tends to be focused on one discipline or a narrow range of target sets. On the other hand, the customers using *Intelink* want the integrated, all-source, fused intelligence data, tailored to their specific level of interest, and to move toward solutions in this area may be *Intelink*'s biggest challenge. Tools to assist such as profiling, filters, data finders, and other Internet technologies move *Intelink* in the direction of satisfying this requirement.

Finally, to put these next steps into their proper perspective, *Intelink* must foster a close association with the Joint Intelligence Virtual Architecture (JIVA) program as well as carefully consider the Intelligence Community-wide vision of the "agile intelligence enterprise" in order to improve the quality, timeliness, and effectiveness of intelligence products.

OTHER CHALLENGES

What are the other *Intelink* challenges? I would speculate that they are as follows:

- Providing broad access to large-scale imagery/maps/special effects type data. *Intelink* can already deal with a small subset of this requirement.

- Providing tools to support imagery and related geospatial filtering functions.
- Improving data finding, push (profiling) and fusion capabilities.
- Dealing with the stress of wartime load levels down to lower command levels.
- Moving more in the direction of multilevel security (a difficult requirement).
- Improving security functionality to prevent unauthorized field access during conflict/warfighting.
- Developing the ability to deal with *Information Warfare* threats, and degrading gracefully when under attack.

The *Intelink* Management Office represents a modest but critically important force in intelligence. Given the enormous potential for *Intelink*, the program is likely currently underfunded—despite recent increases—but competition for scarce resources is tight in today's Intelligence Community. *Intelink* is important because of its reach, flexibility, and continuing potential to satisfy customer critical and diverse intelligence needs. In this book, Fredrick Thomas Martin has provided us with a rich description of the range of architecture, technology and studies efforts inspired by *Intelink*. I predict a bright and successful future for *Intelink* as it strives to meet the challenges of functionality and customer needs.

Admiral William O. Studeman, USN-Retired
Former Deputy Director of Central Intelligence,
Director of the National Security Agency, and
Director of Naval Intelligence

Part One
Introduction to *Intelink*

Chapter 1

Intelink—the Intranet of the U.S. Intelligence Community

*C*onsider the following scenario:

The year is 2005. Tensions in the world have been steadily increasing for the past 16 months, as a former Soviet bloc country with significant nuclear weapons capabilities has entered into a defensive agreement with a coalition of several suspected Middle East-based terrorist organizations that combined forces shortly after the turn of the millennium.

For the past two weeks, the U.S. Intelligence Community has been operating under their highest state of alert. It is two and a half hours past midnight in Washington, D.C. National Imagery and Mapping Agency analysts have been monitoring troop movements from satellite imagery for the past two days. Major Jay Franklin, a U.S. Army intelligence analyst stationed at the Defense Intelligence Agency, receives an emergency call from the commander of an elite special forces unit in the Middle East.

At approximately the same time, the watch officer in the National Security Operations Center of the National Security Agency receives an automated, high priority signal from a special array of sensors. The signal comes from one of its computers at a remote classified location in Eastern Europe, alerting the U.S. Intelligence Community of possible impending troop movements. Meanwhile, analysts at the Central Intelligence Agency have been alerted to a possible attack scenario involving both chemical and nuclear weapons...

This is clearly a scenario with the potential for worldwide catastrophe. The important question to ask is whether U.S. Intelligence could *respond* and appropriately *adjust* its collection, exploitation, and analysis capabilities, i.e., just how *agile* is U.S. Intelligence?

Throughout this book we shall examine this question. We will learn about the beginnings of a new paradigm, based on intranet technology and the principles of open information management. This is the progress made by the U.S. Intelligence Community, an enterprise that has the *ultimate* at risk—the national security of the United States. In Chapter 10 we shall revisit this scenario, demonstrating the progress that they have made. In addition, we will show the relationships of their efforts to the corporate or business enterprise.

Chapter 1 sets the stage for our discussions in this book and contains a brief introduction to the *Intelink* Community by providing some degree of insight into just who *uses* (i.e., intelligence customers) and who *produces* U.S. intelligence.[1] Chapter 1 defines the *Intelink* concept and its related technologies, including a brief discussion of the evolution of the Internet, the World Wide Web, and the role of standards such as SGML (Standard Generalized Markup Language), HTML (Hypertext Markup Language), and the new XML (eXtensible Markup Language). We will also explain the problem that *Intelink* addresses, i.e., why did we need it? We conclude with some rationale as to why an intranet/extranet solution was used, i.e., why this technology was the right solution.

---

[1] Refer to the Introduction to this book for background material on the US Intelligence Community.

1.1 WHAT IS *INTELINK*?

1.1.1 The Beginning

Like many businesses, the Intelligence Community consists of a number of discrete organizations that perform distinct missions for overlapping sets of customers. These separate organizations, which contain the various operations that collect, process, and exploit intelligence data, are frequently referred to as "stovepipes," which connote the image of a large number of individual chimneys all heating the same building.

By 1994, the "stovepipe" method of operations that was used by the various elements of the U.S. Intelligence Community was beginning to create an adverse impact on the development and operation of the nation's intelligence systems. In a joint proclamation in 1994, then Director of Central Intelligence James Woolsey and Deputy Secretary of Defense John Deutch established an important new mechanism to help alleviate this concern—the *Intelligence Systems Board* (ISB). The purpose of the ISB is to improve the interoperability of all automated information systems supporting intelligence operations—regardless of organization—not only within the Intelligence Community itself, but also between the Intelligence Community and the many military commands, agencies, and operations that it serves. This new ISB was initially chaired by Richard Haver and Keith R. Hall, currently Director of the National Reconnaissance Office. The mission of the ISB is carried out by a senior level, permanent staff element known as the *Intelligence Systems Secretariat* (ISS).

The first Director of the ISS, Steven T. Schanzer, decided that an inter-community electronic information service for intelligence information should be his principal mechanism for implementing the goals, operating efficiencies, and cost savings envisioned by the new ISB. Generally considered to be the "father" of Intelink, Schanzer held a series of discussions with Haver and Hall, as well as officials such as Victor A. DeMarines, President of the MITRE Corporation, and other experts affiliated with the CIA. These early discussions helped to form his vision of a secure communications and processing environment for intelligence dissemination and collaboration. Schanzer and the Deputy Director of the ISS, Fred Harrison, assembled a small team of experts to develop a prototype that Harrison later named "Intelink." The initial team included Franklin E. White, Jr., William Brindley, James Davidson, Edward

Engle, Janet Gale, Paul Hyland, and Sherry Johnson. Starting with this proof-of-concept prototype in April 1994, Intelink was operational by the end of that year.

1.1.2 Definition

In short, *Intelink* is a secure, private collection of networks implemented on existing government and commercial communications networks (Figure 1-1). These networks employ Web-based technology, use well-established networking protocols, and are protected by firewalls to prevent external use. In order to begin to grasp the concept of *Intelink*, we will need to spend the rest of this chapter refining these terms and explaining their relationship to the phenomenon known as the "Internet."

Within the Intelligence Community today, *Intelink* is commonly perceived as simply the intranet (or the extranet, as we shall define later) that interconnects various intelligence organizations and operations, i.e., connects the various providers and users of intelligence information. It is this and more: *Intelink* is actually a full suite of information services that have been put in place by various government organizations for their authorized users. It uses advanced technology such as commercial Internet applications and protocols, all operating on existing U.S. Government as well as commercial telecommunications resources. The ultimate purpose of *Intelink* is to provide robust and timely access to all available intelligence information, regardless of location, medium, or format, for all interested users that are authorized access to the various available security levels of *Intelink* service.

By using standard commercial World Wide Web browsers, such as *Netscape Navigator* or *Microsoft Internet Explorer*, users can access intelligence products over the *Intelink* family of networks.[2] They can exchange e-mail, access on-screen "video-on-demand," conduct video teleconferences, and use other tools that allow users to collaborate in real-time.

As such, *Intelink* captures the essence of current advanced network technology and applies it to the production, use, and dissemination of classified

---

[2] The availability of many different browsers is itself a major concern of *Intelink* today, as we will discuss later.

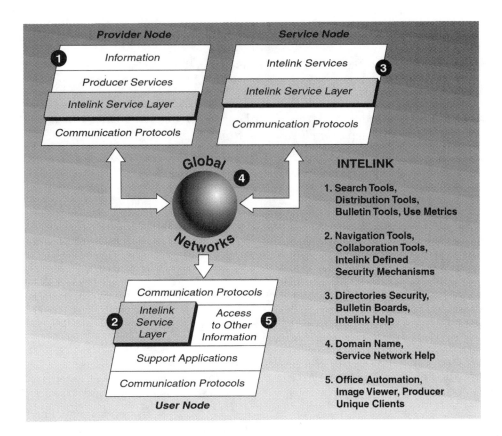

Figure 1-1 Early Intelink Architecture.

and unclassified multimedia data among this nation's intelligence resources. Close examination of the exciting *Intelink* community will reap significant rewards: *Intelink* encompasses one of the world's largest data repositories, and addresses demanding data management issues that are at the very extreme of what an enterprise normally encounters.

1.1.3 Recognition of *Intelink*

Intelink has been recognized throughout the federal government, from Vice President Gore, the Deputy Secretary of Defense, the Director of Central

Intelligence, the information technology industry, and even the mainstream media.

In April 1994, then Director of Central Intelligence James Woolsey was so impressed with a demonstration of the initial *Intelink* capabilities that he initiated actions to deploy this new technology. In August 1994, then Deputy Secretary of Defense John Deutch and Director of Central Intelligence James Woolsey jointly declared *Intelink* as the *strategic direction* for all Intelligence Community "finished intelligence" dissemination systems.[3]

In March of 1996, Steve Schanzer, his deputy Fred Harrison, and the entire *Intelink* implementation team received the prestigious "Hammer Award," presented by Vice President Al Gore. The National Performance Review (NPR) is the special program established by the Vice President to recognize significant contributions to the objectives of President Clinton's government-wide initiative to "reinvent government." In the words of Bob Stone, the Director of the National Performance Review, the *Hammer Award* is "the Vice President's answer to the government of yesterday and its [overpriced] $400 hammer." In presenting the award to Schanzer and his team, Vice-President Gore stated, "Intelink is a brilliant use of cyberspace... It is bringing the Intelligence Community closer together than ever before, delivering state-of-the-art services, and the team behind Intelink is truly world-class" (Figure 1-2).

The Intelligence Community, which typically shuns any type of publicity, contributed to a March 1995 article in Time Magazine on *Intelink*. Entitled "Spies in Cyberspace," the article explained the purpose of *Intelink* and pointed out its similarities to the global Internet. In October 1997, *Intelink* was honored by being included in the list of "Best Information Technology Practices in the Federal Government," a report issued jointly by the Chief Information Officers Council and the Industry Advisory Council.

However, despite the impressive list of accolades, the most important recognition has been the widespread acceptance and usage of *Intelink* by the entire U.S. Intelligence Community. For example, during the Gulf War General

---

[3] "Finished intelligence" or "end-product" refers to the various reports and studies that are disseminated to the customer or end-user, and collectively represent the output of the intelligence process. A threat projection, technology summary, capability study, scientific handbook, detailed national intelligence estimate on some subject, or even an individual translation, are all examples of finished intelligence.

Figure 1-2 Vice President Gore Presents the *Hammer Award* to Intelink Team.

H. Norman Schwarzkopf complained of receiving late or incomplete intelligence reports that impacted on his ability to prepare for combat. His ground commanders did not always have timely satellite surveillance photos partially because the various computer systems could not talk to one another. Thus, participation is no longer simply a fear of being "left out" of the new market, as former Director Schanzer had stated earlier, but, according to current Director James P. Peak, genuine Intelligence Community recognition of the value of this tool.

Since *Intelink* is patterned after the global Internet, we now turn to a brief discussion of its evolution, including the advent of the World Wide Web, and the role of standards such as SGML, HTML, and the new XML.

1.2 EVOLUTION OF THE INTERNET

The Internet: It has been with U.S. now for over twenty years, and in terms of actual and perceived societal impact, there may not be a peer. The global computer network that became the backbone of the Internet was originally built in the 1970's by the Defense Advanced Research Projects Agency (DARPA) of the U.S. Government to connect U.S. military and academic research institutions. Many believe that one of its original purposes was to reduce the impact of a nuclear confrontation, since the capability to withstand losses of large portions of the underlying networks was a natural product of the Internet design.

> **Definition:** The Internet is a global network of individual networks interconnected through a specific set of conventions that allow communication to take place between two separate machines. It is characterized by ubiquitous access by the public with variable security.

Thus, the Internet has evolved into a massive global infrastructure with a universally accessible collection of networks supporting culture, diversity, academia, and business, and now has over 40 million users. Many experts believe that it will grow to over 200 million users by the turn of the century. It is the amalgamation of the telegraph, telephone, radio, television, satellite, and computer industries into a single entity. This same commercial world continues to push the limits of the Internet. It has already revolutionized, and will continue to change, not just the computer and communications worlds, but the world that directly affects U.S. as individuals, every day. For example, electronic mail, and the resulting presence of "ordinary users," has helped to make the Internet a household term. Commercial services and so-called "Internet Service Providers" have had to scramble to attempt to meet the demand for high-speed information services. In fact, this demand continues to grow at an exponential rate (Figure 1-3).

Although the Internet architecture was originally intended to provide a robust communications network for select research institutions in the United States, the development effort that produced it also gave birth to several key technologies that are fundamental to networks today. Thus, it is important to have at least a basic understanding of this architecture since an intranet, as we shall formally define later, is really a private network that uses the methodology, tools, and protocols of the global Internet.

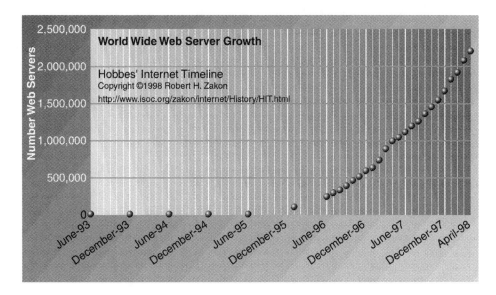

Figure 1-3 Global Internet Growth.

1.2.1 Packets: The Basis of Computer Network Communications

Before the Internet came into existence, when one thought of an example of a network, it was probably of the public telephone system. Here was something that interconnected the homes of millions of people from coast to coast and allowed easy communications for everyone. The reason that the phone system can provide service to so many customers is because its network is based on the concept of "circuit-switching." Circuit-switched networks operate by creating a dedicated path, or *circuit*, between the originating caller and the person that answers on the other end (Figure 1-4).

The primary advantage of this kind of approach is that once a circuit has been formed, its performance will not degrade as a function of the total number of circuits that might exist in the network at that given moment in time (assuming, of course, that the maximum number of physically allowable circuits has not been reached). This is important for voice communication, in

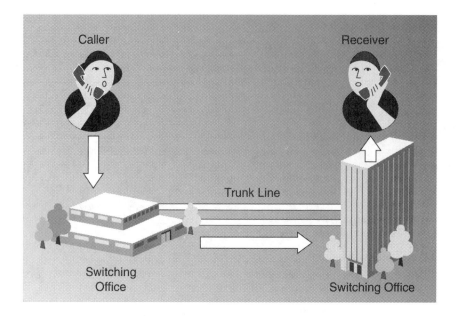

Figure 1-4 Circuit Switched Networks.

which any amount of delay in response time can be disconcerting. Consider the annoying delay that arises from using satellites to relay, say, a live news interview from some isolated region of the world: the time lag may be only less than second, but it is still disruptive to try to speak to someone under those conditions.

For the kind of continuous voice traffic that has traditionally been sent over the telephone network, in which the transmission capacity—consider this as the "size" of the circuit—is a known and fixed amount, circuit-switching works quite well. However, it turns out that this approach is not particularly efficient for the kind of traffic that a computer produces. First of all, when two computers communicate, they do not need to send information to each other on a continuous basis during the entire session. Therefore, setting up a dedicated path implies that there would be some amount of time during the communications session in which the circuit would be idle. Chances are that the network would quickly run out of available circuits in this situation. Secondly, since the transmission capacity of a circuit is fixed, this would force the two computers to transmit and receive data at the same rate. While this would be acceptable for many situations, it still limits the usefulness of the network in providing connections for the wide variety of computers in existence today.

Fortunately, there is a solution that addresses these issues. By their design, computers perform functions on blocks of data that are all the same size. As such, it makes sense to break down a long communications session between computers on a network into more manageable pieces; in this context, these pieces are most commonly referred to as *packets*, and the networks upon which they are used are called packet-switched networks. This concept of packets may seem trivial today, but it actually revolutionized data communications: each packet includes certain identifying information along with its payload of actual data, such as where it came from and where it is supposed to go (referred to as the *source address* and *destination address*, respectively). Carrying this additional information means that a packet does not have to be sent down any particular fixed path on the network. In fact, packets do not even need to be sent in order, provided that there is a mechanism in place for properly rearranging them in the end.

Using packets, then, addresses the problems inherent in using circuit-switched networks for computer communication. First, transmitted packets can be temporarily stored at points along the way to their destination, and then be sent as a group in order to reduce the overall time that a communications path is idle. Secondly, with packets two computers no longer have to send and receive at the same rate, thus allowing total flexibility in connecting different kinds of computers to the network. These are key issues that have allowed the Internet to flourish and likewise will allow *Intelink* and networks like it to grow as well.

As a way to visualize a packet-switched network, consider the postal system. When someone wants to send a package, they stamp it with the destination address and a return address and then send it on its merry way. Along the way, it may be transported in any number of ways and travel through any number of paths, until it finally (hopefully...) arrives at its intended destination (Figure 1-5).

There is a downside, of course. The primary disadvantage of a packet-switched network is that the transmission capacities of various commun-ication paths are very much dependent upon the number of packets being sent through the network at that time. Indeed, when all communication paths in a network are at full capacity, the network's users have little choice but to wait until it ceases being saturated with activity. This situation would be unacceptable if it were how the public telephone system worked—imagine trying to talk to some one on the phone if every other word was dropped out of the conversation! Obviously, the capacity must be guaranteed in that context. Yet, in the world of computers, the capacity issue is much more forgiving. As long as all the packets arrive intact at their intended destination, it really does not matter if it

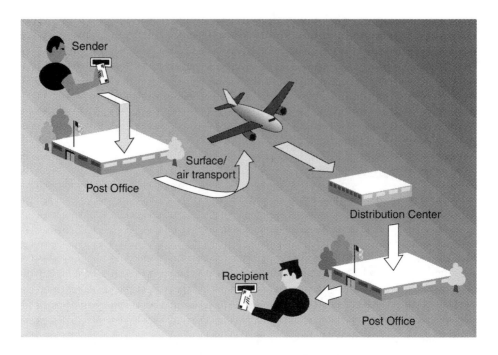

Figure 1-5 U.S. Postal Service Switched Network Analogy.

takes five seconds or a minute (although the sooner the better, of course!). As long as networks continue to be upgraded to support higher capacities and more users, the versatility of the packet-switched approach makes it the logical choice for computer networks like the Internet and Intelink.

One final note that highlights the usefulness of packet-switched networks: a service that is just beginning to be taken seriously is *Internet telephony*, which allows a caller to use a packet-switched computer network to make regular telephone calls. It remains to be seen how easy such a system would be to use, but if it could be made as simple to use as it is to pick up a traditional phone today, Internet telephony could cause a radical shift in how the telecommunications industry provides its services.[4]

---

[4] For a more thorough treatment of the subject of circuit-switched and packet-switched networks, please refer to the text by William Stallings, *Data and Computer Communications.*

1.2.2 Communication Protocols and the OSI Model

Another important aspect to understand about the Internet is the concept of a communications protocol and how it is used in the network. A protocol is simply a set of rules that govern how two entities—in this case, computers—will communicate. An excellent example of this is "TCP/IP," which in reality is a combination of two separate protocols: the Transmission Control Protocol (TCP) and the Internet Protocol (IP). Each of these two parts can work independently of the other, yet they are most commonly used in tandem to communicate across sets of interconnected networks. TCP/IP is actually the foundation upon which a whole group of protocols has been built. Commonly called the Internet Protocol suite, this group of protocols provides specifications for many other necessary common applications such as electronic mail, terminal emulation, and file transfer; and, since it is equally well-suited for both local-area networks (LANs) and wide-area networks (WANs), it is also ideal for intranets and extranets.

As popular as TCP/IP is today, there will probably always be alternative protocols available on the market. Therefore, as we attempt to develop a network, how do we deal with the fact that every manufacturer might have its own unique way of implementing its products, whether through innovation, through a belief that it will enhance competitiveness, or maybe through a desire to avoid a patent infringement lawsuit? The answer is simple: *standardization.* If there were a common framework upon which everyone must build network applications, then there would be no proprietary stumbling blocks and no issue of incompatibility.

The standard Opens Systems Interconnection (OSI) reference model produced in 1974 by the International Standards Organization (ISO) attempts to encapsulate this idea for networks. Specifically, it suggests a method in which the many functions involved in network communication may be split into multiple modules, or *layers.* Implemented correctly, it would then be possible to substitute among any of the protocols written for the same layer, without needing to correspondingly replace any of the protocols at the other layers. The primary usefulness of this notion of modularity is that the various application programs that may exist on completely different network systems would be able to communicate seamlessly with each other, as though they were on the same system. It is important to keep in mind that while the OSI Model has seven layers, many commercially available network products tend to have their own view of how the layers should be defined and may use an alternative approach containing a different number of layers. Nevertheless, the model provides the needed framework for the coordination of open systems standards development: it encourages vendors to work under a common framework and avoid proprietary efforts including implementation of their own sets of protocols. To encourage understanding of the various Internet protocols, it is useful to compare them against the full OSI Model. The following provides a brief summary of the seven layers of the OSI Model: [5]

1) Physical Layer

This layer is concerned with the signals, the physical and electrical interfaces between the user equipment and the network terminating equipment necessary to establish, maintain, and terminate the physical connection.

2) Data Link Layer

The function of this layer is to provide a reliable means to transfer data between the networks. This includes responsibility for functions such as error detection and, in the event of transmission errors, the retransmission of messages.

3) Network Layer

This layer is responsible for the exchange of data between the networks. This includes establishing, maintaining, and terminating the specific network connections, and includes functions like network routing (addressing).

4) Transport Layer

This layer provides reliable, transparent delivery of data, including error recovery and flow control.

---

[5] For additional details on the OSI Model, see the Uyless Black text, *OSI - A Model for Computer Communications Standards*, Prentice-Hall, 1991.

5) Session Layer

This layer allows two application layer protocol entities to organize and synchronize their dialog, for the duration of the complete network transaction.

6) Presentation Layer

This layer is concerned with the syntax or format representation of data during transfer between two communicating application processes, including data conversion services such as encryption or compression.

7) Application Layer

This layer provides the user interface (perhaps an application program or some process) to the range of network-wide distributed information services. Examples include file transfer access and management, as well as general document and message interchange services such as electronic mail.

Fortunately, for the business-oriented reader as well as others, we can narrow the seven layers of the OSI Model. For the purposes of this book, we will use an abbreviated version, rather than getting bogged down into the details of all seven layers. This will facilitate understanding the global Internet and intranet applications based on the global Internet such as Intelink. Therefore, consider the following three subsets shown on the next page.

1) *The Bottom Layer*

This is just the physical layer renamed. It is the most fundamental aspect, though, and one of two that can actually be seen and touched by the user. Ethernet is a good example of a standard that has been developed for this layer. It is an implementation that typically uses electricity on coaxial cable to send its packets. It works under the principle of "best-effort delivery," which means that the sender is given no indication as to whether the packets that it sent were received at the intended destination. So if, for example, the machine on the receiving end were shut down, the sending machine would have no idea what was going on. Other examples of this layer are FDDI (Fiber Distributed Data Interconnect) and ATM (Asynchronous Transfer Mode), both of which use optical fiber in order to provide higher transmission rates than Ethernet.

2) *The "Middle Layers"*

These—corresponding to layers 2 through 6 on the OSI Model—may not be so easily evident to the typical user. TCP/IP falls into this category. Its function is to build upon physical layer implementations like Ethernet and provide the additional functionality needed to make a computer network useful. Specifically, they work together to provide the additional structure and rules needed to make packet communication occur in a reliable way. The primary advantage of TCP/IP is that packets can be routed along different paths and lost or duplicate packets can be dealt with accordingly.

3) *The Top Layer*

This is the other layer that is most easily identified by the average user, since this is where the high-level applications reside. By relying on all of the lower layers to take care of the specific details of communication, applications can then provide the kinds of functions that make networks so useful as a tool. For example, electronic mail (or "e-mail") is a common application in which one can send text and other forms of data anywhere on the network. Another example of an application is FTP (File Transfer Protocol), which provides access to files on remote computers. Using FTP, then, a person could electronically upload a draft document to a remote machine so that another user there might review it; then, that same person could turn around and download the edited file again at a later time.

Many consider the Internet today as the forerunner of the *National Information Infrastructure* or the "Information Superhighway" often touted by Vice President Gore and others in the Clinton administration. Indeed, the Internet is truly the *Global Information Infrastructure*, with connecting networks literally spanning the globe. Just as the Internet is a "prototype" of the National/Global Information Infrastructure, we will learn how *Intelink* is the "prototype" of *Virtual Intelligence*, the "agile" intelligence environment of the future for the U.S. Intelligence Community.

An excellent summary of the early history of the Internet was written by a team of early pioneers involved in its development, evolution, and implementation. The team, which included Vinton G. Cerf (a pioneer developer of the TCP/IP protocol suite) and colleagues, has posted their paper, entitled, "A Brief History of the Internet," on the home page of the Internet Society (http://www.isoc.org). The Internet Society, headquartered in Reston, Virginia, is a nonprofit, nongovernmental, international professional membership organization with over 100 organizations and 7000 individuals dedicated to supporting the growth and progress of the Internet.

1.2.3 The World Wide Web

As profound as the development of the set of interconnecting computer networks known as the Internet, we now have yet another phenomenon, the World Wide Web. The World Wide Web (or WWW or the "Web" as it is known) was conceived in 1989 at what is now known as the European Particle Physics Laboratory, located on the Franco-Swiss border near Geneva, Switzerland. This laboratory is better known as CERN, an acronym of its former French name, *the Centre Europeenne pour la Recherche Nucleaire.* The inventor of the Web is Tim Berners-Lee, who led the development while employed at CERN. Today, Berners-Lee is affiliated with the Computer Science Laboratory at the Massachusetts Institute of Technology, and serves as Chairman of the World Wide Web Consortium, normally referred to as the "W3C."

The Web started out slowly as basically a medium to broadcast read-only material from corporate servers at CERN. "Web-browsing" technology continued to be in its infancy in the early 1990's, but then in 1993, Marc Andreessen from the National Center for Supercomputing Applications located at the University of Illinois, developed a new browser known as "Mosaic" that became an overnight sensation with its installation ease and power. This resulted in widespread usage of the Web, beginning around 1994. The Web has matured significantly since 1994, especially with the advent of newer, and much more powerful browsers such as Netscape (the follow-on to Mosaic) and Internet Explorer (the Microsoft version that was developed literally in a matter of months after Bill Gates realized the potential of the Web). The result of all of this is that the Web has become a major catalyst for the Internet, becoming its primary application for many users today. Indeed, many people today use the terms Internet and the Web synonymously, with little understanding of their difference.

1.2.4 Standards: Role of SGML, HTML, and XML

Just as standardization using the OSI Model facilitated the development of a common framework upon which network applications were built, standards were needed to process the information that would be carried over the Web. But even before Berners-Lee and others at CERN developed their concept of the World Wide Web, progress was being made in another problem area that would ultimately ensure the Web's success: getting computers to recognize the *structure* and *content* of information, not just its presentation *format*.

Back in the late 1960's at IBM, this was recognized by Charles F. Goldfarb, Edward Mosher, and Raymond Lorie. They were trying to manipulate and integrate legal documents among various processing programs of the time. Together they developed a technique to share documents among mainframe computers that was based on document markup "tags" that explicitly described the structure of a document rather than the format. The tags would label a particular element of the document with its purpose or function as a heading, paragraph, or item in a list. The computer could then automatically process the information in a number of different applications. For example, if you needed to present the same information in a different format, or if your style requirements changed, massive revision of the data was no longer necessary. And now you could reuse the same information in a variety of different applications: the information in a paper document could become part of an online service, or as we would learn later, could be produced on a CD-ROM or published on the Web. They cleverly named their new approach for document markup "GML" which could be an acronym for the last names of the inventors, or "Generalized Markup Language" as it came to be known.

1.2.4.1 The Standard Generalized Markup
Language—SGML

After adoption by IBM, Goldfarb continued to refine and improve the basic concepts of GML, eventually inventing in 1974 what is known today as SGML, or the *Standard Generalized Markup Language.* He then led the International Standards Organization (ISO) effort to develop SGML as an International Standard—and it became ISO 8879 in 1986.

The underlying premise of SGML automated markup is the concept of a "document type definition," or DTD. The DTD prescribes the specific rules that SGML will use to process a set or category of documents. For example, the DTD will define the various element types whose identifying "tags" will be used to markup a document, it will dictate the set of rules under which these element types can occur, and it will define the relationships among the various element types. This results in consistent and logical structures for all documents. Of course, all of this can be transparent to the user, thanks to a large number of commercially available SGML authoring tools and other products that produce text and verify the DTD itself as well as conformance to the DTD.

SGML itself does not specify any presentation style, so the file containing the final appearance of an SGML document is frequently in some proprietary format. One effort to produce a standard set of presentation formats, or "style sheets" has culminated in the development of another ISO Standard, the Document Style Semantics and Specification Language (DSSSL)—pronounced "dissel" —released in 1996 as ISO 10179. The Department of Defense developed its own style standard as part of the "Continuous Acquisition and Life-cycle Support" or "CALS" initiative. Their standard, known as the "Output Specification," provided for a style sheet known as a "Format Output Specification Instance," or FOSI—pronounced "fossy."[6] Each individual FOSI specifies the format for every element type in a specific DTD. Together they become the ideal mechanism for computer processing in both paper and electronic media.

Over the years, SGML has gained a wide acceptance throughout the U.S. Government, and among large-scale document users in the private sector. A big boost towards U.S. Government SGML usage occurred in 1987 when SGML

---

[6] This initiative, which dates from the late 1980's and mandated the use of SGML, greatly enhanced the stature of SGML.

was mandated by the Department of Defense for the CALS Program. In 1996, the DoD's "Joint Technical Architecture," which we describe in Part Two of the book, endorsed the use of SGML. Within the Intelligence Community, SGML was implemented in a number of programs, including the CIA's Foreign Broadcast Information Service (FBIS) as early as 1988.[7] In 1993, the CIA accepted SGML as its information processing "standard," although organizations were still permitted to use proprietary solutions. In 1994, the CIA also established the "SGML Resource Center" which facilitated the use of SGML throughout the Intelligence Community. Soon after the inauguration of *Intelink* in 1994, it was decided that *Intelink* documents should be tagged in SGML, and this led to a number of SGML implementation efforts.[8]

1.2.4.2 The Hypertext Markup Language—HTML
The eXtensible Markup Language—XML

When Berners-Lee and his colleagues were choosing the method they would use to handle hypertext and other Web applications, they knew that they wanted to turn to SGML due to its wide acceptance in the document management community. They also wanted to keep the implementation simple and ended up developing a unique SGML DTD that was called the Hypertext Markup Language (HTML). The job of HTML was to define the necessary syntax to display the contents of a complete document, including text, pictures or other images, and any other supporting media. The key to this new language, however, was its ability to create special hypertext links between the document and other documents on the Internet. In the end, HTML was designed for overall simplicity, and the ease with which it combined pictures and text.

So even though HTML is an outstanding mechanism for publishing simple documents, its simplicity constrains the ability to produce complex applications on the Web. In many applications, however, the power of customized SGML DTDs is really needed. When this situation arises, since the most popular Web browsers today do not provide support to all of the broad and powerful options offered by SGML, most World Wide Web publishing applications deliver their customized SGML document types over the Web by

---

[7] Additional details of the use of SGML by the FBIS are provided in Chapter 8.

[8] Several of these efforts are detailed as *case studies* in Chapter 8.

first converting the documents to HTML. Indeed, in most SGML authoring software, all that is needed to publish on the Web is the HTML DTD. Unfortunately, this conversion tends to remove most of the intelligence of the original SGML information. Most importantly, this lost intelligence virtually eliminates information flexibility and poses a significant barrier to information reuse, exchange, and automation. Despite its shortcomings, HTML currently remains the preferred data format or "notation" for publishing information on the World Wide Web. But help is on the way!

XML, or the *eXtensible Markup Language*, made its debut at the SGML Conference held in Boston in November 1996. The development was led by Jon Bosak from Sun Microsystems, and the specification was edited by Tim Bray from Textuality, C. M. Sperberg-McQueen of the University of Chicago, and Jean Paoli of Microsoft.

It is important to understand that XML is a *subset* of SGML, while HTML is an *application* of SGML. Indeed, the purpose of XML is to create a mechanism for delivery of SGML information over the World Wide Web. Thought of by many as "SGML-Lite," XML has the functionality of the most popular and widely supported capabilities of the SGML standard, and therefore the ability to overcome the limitations of HTML. According to Michael Krantz writing for the Technology Section of Time Magazine in November 1997, both Microsoft and Netscape have agreed to adopt XML in their browser software.

The March 1998 issue of BYTE Magazine had an interesting cover article on XML—"Weaving a Better Web: The features that made HTML so popular are causing the Web to fall apart. What's next?" The article covered XML in some detail—including explanations of how XML handles DTDs, and XML's companion specifications XSL (Extensible Style Language) and XLink (Extensible Link Language). It also explained why XML is needed ("What's Wrong with HTML"), described applications that "will drive XML acceptance," and noted some of the XML tools on the horizon. The article predicted "major changes in the Web starting at the end of this year as sites start using XML." An article by Bill Gates in the same issue reiterated that Microsoft considered XML as its initial answer to problems of data representation.

P. G. Bartlett, currently Vice President of Marketing for ArborText, a leading supplier of SGML solutions, expresses the feelings of many industry experts when he says, "XML is inevitably destined to become the mainstream technology for powering broadly functional and highly valuable business applications on the Internet, intranets, and extranets." As cited later in Chapter 8, XML is being watched closely. It is being looked at by the *Intelink* Management Office, and is being considered by most Intelligence Community organizations that are developing applications for *Intelink.*

1.3 WHAT IS AN *INTRANET*?

Now that we have some familiarity with terms like TCP/IP, packet switching, and the Web, we can begin to understand the concept of an intranet. An intranet is a private, unique network implementation based on the technology, services, protocols (such as TCP/IP), and applications (such as the Web) of the Internet. Its purpose is to support an internal information system, and it is either physically separate, or protects itself from the outside world through the use of some security system, e.g., a "firewall," a hardware device or software that restricts the types of traffic or access to a network.

Intranets have become another phenomenon of this decade, a natural follow-on to the success of the Web. Every forward thinking company or element on the planet has realized the potential and has implemented or is in the process of implementing its own "Internet." Pacific Gas and Electric Company, Hewlett-Packard Corporation, and Bechtel Manufacturing are all examples of very large and successful intranet applications that have improved operations and productivity.

Indeed, a recent study by Palo Alto, California, research firm *Creative Networks, Inc.* found that the use of corporate intranets is exploding, as companies find that they save time and money. The survey, one of the first major studies of intranets according to the Wall Street Journal, concluded that intranet usage would more than double during 1997 over 1996.

1.4 WHAT IS AN *EXTRANET*?

There is much hype and a seemingly unending supply of "buzzwords" surrounding the Internet and its related technologies. These loosely defined terms create confusion among the managers, organizations, and perhaps especially among the users. The term extranet is a recent buzzword that really describes a special type of intranet. While *intranets* are internal systems designed to connect users within a specific "community of interest" (such as *Intelink* in the case of the U.S. Intelligence Community), *extranets* are extended intranets that connect to outside customers and other more strategic partners. There must be some sort of security associated with this connection, of course, and frequently this is accomplished through the use of passwords or other application level mechanisms. Therefore, a typical extranet strategy might be two discrete intranets with a secure link between them.

For example, the Mobil Corporation has developed its own extranet. This company is one of the leading oil, gas, and petrochemical companies in the world, with operations in over 100 countries. No stranger to network technologies, they make extensive use of SGML to coordinate the construction of their oil and gas facilities and were chronicled in the Chet Ensign book, *$GML the Billion Dollar Secret*. Their extranet connects all of their lubricant distributors around the world, using the Internet, to their intranet so that they can submit purchase orders, billing information, etc. Most extranet applications today are centered on some type of electronic commerce appli-cation.

In fact, one could view *Intelink* as an extranet. If you think of the entire Intelligence Community as a set of separate organizations, each with their own internal intranet serving their own domain, then Intelink could be thought of as the common mechanism, the extranet that connects them. The primary difference, of course, is that none of this occurs over the public Internet, and is based on a characterization of multiple security levels that is more formal, as we shall learn. And, the concept of electronic commerce does not enter in. Nevertheless, the concerns are exactly the same as the private sector.

1.5 THE INTELINK COMMUNITY

The "*Intelink* Community" is quite large and spans a broad spectrum of users since it consists of both intelligence "producers" and intelligence "user" organizations. Indeed, the *Intelink* Community is considered by many to be the "ultimate information producers" in terms of volume, number of users, and mission: to support efforts to ensure and maintain the security of this nation.

As you would expect, at the top of the *Intelink* Community is the Office of the President in the White House (Figure 1-6). And, in addition to the President, you might expect the 13 agencies of the U.S. Intelligence Community, including the Central Intelligence Agency, the National Security Agency, the

Figure 1-6 White House—Consumer of U.S. Intelligence.

Defense Intelligence Agency, and the recently created National Imagery and Mapping Agency (NIMA). But the *Intelink* Community also includes cabinet level organizations such as the Departments of Defense, Treasury, Energy, Justice, State, and Transportation, and the military service intelligence centers, commands, as well as other supporting organizations that may have access to one or more service levels provided by *Intelink*.

Figure 1-7 and the below chart depict many of the organizations within the *Intelink* Community, reflecting organizations that support intelligence operations from the "warfighter" in the cockpit or foxhole, through the intelligence analyst, to the senior policy makers of the U.S. Government. In DoD parlance, the term *warfighter* refers to the individual on the front lines of a conflict or potential conflict, and therefore an important end-user of information.

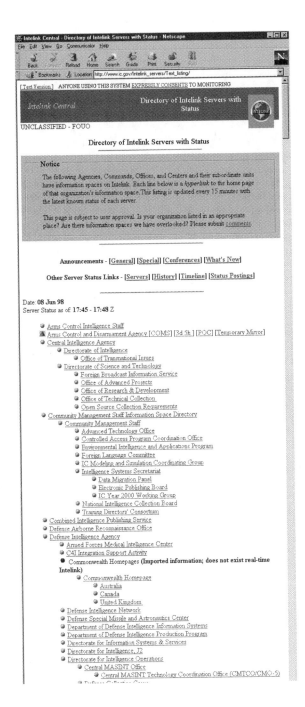

Figure 1-7 Screen Shot of the Intelink Community.

- Central MASINT Technology Coordination Office (CMTCO/CMO-5)
  - Defense Collection Group
  - Defense HUMINT Service
- Directorate for Intelligence Production
- Humint Imagery Server
- Joint Intelligence Virtual Architecture (JIVA)
- Joint Military Intelligence College
- Joint Military Intelligence Training Center
- Missile and Space Intelligence Center
- Office Of Technical Services
- US Defense Intelligence Liaison Office, London
- Department of Defense Office of the Space Architect
- Department of Energy, Office of Intelligence
- Department of State Bureau of Intelligence and Research
- Deputy Assistant Secretary of Defense Intelligence and Security
- Director of Central Intelligence
  - Balkan Task Force
  - Foreign Intelligence Relationships
  - National Intelligence Council
    - Tier II Project
- Intelligence Community Librarians' Committee
- Intelink Management Office
  - Intelink Information Management Directorate
  - Intelink Service Management Center
  - Security Policy and Plans Directorate
- Joint Reserve Intelligence Program
  - Joint Reserve Intelligence Connectivity Program
    - Fort Sheridan
  - Reserve Intelligence Integration Division (RIID)
- Joint Spectrum Center
- Joint Tactical Exploitation of National Systems
- National Counterintelligence Center
- National HUMINT Requirements Tasking Center
- National Imagery and Mapping Agency
  - National Imagery and Geospatial Policies
  - NIMA Imagery Intelligence
  - NIMA Geospatial Information
    - NIMA St Louis Targets-Gridded Products-Airfields
      - NIMA5D-St Louis Image Server
- National Military Command Center
- National Reconnaissance Office
- National Security Agency
  - Fort Gordon Regional SIGINT Operations Center
  - Unified Cryptologic Architecture for USCS 2010
- National SIGINT Committee
- Nonproliferation Center
- Nonproliferation and Arms Control Technical Working Group [COMS] [3d 5h] [POC] [Temporary Mirror]
- On-Site Inspection Agency
- Overhead Collection Management Center
- **Unified Commands**
  - Joint Command and Control Warfare Center
    - Warfighter Information Operations
  - Joint Warfare Analysis Center
  - US Atlantic Command USACOM
    - Atlantic Intelligence Command
    - US Army Forces Command FORSCOM
      - Ground Intelligence Support Activity-CONUS
        - III US Armored Corps-III CORPS
    - US Marine Forces, Atlantic MARFORLANT
    - US Atlantic Fleet LANTFLT
    - Special Operations Command Atlantic Command
  - US Central Command
    - ARCENT
    - **CENTAF** (server temporarily unavailable)
    - Joint Task Force Southwest Asia
    - COMUSNAVCENT/COMFIFTHFLT
  - US European Command
    - HQ USEUCOM
    - USEUCOM J2 Joint Analysis Center
    - Combined Task Force - Operation Northern Watch
    - United States Air Force, Europe
      - CAOC - National Intelligence Cell (NIC)
    - United States Army, Europe
      - USAREUR Combat Intelligence Readiness Facility
        - 66th MI GRP Requirements Management
          - AETCAE

Figure 1-7 *(Continued).*

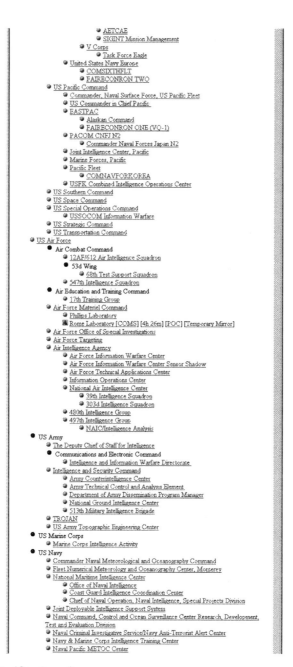

Figure 1-7 *(Continued).*

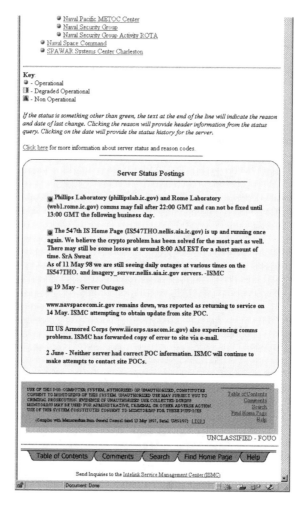

Figure 1-7 *(Continued).*

This person could be the pilot of a plane, the commander of a ship at sea, the operator of a tank, or a soldier in the field or foxhole.

US Intelligence Community Agencies
Central Intelligence Agency
    Directorate of Intelligence
    Directorate of Science and Technology

Foreign Broadcast Information Service
National Security Agency
Defense Intelligence Agency
National Reconnaissance Office
National Imagery and Mapping Agency
    National Imagery and Geospatial Policies
    Imagery Intelligence
    Geospatial Information
Army Intelligence
    Deputy Chief of Staff for Intelligence
    Army Intelligence and Security Command
    National Ground Intelligence Center
Naval Intelligence
    Office of Naval Intelligence
    Naval Security Group
    National Maritime Intelligence Center
Marine Corps Intelligence
    Marine Corps Intelligence Activity
Air Force Intelligence
    National Air Intelligence Center
Department of State
    Bureau of Intelligence and Research
Department of Energy
    Office of Energy Intelligence
Department of the Treasury
    Office of Intelligence Support
Federal Bureau of Investigation

US Air Force
    Air Combat Command
    Air Education and Training Command
    Air Force Material Command
    Office of Special Investigations

US Army
    Communications and Electronic Command
    Topographic Engineering Center

US Navy

    Meteorological and Oceanography Command
    Meteorology and Oceanography Center, Monterey
    Command, Control and Ocean Surveillance Center

DoD Unified and other Commands

    Atlantic Command
        US Army Forces Command
        US Marine Forces, Atlantic
        US Atlantic Fleet
        Special Operations Command, Atlantic
    Central Command
        Joint Task Force, South West Asia
    European Command
        Headquarters, European Command
        J2 Joint Analysis Center
        Combined Task Force
        US Army, Europe
        US Navy, Europe
    Pacific Command
        Naval Surface Force
        Alaskan Command
        Commander Naval Forces Japan
        Joint Intelligence Center, Pacific (JICPAC)
        Pacific Fleet
        Combined Intelligence Operations Center
    Southern Command
    US Space Command
    US Special Operations Command
        Information Warfare
    US Strategic Command
    US Transportation Command

Other Intelligence Related Organizations, Laboratories, and Task Forces

    Arms Control Intelligence Staff
    Community Management Staff
        Advanced Technology Office

Intelligence Systems Secretariat
Intelink Management Office
Information Management Directorate
Service Management Center
Security Policy and Plans Directorate
National SIGINT Committee
Combined Intelligence Publishing Service
Rome Laboratory
Nonproliferation and Arms Control Technical Working Group

It is clear from this partial listing that Intelink has the potential to touch every aspect of the warfighter of today. Remember Captain Scott O'Grady? He was the U.S. Air Force F-16 (Figure 1-8) pilot whose jet was downed on a mountainside in Bosnia in June 1995. Later, it was revealed that anti-aircraft missile batteries had previously been detected in the area that Captain O'Grady was supposed to fly, but the intelligence information failed to reach him in time. Similar to concerns expressed by General H. Norman Schwarzkopf after the 1991 Persian Gulf War, the failure of intelligence information to reach the warfighter at the time it is needed constitutes a long-standing and haunting intelligence dissemination issue. It has become clear that Intelink will play a major role in alleviating this problem.

1.6 WHAT IS THE PROBLEM TO BE SOLVED?

Why build an intranet? As the ultimate information producers spending billions of dollars annually, the Intelligence Community has always faced enormous in formation management challenges in the collection, processing, and dissemination of intelligence. In this ever-changing environment, they needed several things: an architectural framework that allowed for sharing of intelligence data, products, and information across the various intelligence organizations; a methodology for collaboration to facilitate their production; and an improved mechanism for their dissemination electronically.

On a personal note, I can still recall my assignment as a linguist to a remote outpost in the Middle East in 1962 during the Cuban Missile Crisis. All coordination of our intelligence collection requirements, all target research, dev-

Figure 1-8 U.S. Air Force F-16 Aircraft.

elopment and forwarding of time-sensitive information, indeed all processing and dissemination of our finished intelligence was accomplished over cumbersome, teletype circuits and other relatively low-speed communications media. Collaboration with our counterparts elsewhere and with NSA Headquarters meant asking a question, forwarding it on a special teletype circuit, and waiting until your shift the next day (if you were lucky) for the reply. Although many improvements were made to this basic approach over the next 30 years, the fundamental set of dissemination and collaboration problems remained.

A number of important factors have shaped and intensified the contemporary need for the information sharing and collaboration of intelligence information offered by the use of intranet technology. These factors were used in the development of *Intelink*.

1) Broadening Intelligence Dissemination Base

The customer set of the U.S. Intelligence Community requires a much broader base of intelligence dissemination today and in the foreseeable future. The world is no less dangerous today than it was during the Cold War. However, the wide diversity of U.S. intelligence requirements for the modern warfighter today sharply contrast the days of the Cold War, when there was essentially one adversary, the former Soviet Union. We once feared a global thermonuclear war that had the potential to destroy most of the planet in a single confrontation. However, today the focus is on a wide variety of potential adversaries and problems that range from control of weapons of mass destruction and terrorist activities, to economic and information warfare. Since the end of the Cold War, the intelligence mission also includes international law enforcement activities such as drug trafficking.

2) Increase in Exploitable Data/Information

A true information explosion has occurred. The amount of information available to intelligence producers continues to increase exponentially. Since not all information can be processed, smart tools and methods of sorting and determining which information we can use must be developed.

3) Government "Cutbacks"

Downsizing or "rightsizing" has become a way of life in the federal government this decade, and the Intelligence Community is no exception. Base closures, consolidations, and decreasing resources in terms of both funds and people continue to have the potential to adversely impact intelligence operations.

4) Need for Intelligence Community to Become ore "Agile"

This is perhaps the single most important factor. The Intelligence Community must become adaptive, flexible, and more "agile" as an enterprise in order respond to new and unexpected intelligence situations. They must be able to manage and share all of their information across the entire Intelligence Community, to include both the intelligence users as well as the intelligence producers. The current way of doing business simply cannot adapt fast enough.

While collectively these four factors became the basis of our migration to this exciting new technology, and resulted in the development of *Intelink*, there also was a general consensus among senior intelligence officials that this approach would provide the basis for improved management of our intelligence information. And, as the story of *Intelink* unfolds in this book, we can easily envision this intranet as the prototype of the "agile" intelligence enterprise of the 21st Century. We will examine how the government plans to accomplish this in Part Three of this book.

1.7 WHY IS AN INTRANET THE RIGHT SOLUTION?

Will an intranet help the Intelligence Community achieve its information sharing and collaborative needs as shaped by the four factors cited above? Timing is everything. Intranet and Web-based technology development have come on the scene and are maturing at precisely the right time to play a key role in managing information for the Intelligence Community, and indeed, the entire federal government. Several reasons point to an intranet as the right solution:

1) "Killer App:" Electronic Publishing

Every new automated capability needs a "killer application," the one area that single-handedly eclipses all other uses and proves its usefulness. For the Intelligence Community, this is *electronic publishing*. The Intelligence Community knew it had to improve the way in which it managed its information, including the way in which it was distributed to the ultimate consumer. *Intelink* provided a new strategic direction for intelligence dissemination. In addition, they realized that there are many other critical mission applications and other distribution systems that intranet technology had the potential to enhance such as the use of search engines, directory services, and other analytical tools.

2) Functionality: Multisecurity Level Collaborative Environment

In addition to electronic publishing, the Intelligence Community realized that it needed to foster interaction and collaboration among its analysts and users, all within a multiple security level environment. This included the need to search and retrieve information classified at various levels, across both database and organizational boundaries. System users needed rapid access to information regardless of their physical location, location of the data, or classification level of the data.

3) Other Advantages of this Technology

There are a number of other clear advantages that the Intelligence Community seniors evaluated in making their decision to invest in *Intelink*. They included:

• *Lower Costs*

One generally thinks of two business models in justifying the use of new technology:

- Save Money
- Improve Quality of Product

Web and intranet technology related tools continue to increase in speed and capacity while constantly decreasing in cost. However, in the case of *Intelink,* improving the way in which intelligence is produced always wins out over saving money. Nevertheless, productivity improvements and even material savings, such as reduced paper costs, in the distribution of intelligence must not be discounted.

• *Ease of Use*

The ability to share information easily on an intranet application like *Intelink,* is critical to its success. The ease of use today is based on the use of International Standards such as the Standard Generalized Markup Language (SGML), and the proliferation of commercially available tools. The simplicity and power of multimedia Web browsers developed in the past few years have had a profound impact on intranet development.

● *Shorter Tool Development Cycles*

The global Internet's dramatic emergence and phenomenal growth are fundamentally changing the way we work, our educational opportunities, and even the way in which we are entertained. With this growth has come correspondingly robust opportunities to exploit this high value market. As a result, the application development vendor community continues to turn out new tools and technologies at an ever-increasing rate—improved tools that can be integrated immediately (or at least relatively easy) into an existing environment.

● *Use of Existing Hardware/Software/Network Infrastructures*

Intelink was implemented initially on existing Department of Defense and Intelligence Community networks. The ability to take advantage of an existing, secure networking environment was a key advantage for *Intelink* deployment.

The bottom line is clear: when one examines the functions that are delivered by *Intelink,* (i.e., what *Intelink* actually does), and its content (i.e., the information available on *Intelink*), a compelling business case can be made that shows that *Intelink* improves intelligence production and distribution. As a prototype of the future world of intelligence, ("Virtual Intelligence"), *Intelink* has become *the* strategic tool for open information management within the U.S. Intelligence Community.

Chapter 2

A High-Level Look at *Intelink*

We know that Intelink is the intranet of the U.S. Intelligence Community—a secure, private collection of networks implemented on existing government and commercial communications facilities. We begin our examination of Intelink in this chapter with a high-level look at its functions, services, tools, security levels, and operating environments. This is followed by an explanation of the specific levels— "classes" or instantiations of Intelink. The chapter concludes with discussion of the implementation philosophy of Intelink—its security tenets, use of open systems as well as commercial off-the-shelf products, and migration to a fully Web-based environment using the concept of an "information space."

2.1 INTELINK SUPPORT FRAMEWORK

The overall support framework for Intelink addresses a number of issues and concerns related to the methods used for the exchange, collaboration, analysis, production, and dissemination of intelligence. The intent was to unify these various methods and allow system users to search, discover, and retrieve information, while permitting collaboration among various "communities of interest." Indeed, a goal of Intelink is to improve the interoperability of existing automated intelligence systems, across organizational boundaries, while not adversely impacting on the internal architectures of the military services and national agencies (Figure 2-1).

2.1.1 Categories of Intelink Service

To accomplish this goal, Intelink has been implemented with a "standards-based" architecture[9] and provides support to intelligence producers, users, and decision-makers in four primary service areas:

1) Intelligence Product (Finished Intelligence) Dissemination

The "killer app" for Intelink, this includes publishing and distribution of multimedia intelligence information electronically, rather than in a paper-based, text-only message or report. Intelink provides near real-time access to all available information on a particular topic, no matter where it originates, and no matter where the user is located. And they can access this information exactly when it is needed, rather than having it sent to them automatically and then not be able to locate it.

2) Analytical Research Support

Databases are now on-line for both research and production with very sophisticated search and retrieval tools allowing information access across not only organizational boundaries, but across the boundaries of

---

[9] Additional detail is provided in Chapter 3.

Figure 2-1 Official Intelink Icon.

the databases themselves. In addition, access to all types of information sources is now available electronically, providing a rich source of unclassified or "open source" information, as well as library functions and other assistance.

3) Collaboration Facilities

Intelink users are able to collaborate within their own "communities of interest" while actually viewing common data or reports and graphics right at their own computer terminals. Analysts are able, for example, to annotate reports on-line, or discuss potential changes by voice or even video exchange. This real-time, live exchange greatly enhances the interaction of analysts as well as reporters and users of intelligence.

4) Training and Administration

Intelink provides the capability for various multimedia training, education services, and "just-in-time" training for intelligence operations. Current training offerings range from on-line information hyperlinks provided by the central Intelink Office to formal courses "posted" to Intelink by the various participating Intelligence Agencies.

2.1.2 Early Intelink Management Structure

After discussions with then Director of Central Intelligence James Woolsey, founding father Steve Schanzer knew that furthering the business aims of the Intelligence Community was a key objective of the implementation of Intelink. Those business aims included creating a *market environment*—a high demand for intelligence products and services so that Intelligence Community customers could better fulfill their own individual business objectives. Schanzer felt that in order to create this market environment, he would need to do two things:

1) Focus on the *content* of intelligence information—not get caught up in the hype or glitz that might surround a new, high technology initiative. Indeed, Intelink was the first real attempt to manage content across the Intelligence Community.

2) Create a "Virtual Intelligence Analyst," i.e., give all intelligence analysts in the Intelligence Community the ability to share information, collaborate on issues of common interest, and electronically disseminate the results of their analysis.

As a result, Schanzer formed three groups to implement Intelink and to ensure the management of the content of intelligence information:

• Information Management Group

Schanzer and his deputy, Fred Harrison assumed full control of these early efforts, which were conducted within the Intelligence Systems Secretariat at the CIA.

• Engineering Group

This group, headed by Dennis Eshoo of the NSA, was responsible for new technology development for Intelink.

• **Operations Group—the "Intelink Service Management Center" (see below).**

The Information Management Group and the Engineering Group were subsequently folded into the new Intelink Management Office (IMO). But with the establishment of this early structure, Intelink was on the road to success.

2.1.3 The ISMC: Intelink Service Management Center

Steve Schanzer and Fred Harrison immediately began to assemble a cadre of top-notch talent to handle the day-to-day chores of Intelink. The result was the *"Intelink Service Management Center"* (ISMC: pronounced Iz–Mick) —located at the National Security Agency at Fort Meade, Maryland. All Intelink operations are now supported and monitored by the ISMC (Figure 2-2), which operates on a full 24-hour, seven-days-a-week basis. Essentially, the ISMC maintains all network services, assists Intelink subscribers with their operational questions/needs as required, and administers all security mechanisms and procedures. These activities ensure the stability, security, and availability of Intelink as an information service (Figure 2-3).

Early on, the ISMC was the only full-time Intelink staff, so the center staff also participated in all development and planning activities. Even today, the ISMC has a special role in that it leads the efforts for technology insertion for the Intelink Community—ensuring that they can take advantage of the benefits of new information technology from both the government as well as the commercial sector. It can be said that the concept of a service management center—like ISMC—is what separates an intranet—like Intelink—from the unregulated global Internet. Intelink users always have a support staff to which they can turn for problems, advice, and the latest technology.

The ISMC staff—or "ISMCians (pronounced Iz-Mick-ee-ans)—are a professional, dedicated staff. As part of an Intelligence Community-wide project, they are on "loan" from their originating agencies, which continue to pay their salaries. And they tend to stay a long time. All of the founding partners and original team chiefs of the ISMC—they were present when Vice-President Gore presented the "Hammer Award" to Intelink—remained in their

Figure 2-2 Official ISMC Icon.

jobs as this book was published. For example, Bill Campbell, the head of the ISMC, delayed his government retirement because he was "having so much fun." He also strongly feels that the early successes of Intelink were a result of the dedicated ISMC staff and their freedom to operate "independently," outside of the conventional Intelligence Community oversight mechanisms.

Figure 2-3 ISMC Operations—Control Panel.

Campbell has stated

In the beginning, Intelink was not implemented using formal U.S. Government "Project Management" methods. Since Intelink crossed nearly all organizational boundaries within the Intelligence Community, trying to get agreement on policies, practices or even which intranet tools to employ, would have been too cumbersome, time consuming, and mostly likely would have led to failure. Schanzer and Harrison convinced NSA to host the ISMC. To the credit of NSA senior management, operation of Intelink was left as the responsibility of the site manager, with no technical or management oversight. The individuals initially selected for this job left their individual Agency allegiances behind, took on a corporate Intelligence Community persona, and endeavored to adopt the tools, services, and policies that were best for the Intelligence Community as a whole. New tools, services, and capabilities were implemented based upon technical merit. During this initial period, the ISMC did not seek a vote of approval from the broader Community and relied upon user acceptance to determine success.

The synergistic effect of this team is obvious: Campbell, Randy Marks, the Technical Team leader; Susanne Rosewell, the Intelink *Information System Security Officer* (ISSO); and Rene Cook, CIA liaison; all continue to communicate regularly with Steve Schanzer. And as the Chief Operating Officer of his new organization, Schanzer has implemented another Intelink-like intranet for the U.S. Defense Investigative Service.

2.1.3.1 ISMC Responsibilities

Exactly what does the ISMC do? There are four general areas of responsibility that ensure the necessary daily operations, assistance to users, security administration, and future viability of Intelink. These four areas are:

1) **Intelink's "Central Services," or Around-the-Clock Operations**

• Developing and maintaining all "central services" including the Intelink "Home Page," which is its focal point for access (Figure 2-4);

• Providing the Intelink Help Desk and related functions;

• Processing all service trouble reports;

• Maintaining an accounting database containing usage and performance statistics for Intelink management as well as users and producers.

2) **Maintenance of Operational Hardware/Software Configuration**

• Acquiring and ensuring operational readiness of all ISMC hardware and software, including all centrally-managed Intelink equipment;

Figure 2-4 Official Intelink Central Icon.

• Maintaining a software and information distribution facility, including a software repository capable of electronically distributing all Intelink software to interested users.

3) Management of the Security Infrastructure

• Performing ISMC security assessments and administering operational security, including investigating and reporting all security incidents, and issuing advisory warnings;

• Managing the Intelink security certificate infrastructure;[10]

• Providing ad hoc security assistance to the Intelink Community;

• Facilitating the creation of classified "communities of interest" on a particular target or interest area.

4) Management of the Intelink Technology Program

• Ensuring that the Intelink Community benefits from the identification, evaluation, and early introduction of new information technology

---

[10] For additional detail, see Chapter 5.

from the government as well as industry (includes, for example, the latest security products and new collaborative tools);

• Operating the *Intelink Technology Working Group* (ITWG) with membership from the major Intelink participating agencies such as the NSA, CIA, DIA, NIMA, and the NRO;

• Maintaining the interconnected set of research and development computers from the various laboratories from across the Intelink Community;

• Maintaining a separate commercial technology test computer that can be used by all interested Intelink users to try out the latest commercial off-the-shelf software deemed useful in Intelink operations.

2.1.4 The IMO: Intelink Management Office

Intelink began to grow rapidly after its initial operations began in earnest in 1995. By the time that Ronald D. Elliott—the successor to Steve Schanzer—arrived as the second Director of the Intelligence Systems Secretariat (ISS), Intelink operations had become a full-time job. Ron Elliott knew that Intelink operations, planning, and engineering activities needed to be focused. Other Intelligence Community leaders agreed, realizing that what was needed was a separate program office—managed by the ISS for the Intelligence Community as a whole—tasked with the management, development, and enhancement of the Intelink family of services.

The result was the formation of the *Intelink Management Office* (IMO). The overall objective of the IMO is to manage the operations and growth of the Intelink concept, ensuring that appropriate strategic resource investment and commitment are made to maintain its viability and importance. Oversight of the IMO is provided by a special *Senior Information Managers* (SIM) Panel chaired by the ISS Director. The SIM Panel, which consists of the *Corporate Information Officers* or other senior members of each of the Intelligence Community Agencies and elements, meets on a monthly basis to discuss Intelink related issues and other areas of common concern. According to the 1997 *IMO Management Plan*, other IMO objectives include the following, as shown on the next page.

• Fostering the integration of Intelink into the daily operations of the Intelligence Community in order to broaden Intelink's contribution to achieving the intelligence mission;

• Establishing new funding mechanisms to facilitate and sustain future growth;

• Managing the day-to-day operations of Intelink;

• Enhancing Intelink capabilities so that a greater amount and variety of information is available;

• Establishing a viable security program that supports service and information access controls, auditing capabilities; ultimately, the creation of a single Intelink for all levels of security classification;

• Establishing a viable information management program that improves the user's ability to find information and applies the notion of information labeling to facilitate security and information management activities;

• Enhancing support infrastructures to ensure that future Intelink services enjoy the stability of a robust and well-administered information environment;

• Establishing a viable training program to ensure that all producers and users can effectively use existing and new services;

• Developing a technology integration program to ensure that Intelink enjoys the benefits of early introduction of new information technology;

• Establishing standard/preferred products and mechanisms for sharing these products through licensing agreements across the Intelink Community.

The overall strategy is to develop a strong and viable "federation" of intelligence users, producers, and service providers that will contribute to the achievement of these objectives.

2.1.4.1 IMO Structure

The structure of the Intelink Management Office contains the office of the Intelink Director (currently James P. Peak from the Defense Intelligence Agency), the Deputy Director (currently Janice Hite from the NSA), and the Associate Director (currently Mac Schuler from the CIA). Originally, the IMO reported directly to the SIM Panel, chaired by the Director of the Intelligence Systems Secretariat. It now reports to a special Intelligence Community Board of Directors known as the *Intelink Management Group*. The IMG is currently chaired by John Dahms, the *Corporate Information Officer* of the Central Intelligence Agency. The SIM Panel has decreed that the Director position shall be a two-year tour alternating between the CIA and the DIA. The Deputy Director on the other hand, will always be selected from the NSA. Together they are responsible for the overall management and guidance of all Intelink services.

The IMO, as presently configured, consists of three primary sub-components; the original Intelink Service Management Center (ISMC) discussed earlier, and two additional directorates:

1) Security and Policy and Plans Directorate

This Directorate, currently managed by Jack Torok from the CIA, is charged with establishing a comprehensive yet pragmatic security environment for Intelink, by developing and coordinating all security plans, policies, architecture, and standards. With the concept of *risk management* as the overall guide, this Intelink security environment must strike a balance between security requirements and information access. Example tasks include security education and training, participating in government certification and accreditation activities, and assessing the security solutions for other Intelink related programs such as the *Global Command and Control System* (GCCS). GCCS is the new DoD system for efficiently delivering command and control capabilities to the warfighter. One of the mission applications of GCCS includes part of Intelink.

2) Information Management Directorate

Improved information management is a primary goal of Intelink. The Information Management Directorate, currently headed by William

Fleming from DIA, is engaged in improving the process of organizing and structuring information for Intelink and managing its overall *information space*, while remaining responsive to technical innovation. It essentially provides a forum for intelligence users and producers with separate teams in three primary areas:

• **Information Organization and Process Team**

This team is responsible for developing and maintaining a complete current model of all information flow and organization. Thus, it provides the "big picture" of the overall landscape of the information within a particular area.

• **Consumer Requirements Team**

This team gathers, reviews, and responds to all customer requirements that are received, making them the lead consumer advocate for the Intelink Community. Through telephone calls, personal on-site visits, video teleconferencing, e-mail, and specific Intelink User Conferences, they are able to obtain an in-depth understanding of how users interact with Intelink. This allows them to respond rapidly and inform, educate, and train users on new and existing Intelink products and services.

• **Production Support Team**

This team works primarily with the intelligence producers. They ensure that the intelligence production and publication operations—the electronic publishing community—have everything they need. Example activities include the incorporation of appropriate hyperlinks into finished intelligence, the integration and standardization of metadata, the application of security classification labeling on reports, the standardization of the home pages of producers, and even the development of new Web-based software products.

2.1.4.2 Industry Liaison Program

Jim Peak and his IMO have also established a very strong private industry liaison program in an attempt to influence the functionality of commercial products to support the Intelink mission. Of course, this also allows them to maintain a leading-edge knowledge of emerging technology. To respond to this need, an ad hoc and unofficial fourth organization has emerged in the IMO, known as the Technology Integration Directorate, which is headed by Randy Marks from the ISMC.

A recent example of IMO industry partnering was a project named *Spitfire*. In Spitfire, the IMO teamed with perhaps the most prominent purveyor of Internet "push" technology, *PointCast*. The idea was to potentially enhance the relevance of intelligence information by automatically "pushing" various classes of intelligence to predetermined subscribers. The application of *PointCast* to Intelink is discussed in more detail in Chapter 7.

2.1.5 How Does this Relate to Business?

Let's step back a moment and assess the basic support framework of Intelink by examining its relationship to the business leader of today. We can do this by summarizing a number of basic organizational attributes that led to the success of Intelink. For example:

• **The overall organizational structure was essential to the success of Intelink.**

Starting with the Intelligence Community Management Staff, through the Intelligence Systems Secretariat, the Intelink Management Office, and the various IMO organizations, there are well coordinated, clear lines of authority and responsibility.

• **Sufficient staffing needs were addressed, and sufficient resources were allocated.**

Despite the fact that Intelink was not initially funded and staffed through the traditional Intelligence Community budgetary mechanisms, the necessary people and money were acquired.

• **The Intelink support framework contains a good balance of hard and soft skills.**

At all levels of the Intelink structure, there are nontechnical intelligence professionals working side-by-side with computer scientists and engineers. This balance has allowed Intelink to take greater advantage of all related technology within its specific intelligence environment.

These are considered to be lessons learned and are recommended for business enterprises.

2.2 INSTANTIATIONS OF INTELINK

With an understanding of the above basic support framework, we can now address the four basic families of Intelink. Classification levels within the Intelligence Community and the U.S. Government at large currently dictate several "flavors" or separate instantiations of Intelink. However, as technological advances in both security level functionality and telecommunications service and capacity mature, it is conceivable that the future Intelink environment will be based on only two simple and basic implementation levels: "Classified" and "Unclassified." In this future environment, those allowed to access certain information will be given permission to do so *transparently*, i.e., there will be no need for extra effort on the part of the user. Those without permission will be denied access.

There are currently three basic families or classes of Intelink under the direct purview of the Intelink Management Office, and a fourth instantiation managed separately by the CIA. Operating primarily on an independent basis today, it is expected that these four versions of Intelink will evolve into a "virtual information space" separated into various segments or "communities of interest" by cryptographic and security level access methods. The four instantiations of Intelink, which operate on nearly 400 discrete servers from nearly 300 physical sites for literally hundreds of thousands of users, are summarized in the following sections.

2.2.1 "Intelink-SCI"

This was the initial capability for the *Intelink* family with operations beginning in December 1994. "SCI" means *Special Compartmented Information* in the

Intelligence world and Intelink-SCI currently has the largest number of intelligence *producers* (and users) accessing and exchanging the largest amount of intelligence information. This information is classified at up through, but no higher than, Top Secret/SCI (some agencies have information that is classified higher than Top Secret/SCI). It can be found at all thirteen national agencies that comprise the Intelligence Community, as well as most major intelligence organizations, DoD military commands, scientific and technical centers, participating law enforcement agencies, and many other intelligence centers. In all, there are over 50,000 Intelink-SCI users operating on nearly 200 servers at over 100 individual physical sites. Access to the system, through the Department of Defense "Joint Worldwide Intelligence Communications System" (JWICS) network operated by the Defense Intelligence Agency, is provided to authorized users with the appropriate security clearances.

2.2.2 "Intelink-SecretNet" or "Intelink-S"

The Intelink-S network is used predominantly for intelligence support to the "warfighters" and supporting military commands, and even in communities outside of DoD, for information classified up through *Secret* only. Access is provided to these intelligence *users* through the "Secret Internet Protocol Router Network," or "SIPRnet," operated by the Defense Information Systems Agency (DISA), the DoD organization responsible for the communications infrastructure for all U.S. warfighters. Intelink-S currently has the largest numbers or servers (nearly 200 on about 160 individual physical sites), and a significant user population growth rate. DISA estimates that the total number of SIPRnet clients with access to Intelink-S is about 265,000. It is true that, as in Intelink-SCI, access is provided to both intelligence information producers and users with the appropriate security clearances. However, the bulk of Intelink-S system users are categorized as intelligence information *users.* Indeed, one could view the primary users and producers on Intelink-SCI as the Intelink *intranet,* and the remote SIPRnet clients on Intelink-S as the Intelink *extranet.*

2.2.3 "Intelink-PolicyNet" or "Intelink-P"

This network, which went operational in 1995, is managed and operated by the CIA. It specifically supports very high-level U.S. Government policy makers, such as the President's National Security Advisor, and the Director of Central Intelligence. It provides this select group with multimedia intelligence products containing extremely sensitive, "compartmented" information. Operating on a private, secure, high bandwidth network, it is used primarily as a method to disseminate special reports and other intelligence products that are not available through any other class of Intelink service. At this time, Intelink-P usage, which includes one-way access into Intelink-SCI, is very limited by security clearance and special approval. Participation includes small numbers of people at the State Department, the National Security Council, the two intelligence committees of the U.S. Congress (House Permanent Select Committee on Intelligence, and the Senate Select Committee on Intelligence), and senior officials at several of the national level intelligence agencies.

2.2.4 "Intelink-UnclassifiedNet" or "Intelink-U"

Intelink-U is the newest network in the Intelink series and at this time clearly has the greatest growth potential. Accessed through a "Virtual Private Network," it is available to all users who are either members of the "Open Source Information Service" (OSIS), or have been approved by OSIS.[11] The new Community Open Source Program Office (COSPO), located at the CIA, is handling the development, coordination, and implementation of OSIS. COSPO, which was established under the authority of the Director of Central Intelligence, is responsible for all aspects of the open source program, including strategic planning, program formulation and representation, sponsorship of new initiatives, operational services, systems architecture, and open source advocacy across the Intelligence Community.

Intelink-U is beginning to employ fiber links to over 50 data bases and other security domains that contain Intelligence Community information that is available from all "open," or unclassified sources. This area is touted to be the single largest data repository in the world.

---

[11] We will discuss *Virtual Private Networks*, which combine the flexibility and cost structure of public networks with the security and performance advantages of a private network, in more detail in Chapter 4.

2.2.5 Other Instantiations

Although these four instantiations of Intelink are generally considered to be the primary family of Intelink services extending to what is generally referred to as the *Intelink Community*, other intranets related to the U.S. Intelligence Community continue to appear.

Perhaps the best example is *Intelink-Commonwealth* or Intelink-C. Intelink-C is the intranet that serves the association of the United States and three of its allies, the United Kingdom, Canada, and Australia, and is not under the formal purview of the Intelink Management Office. Intelink-C is represented in the United States by the Defense Intelligence Agency, in the United Kingdom by the Defence Intelligence Service (DIS), in Canada by the J2/Director General Intelligence (J2/DG Int), and in Australia by the Defence Intelligence Organization (DIO). Intelink-C has its own private, Top Secret-SCI network as part of the *Joint Worldwide Intelligence Communications System* (JWICS). This instantiation of Intelink is especially noteworthy for three primary reasons:

1) The concept of an interactive Web among four U.S. allies that share intelligence information is a major step with tremendous potential for the future.

2) The Senior Information Managers (SIM) Panel of the ISS has declared that it is within their vision to have Intelink-C under the purview of the Intelink Management Office.

3) Intelink-C can serve as the prototype for expansion of this concept to other U.S. allies and coalition partners.

Now that we have a better grasp of the management structure and current instantiations of Intelink, we can examine its implementation philosophy, i.e., the numerous principles that have helped to make Intelink so successful.

2.3 IMPLEMENTATION PHILOSOPHY

The implementation philosophy of Intelink has slowly evolved since its inception in 1994, taking advantage of lessons learned. However, Steve

Schanzer and his successor, Ronald Elliott, and other senior Intelligence Community officials, have adhered to a general set of guiding principles that have fostered acceptance of the Intelink concept and enhanced communications and information exchange. These principles include maximizing the "return on investment," security, the use of standards and commercial products, and attaining full migration to a Web-based environment.

2.3.1 "Return on Investment"

One of the most notable aspects of Intelink implementation was the absence of a large, up-front, dollar investment. By taking advantage of initially low cost browsers—the government, like many users, initially paid for the opportunity to use Mosaic and later Netscape browser software—the Intelligence Community was able to successfully promote the concept. More importantly from a cost perspective, the communications networks and the actual computers and related hardware were already in place. By taking advantage of this installed infrastructure, the Intelligence Systems Secretariat was able to implement Intelink without going through the normal, lengthy, budgetary approval process. This development of a new and literally revolutionary state-of-the-art intelligence dissemination and collaboration tool with no up-front dollar investment produced the best possible "return on investment."

This emphasis on optimizing the funds spent on Intelink continues today. In order to continue smoothly in the implementation of Intelink, the ISS must ensure that the appropriate resources, both funds and human resources, remain available. There must be a firm commitment to a sound fiscal basis across the entire Intelink Community, including all users, producers, and various service providers. Human resources include both government and contractor personnel. Four major intelligence agencies have stepped forward as "hosts" of Intelink: the National Security Agency, the Central Intelligence Agency, the Defense Intelligence Agency, and the National Imagery and Mapping Agency.

Within the Intelink Management Office, funds are currently allocated primarily for contractor support, acquisition of hardware and software, training, and travel. Government personnel are supplied to the IMO at no charge, i.e., on a "non-reimbursable rotation." This means that personnel assigned to an Intelink directorate or center remain employees of their parent agency while on assignment to Intelink. IMO administrative costs are shared by the four host agencies, NSA, CIA, DIA, and NIMA. Likewise, facility and logistical costs are also covered by the four host organizations, depending on the location of the activity. For example, the facility costs of the ISMC are the responsibility of the NSA, since the ISMC is located at NSA Headquarters.

2.3.2 Continued Commitment to "Need-to-Know" Security

True multilevel security has become somewhat of a "Holy Grail"—always around the corner, but never attained.[12] As a result, current implementation of Intelink is based on the four instantiations described above in Section 2.2. Indeed, even before Intelink could begin operations, the long-time Intelligence Community practice of reducing security risks by disseminating information on a "need-to-know" basis—that is, only to those who have been both approved and deemed to actually need the information to perform their job—had to be waived. Seeking and acquiring this permission was no small feat, and ultimately involved the Director of Central Intelligence himself. Permission was finally granted, and Intelink was launched. As one can imagine, there were many pockets of resistance—people who were adamantly opposed to waiving or even relaxing the "need-to-know" principle. But, interestingly, once the success of Intelink had been established, there was no turning back, and very little talk of turning back.

Indeed, now that Intelink has been successfully in operation for some time, a somewhat increasingly common belief is that perhaps Intelink *killed* the need-to-know principle, at least on networks. Current Intelink Director James Peak disagrees. "I'm increasingly suspicious of that common wisdom," he says. "First, the principle of protecting sources and methods has not changed at all, and that, to my mind, was at the center of the need-to-know principle. Second, if the need-to-know principle is, in fact, dead, I think it may have been more a victim of history than of Web technology."

A metaphor originally used by James Woolsey in an appearance to Congress, likened the end of the Cold War and the demise of the Soviet Union to "slaying the dragon." Woolsey compared the future of American foreign

---

[12] This is discussed in more detail in Chapter 5.

policy to living in a jungle inhabited by a bewildering variety of poisonous snakes and stated that, "in many ways, the snakes are harder to keep track of than the dragon ever was." Thus, the biggest problem that faces the implementers and followers of the need-to-know principle is this question: *Who needs to know what and when?*

The world today is characterized by much uncertainty with respect to threats to our national security. In our contemporary unstable geopolitical world, it clearly is no longer a case of a single threat of Communism, or a single target such as the former Soviet Union. The intelligence analysis process of today is very unpredictable, and certainly not hierarchical in nature. International crime, narcotics trafficking, terrorism, even attempts at hostile information warfare, collectively require a re-look at how we implement our security policies. This understanding has become a cornerstone of Intelink development and growth.

2.3.3 Use of Open Systems and Commercial "Off-the-Shelf" Products

From the inception of Intelink, the ISS has mandated both the use of commercial off-the-shelf (COTS) products and the concept of "open systems." Within the Department of Defense (DoD), and within the computer systems development field as a whole, greater use of COTS products has become commonplace. According to the *Software Engineering Institute* (SEI), many groups, from industry, academia, and government, have mandated the practice since the early 1990's. At the same time, according to the SEI, the use of "open systems" has grown significantly.

They should know. As a federally funded research and development center, the Software Engineering Institute has a broad charter to address the transition of software engineering technology. The SEI is an integral component of Carnegie Mellon University and is sponsored by the Office of the Under Secretary of Defense for Acquisition and Technology. The Intelligence Community, particularly the DoD components, has had a special relationship with SEI since SEI's inception in 1984. Indeed, NSA, for example, has regularly participated in SEI activities and normally has a software engineer on-site at Carnegie Mellon in Pittsburgh.

The concept of open systems is often confused with the use of COTS products. Tricia Oberndorf of the SEI offers a brief summary of the key points in this technology:

- The term "COTS" refers to products that one can purchase, ready-made, from a manufacturer. (COTS products can be obtained, for example, from an outlet, catalogue, price list, or from the Internet.) It is understood that one is getting an item that will do the job at hand quickly, efficiently, and at a reasonable price.

- The term "Open System" refers to interacting software, hardware, and human components that satisfy a stated need, with components that are fully defined by, and conform to, the "standard interfaces" that are maintained by various public consensus mechanisms such as the World Wide Web Consortium (W3C).

- One can certainly use COTS products without having an "open system," and can also have an open system without the extensive use of COTS products.

- The use of both COTS products and open systems architectures are important goals that enhance our ability to create systems quickly and cost-effectively, while improving their performance.

The use of this philosophy has significantly improved the implementation of Intelink. A number of COTS products are discussed in follow-on chapters, including the discussion of Intelink tools in Chapter 6, and intranet and SGML tools in Chapter 8.

2.3.4 Migration to Full Web-Based Environment

Another key assumption and implementation principle related to the creation of Intelink is that users, producers, and service providers will work together to ensure a continuous migration of the information services infrastructure, or the Intelink "information space," to a content-rich and Web-based environment. This means a total commitment to continue to move from the first Intelink experiment in 1994 to a robust, multiple security level, total Intelligence Community-wide implementation based on the global Internet. Here are some of the basic tenets that Intelink is using to ensure a successful transition to a Web-based environment:

• Following the W3C

The Intelink Management Office wisely chose to follow the lead of the World Wide Web Consortium. It even joined the W3C, becoming an official member organization. By choosing the activities of the W3C as the benchmark, this means that whenever they change Web standards, Intelink will implement that change six months later. For example, when the W3C announced the adoption of HTML 3.2 at the Sixth International WWW Conference in Santa Clara, California in April 1997, Intelink mandated the use of HTML 3.2 effective October 1997. Likewise, with the W3C announcement in December of its acceptance of the eXtensible Markup Language (XML), the IMO encouraged the adoption of this promising new approach to document management. The reasoning behind their following the W3C is simple: the W3C deliberations are open to the public, the results are accepted by industry, and the enhancement of the World Wide Web is their prime consideration. Following their lead is in the best interests of the Intelink Community.

• Using Metadata Standards

The Intelink Community has launched an ambitious effort to implement the concept of "metadata," or "data about data." Additional detail is provided in Chapter 7, but essentially the idea is to improve the performance of the various "search" engines in use on Intelink by "tagging" items of known interest. Many Intelink users have complained about the difficulty of finding the information that they need, and metadata will help alleviate that problem. While much progress is being made to use the Standard Generalized Markup Language (SGML) or its derivatives such as the new XML—see the case studies in Chapter 8—the fact remains that adopting a set of metadata content tags will provide Intelink with measurable improvement in the interim. Given the use of metadata tags, metadata *standards* ensure that all Intelink users can use the interim process—optimizing the use of search engines.

• Push and Pull Concepts

In the Intelink world, it is not really clear whether the "push" or "smart push" or "pull" metaphor for content will be valid in the long run. The World Wide Web metaphor refers to the ability for Intelink users to "pull" desired reports or other information from the network as desired. In addition, information can be "pushed" to users automatically with available tools that embed an appropriate hypertext link.

Intelink has made a commitment to exploring innovative ways to exploit the Web environment and take advantage of emerging technologies that enhance the way in which content can get through. In Chapter 7, we discuss Project Spitfire, the Intelink experiment with using the popular PointCast commercial product for "smart push" of intelligence information.

We introduced Intelink and provided some necessary background in Chapter 1. In Chapter 2, we have discussed the overall support and management framework of Intelink, including its current instantiations and implementation philosophy. With this high-level look at Intelink, we are now ready to look at Part 2—the issues and challenges such as standards and security, as well as the tools, with which Intelink has grappled. We will conclude Part 2 with Chapter 8—a look at some of the Intelink case studies.

Part Two
Intelink Issues and Challenges

Chapter 3

Closed System, Open Standards

Why are "standards" so important to managing information today? To begin to get an answer, we need only to turn to our everyday life experiences. As we continue to be bombarded by new technology in the home, we are constantly reminded of the presence or absence of standards. Here in the United States, we enjoy a standard interface to our electric power in the form of a two—or three if grounded—pronged plug that fits nicely into our standard wall receptacle. And the power itself is standard—110/115 volts at 60 Hertz—which means that all of our appliances will work. Never mind that in Europe, for example, the standard is 220/230 volts and 50 Hertz. At least we have a standard here. Try to interchange the power cords on the cellular phones of two different manufacturers in your car, however, and you will find that they will fit your car (standard 12-Volt, negative ground, and standard receptacle), but not both phones (no standard). Try to play a VCR tape recorded on equipment in Australia (PAL standard) on your own VCR after you return to the U.S. and you will find that you can't. Mr. William P. Crowell, the former Deputy Director of the National Security Agency, was always fond of pointing out the ramifications to the electronics and home entertainment industry if we did not have this simple standard, acceptable by all, which has been with us for decades. He was referring to the *RCA phono jack*—used on every television, VCR, and stereo equipment to interconnect audio and video components. Without that standard interface, the electronic audio/video component industry certainly would not be enjoying vendor interoperability and the resulting consumer confidence and satisfaction.

In the world of information technology, the need for standards is just as critical. We simply cannot achieve our goals of integration and interoperability of systems without them. All of us who have experienced first hand the shortcomings of what years from now will be referred to as "primitive" home computers, have been faced with a dilemma. While we do not want to stifle competition—while we do not want one man or one company to "rule" the world—we secretly ponder, "Gee, wouldn't it be nice if we had only *one* interface, and everything worked?"

A very analogous situation existed only a few years ago within the DoD, and exists today in many companies in the private sector. In the late 1980's each of the military services had deployed quite a variety of systems, mostly incompatible with one another, that were responsible for the delivery of intelligence information down through the chain of command, to combat units and eventually to the individual warfighter. The interoperability problems became apparent during the Persian Gulf War in 1991, when critical intelligence information did not reach some of the mission support and combat units during the heat of battle. For example, General H. Norman Schwarzkopf, who commanded U.S. forces in the War, complained to Congress as early as June 1991 that imagery intelligence did not reach him in time. One of the big lessons from that war was the need to develop an overarching framework for information systems standards.

This chapter will provide an overview of the standards framework that has been implemented by the DoD, and then relate that framework to the U.S. Intelligence Community and to the implementation of intranets such as Intelink. Specifically, it will discuss the *Technical Architecture Framework for Information Management* (TAFIM), the *Common Operating Environment* (COE), and the *Joint Technical Architecture* (JTA). It will explain how the U.S. Intelligence Community is developing its own "Functional Reference Model" for Intelligence. The chapter will conclude with a brief look at a companion tool to Intelink, the new *Defense Message System* (DMS), and how this new message handling capability will be implemented within the Intelligence Community. It is strongly believed that the utility of intranets, as exemplified by Intelink, is greatly diminished without a strong information technology standards program.

3.1 DEPARTMENT OF DEFENSE STANDARDS

Within the U.S. Department of Defense, responsibility and authority for information management, counter-intelligence, and security counter measures falls to the *Assistant Secretary of Defense for Command, Control, Communications, and Intelligence*, or "C3I" as it is almost universally known. The DoD directive for this position states that the Assistant Secretary of Defense (C3I) is responsible for software policy and practices, (except weapon systems), and for the policy, processes, programs, and *standards* for the "development, acquisition, and operation of automated data processing equipment." This oversight responsibility includes, of course, the various DoD security organizations, but also the Defense intelligence agencies: NSA, DIA, NIMA, NRO, Army, Navy, Air Force, and Marine Corps Intelligence—eight of the 13 components of the U.S. Intelligence Community. Under the previous Assistant Secretary of Defense (C3I), Duane P. Andrews (the incumbent during the Persian Gulf War), and his successor, Emmett Paige, Jr. (1993-1998), the Pentagon explored ways to correct the interoperability problems experienced during the Gulf War. The answer was a series of efforts that resulted in a framework designed to promote the integration of all DoD information systems, including those supporting intelligence operations. This overall framework consists of a number of efforts, including the TAFIM and JTA.

3.1.1 Technical Architecture Framework for Information Management (TAFIM)

Armed with the lessons learned from the Persian Gulf War, the *Technical Architecture Framework for Information Management*, or "TAFIM," is a continuously evolving set of documents that articulate the DoD commitment to an *open systems* environment. Its purpose is to facilitate the development of information systems that are independent of *proprietary* technical solutions. It also emphasizes the need for a *standards-based* architecture that is deemed critical to achieving interoperability. The DoD strongly believes that focusing on these two areas—standards and open systems—will provide the highest payoff in achieving interoperability.

The commitment and rapid evolution of the TAFIM, maintained by the Defense Information Systems Agency, are readily apparent. Version 1.0 was published in June 1994, Version 2.0 in March 1995, and Version 3.0 in April 1996. Version 3.0 consists of eight volumes summarized below:

1) Overview

This volume presents an overview of the TAFIM. It relates information technology and information management guidance published in DoD directives, instructions, and manuals. Volume 1 defines the various levels of the TAFIM Model, including *Enterprise, Mission, Function, and Application* levels, which are referenced in other volumes.

2) Technical Reference Model

This volume defines the *Technical Reference Model* for information systems. Within the context of U.S. Government information systems, a "reference model" is defined to be a mechanism to facilitate agreement on definitions, and identify issues needing resolution. A "Technical Reference Model" establishes a mechanism for relating the various technologies to each other, identifying the key issues such as portability, scalability, and interoperability. The Technical Reference Model is not a specific system design, but establishes common vocabularies for the services and interfaces. For example, it defines a number of "service areas" such as *Software Engineering, User Interfaces, Data Management,* and *Data Interchange.* By establishing and defining these commonalities, it enhances interoperability, portability, and cost reductions.

3) Architecture Concepts and Design Guidance

This volume of the TAFIM provides the framework and a set of architectural concepts, definitions, and guidance principles for the design of information systems. Focusing primarily on technology, it provides a useful set of principles to enhance system development by examining specific areas including computing models, data management, communications, and security.

4) Standards-Based Architecture Planning Guide

Then Deputy Secretary of Defense William J. Perry issued a policy memorandum in October 1993 that called for all DoD components to begin migration toward an open systems and standards-based environment. TAFIM Volume 4 supports this goal by defining a common framework and profile of standards for the computing and communications infrastructure. Essentially, Volume 4 presents a process for developing a standards-based architecture within the DoD.

5) Program Manager's Guide for Open Systems

Volume 5 is a new addition to the TAFIM. It is a guide for applying and integrating TAFIM principles and guidelines as well as other DoD guidance documents, by promoting an open systems environment for information systems. The information provided in Volume 5 is intended to assist information systems program managers in making sound decisions resulting in open systems.

6) DoD Goal Security Architecture

This volume describes the "Department of Defense Goal Security Architecture." Developed in cooperation with the National Security Agency, it specifies desired security principles and target security capabilities, guiding system developers in creating consistent security architectures in their own organizations.

7) Adopted Information Technology Standards (AITS)

Volume 7 contains a specific set of information technology standards that are to be used throughout the DoD. These standards provide consistency across the Enterprise, Mission, Function, and Application levels of the TAFIM Integration Model described in Volume 1. The overall goal of these specific standards is to enhance user productivity by improving system interoperability, portability, and scalability. In addition to improved user productivity, adherence to these standards will:

- Promote vendor independence

- Reduce life cycle costs

- Enhance security

8) Human Computer Interface Style Guide

The purpose of Volume 8 is to provide a common framework for the design and implementation of human-to-computer interfaces. It is expected that this framework will define and document the long-term functional goals, objectives, and requirements of human-to-computer interfaces. By standardizing all interface implementation options, TAFIM-compliant applications will appear and operate in a consistent fashion. In turn, it is expected that productivity will be higher, training can be accomplished in less time, and overall system development time will be reduced.

As each version of the TAFIM was completed, then Assistant Deputy Secretary of Defense (C3I) Emmett Paige, Jr., immediately mandated its use for all DoD elements, including the intelligence agencies. Each new TAFIM version reiterated the commitment to a standards-based, open systems environment, establishing a clear direction towards the long-range goal of interoperability.

3.1.2 Joint Technical Architecture (JTA)

It was clear from the Persian Gulf War that effective military operations required the rapid deployment, on a world-wide basis, of a mix of various military forces from all branches of service—known as "joint" operations. It was also clear from the Persian Gulf War that information system interoperability was absolutely critical to the success of these joint operations. To respond to this need, a number of Department of Defense organizations, the branches of military service, the Defense Information Systems Agency, and various elements of the Intelligence Community collaborated to produce a new item in the overall strategy toward interoperability. Known as the *Joint Technical Architecture* (JTA), it facilitates cost cutting and reduced deployment times through the use of commercial off-the-shelf (COTS) products, hardware independence, and software portability. The idea was that the TAFIM would provide the *general direction* to be taken to achieve the long-range goal of interoperability, but the JTA would establish the specific *path*.

How does the JTA provide the specific path? It mandates a specific set of standards to be used by all DoD components, including the Defense intelligence agencies. These standards were developed by the JTA Working Group, with oversight by a senior steering committee chaired by Emmett Paige, Jr. The JTA Working Group consisted of representatives from each of the military services, the office of the Assistant Secretary of Defense (C3I), the Joint Staff, Defense Information Systems Agency, and various members of the Intelligence Community. The Intelligence Community representation included the *Intelligence Systems Secretariat*, the organization that was responsible for the implementation of Intelink. Other participants included leaders from industry and the Defense Advanced Research Projects Agency (DARPA, also known as ARPA), the developers of the global Internet. The JTA implementation memorandum, dated August 22, 1996, and signed by Emmett Paige, Jr., and Paul G. Kaminski, the then-Under Secretary of Defense for Acquisition and Technology, explains how the JTA provides the path to interoperability:

> *The JTA specifies a set of performance-based, primarily commercial, information processing, transfer, content, format and security standards. These standards specify the logical interfaces in command, control and intelligence systems and the communications and computers that directly support them. The JTA is a practical document, identifying standards where products are available today.*

Thus, the JTA provides the minimum set of standards that permit the flow of information, including intelligence information, to the warfighter. For example, in Section 2 of the JTA (Information Technology Standards), under Data Interchange Services, the use of the *Standard Generalized Markup Language* (SGML) is mandated for long-term storage and electronic dissemination of documents. As we shall see in the case studies in Chapter 8, this was a dominating influence in the adoption of SGML, the Hypertext Markup Language (HTML), and the new eXtensible Markup Language (XML) throughout the Intelligence Community.

3.1.2.1 Scope of the JTA

The latest version of the Joint Technical Architecture, Version 2.0, was released during June 1998. The scope of the new JTA specifically refers to the 21st century vision statement issued by the then-Chairman of the Joint Chiefs of Staff, General John M. Shalikashvili in July of 1996. In this statement, the Chairman unveiled his vision for the Department of Defense to "channel the vitality and innovation of our people and achieve new levels of effectiveness in joint warfighting." Entitled *Joint Vision 2010*, it offers a template for a common direction to the various military services to develop their individual capabilities within a joint framework. General Shalikashvili stated, "The nature of modern warfare demands that we fight as a joint team...*Joint Vision 2010* provides an operationally based template for the evolution of the Armed Forces for a challenging and uncertain future...a benchmark for Service and Unified Command visions."

Responding to Joint Vision 2010, the JTA defines an overall framework, or interrelated set of three basic architectures into which all interfaces, standards, and recommended guidelines fall. It is worth understanding this framework not only to gain perspective into the issues of standards with Intelink, but as a useful guide for anyone involved in automated systems that produce, use, or exchange information. The framework begins with the Institute for Electrical and Electronics Engineers (IEEE) definition in their *Standard Glossary of Software Engineering Terminology* (IEEE 610.12-1990). An "architecture" is defined as the organizational structure of a system or component, their relationships, and the principles and guidelines governing their design and evolution over time. Expanding this IEEE definition, the JTA has defined the following set of three interrelated architectures (Figure 3-1).

1) Operational Architectures

The Operational Architecture describes the "big picture." It provides the operational elements, assigned tasks, and various information flows

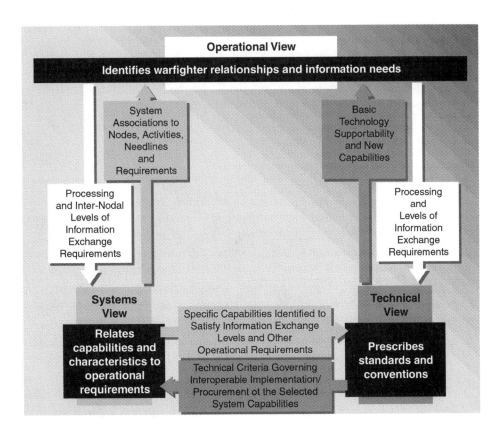

Figure 3-1 JTA Architectural Relationships.

that are required to accomplish or support the warfighting function. It defines, often in a graphical format, the various tasks that are supported, including the types of information and frequency of exchange.

2) Systems Architecture

The Systems Architecture can be viewed as the mechanism that relates the detailed standards (contained in the Technical Architecture) to satisfying the overall requirements given in the Operational Architecture. To do this, the Systems Architecture contains a description, frequently including graphics, of the supporting systems and interfaces that provide support to the warfighting functions. Specifically, the Systems Architecture defines the physical connections; identifies the key nodes, circuits, networks, and warfighting platforms; and shows the linkages of multiple systems within a subject area. It could include, for example, descriptions of the necessary access providers, mission management functions, and even personnel resources.

3) Technical Architecture

This refers to a set of rules that govern the interaction or inter-dependence of a system to ensure that it conforms to its stated requirements. The Technical Architecture identifies the various services, interfaces, standards, and their relationships. It provides technical guidelines for the implementation of systems, and can include engineering specifications, common building blocks, and specific product lines. It could include, for example, specific standards for security functions, or perhaps networking or other common services.

3.1.2.2 Organization of the JTA

Given the framework of these three architectures, the JTA is able to address commercial and government standards relating to information technology that are to be used for new or upgraded information systems. This is done in five specific JTA sections as follows (Figure 3-2).

1) Information Processing Standards

Government and commercial information processing standards that will be used to develop "integrated, interoperable systems that meet the warfighter's information processing requirements" are mandated in this section. The section also describes individual processing standards and the concept of a "common operating environment," explained below.

2) Information Transfer Standards

The information transfer standards and profiles essential for inter-operability and seamless communications are described in this section.

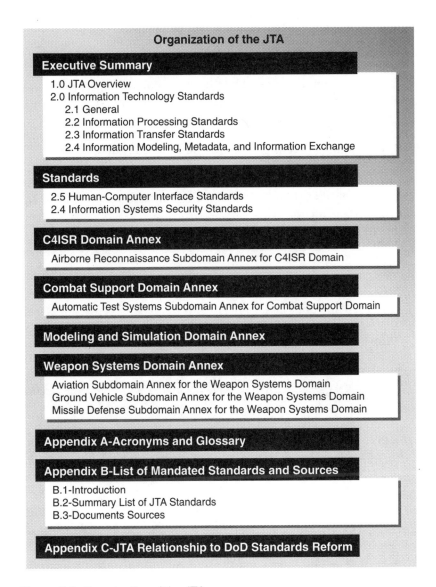

Organization of the JTA

Executive Summary

1.0 JTA Overview
2.0 Information Technology Standards
    2.1 General
    2.2 Information Processing Standards
    2.3 Information Transfer Standards
    2.4 Information Modeling, Metadata, and Information Exchange

Standards

2.5 Human-Computer Interface Standards
2.4 Information Systems Security Standards

C4ISR Domain Annex

Airborne Reconnaissance Subdomain Annex for C4ISR Domain

Combat Support Domain Annex

Automatic Test Systems Subdomain Annex for Combat Support Domain

Modeling and Simulation Domain Annex

Weapon Systems Domain Annex

Aviation Subdomain Annex for the Weapon Systems Domain
Ground Vehicle Subdomain Annex for the Weapon Systems Domain
Missile Defense Subdomain Annex for the Weapon Systems Domain

Appendix A-Acronyms and Glossary

Appendix B-List of Mandated Standards and Sources

B.1-Introduction
B.2-Summary List of JTA Standards
B.3-Documents Sources

Appendix C-JTA Relationship to DoD Standards Reform

Figure 3-2 Organization of the JTA.

In addition, this section mandates the use of open systems standards for networks that use the Internet Protocol (IP) suite, such as the global Internet and the Defense Information Systems Network (DISN), which is used by Intelink. The Internet Protocol (IP) suite provides communications interoperability between information systems that are on different platforms or communications networks.

3) Information Modeling and Information Standards

The use of applicable integrated information modeling standards is mandated in this section. This section also includes required message formatting standards.

4) Human-Computer Interfaces

The objective of this section is to standardize user interface implementation options, enabling applications to appear and behave in a reasonably consistent manner.

5) Information Systems Security Standards

This section prescribes the standards and protocols to be used to satisfy security requirements, provides both mandated and emerging security standards.

The JTA refers to and builds upon the TAFIM. It gets complicated here, but one of the ways it builds upon the TAFIM is by relating the five JTA sections to the seven "service areas" that are defined in Volume 2 of the TAFIM, which contains the DoD "Technical Reference Model." The seven major Technical Reference Model (TRM) service areas are: (1) Software Engineering, (2) User Interfaces, (3) Data Management, (4) Data Interchange, (5) Graphics, (6) Communications and (7) Operating System Services. As the JTA evolves, it is carefully defining the relationship between its interfaces and standards and the TRM major service areas. These relationships are shown in the following chart:

- JTA Information Processing Standards relate to:
   Software Engineering, User Interfaces, Data Management, Data Interchange, Graphics, and Operating Systems

- JTA Information Transfer Standards relate to:
    - Communications
- JTA Information Modeling and Information Standards relate to:
    - (Various mission areas)
- JTA Human-Computer Interfaces:
    - User Interfaces
- JTA Information Security Standards:
    - (Refer to all service areas of the TRM)

3.1.2.3 Related Initiative: Common Operating Environment

To fully realize the magnitude of standards efforts within the Department of Defense, it is useful to briefly examine an important effort related to the JTA known as the Defense Information Infrastructure Common Operating Environment (DII COE). The terms National Information Infrastructure (NII) and Defense Information Infrastructure (DII) originally became popular as a result of efforts within the Clinton administration. In September 1993, President Clinton presented his vision of a "National Information Infrastructure" for the 21st Century in Washington, D.C. to the National Telecommunications and Information Administration. He articulated the benefits and the profound impact that it would have on our society by making a vast array of information, communications, and other services readily available to all Americans at affordable prices. As this concept grew, the NII generally was referred to as the total collection of networks, computers, software, and related components that collectively meet the information processing and transport requirements of this nation. Similarly, the DII came to be known as the analogous equipment and capabilities that collectively meet the information requirements of the DoD.

The DII COE concept got its start during the same soul searching phase after the Persian Gulf War that resulted in the TAFIM. In this case, analysts realized that there was tremendous overlap and redundancy in the various functions that constituted all "Command and Control" (C2) information systems. Indeed, certain functions such as mapping, communications interfaces, mapping programs, and the like were required in virtually every C2 system. And everybody was building them for the DoD in a different way, literally starting over each time. When the time came to begin work on a replacement system for one of the most critical C2 systems, the Defense Information Systems Agency (DISA) began to search for a better way.

The information system that DISA was replacing was the *World-Wide Military Command and Control System* (WWMCCS: pronounced "whim-mix"). WWMCCS, a large-scale "mainframe" system based on technology from the 1970's, served its nation well for decades as the "war command and control" system for military planning and deployment. It was upgraded and modernized in the 1980's, but grew cumbersome and unwieldy nevertheless, as the list of unfulfilled warfighter requirements continued to grow. In September 1992, the WWMCCS "modernization program" was terminated and a decision was made to build an entirely new system. Rather than build the replacement system, known as the *Global Command and Control System* (GCCS), using traditional approaches, DISA was directed to build GCCS using standards and commercial and government "off-the-shelf" products wherever possible. In addition, this new approach included a continuous refinement process to *ensure* responsiveness to military requirements. GCCS was to become the *modus operandi* for all future DoD information systems developments. The new methodology is embodied in the DII COE.

According to DISA, the DII COE "provides a standard environment, off-the-shelf software, and a set of programming standards that describe in detail how mission applications will operate in the environment. The [DII] COE contains common support applications and platform services required by mission applications. Each application that is migrated to the common environment must comply with published guidance..."

Although it got its start with the development of GCCS, the DII COE has become a large collection of reusable software components capable of supporting many mission application areas. Today, COE specifications describe how to reuse existing software and build new software applications that are capable of being integrated seamlessly, and to a large degree, in an automated fashion.

How does the DII COE relate to the JTA? Each standards effort refers to the other. In an implementation memorandum dated May 23, 1997, Emmett Paige, Jr. stated that the COE "would evolve as necessary to maintain compliance with the JTA." The recently released Version 2.0 of the JTA refers to the various DII COE compliance levels. The JTA is mandatory within the Department of Defense for all emerging systems and system upgrades. Thus the

JTA and the DII COE have become powerful tools in meeting the long-range DoD goal of interoperability for its information systems.

3.2 INTELLIGENCE COMMUNITY STANDARDS

Standards that are mandated by the Department of Defense apply to only eight of the thirteen members of the U.S. Intelligence Community: NSA, DIA, NRO, and NIMA, as well as the four military agencies (Air Force, Navy, Army, and Marine Corps). The four non-defense agencies (Departments of State, Treasury, and Energy, and the FBI), and the CIA as an independent agency, do not fall under the DoD mandate. A number of efforts, however, have ensured that the Intelligence Community at large could take full advantage of the large-scale standards efforts of the DoD. These efforts include the definition of a "Functional Reference Model" for Intelligence, (akin to the *Technical Reference Model* concept in Volume 2 of the TAFIM) and the development of a unified, overarching architecture for all cryptologic operations within the U.S. Intelligence Community.

3.2.1 Functional Reference Model for Intelligence

Volume 2 of the TAFIM defines "reference model" as a mechanism to facilitate agreement on definitions, and identify issues needing resolution relating to information systems. Along these same lines, the Systems Integration Management Office within the Defense Intelligence Agency has developed a "*Functional Reference Model for Intelligence*" that has received wide acceptance. The model defined in this effort contains a framework and methodology for documenting the relationships among the organizational missions and various intelligence functions, including the specific tools, data, and infrastructure deemed necessary. This model bridges the gap between the very broadly defined intelligence functions (such as "produce military intelligence") and the specific activities carried out by a given intelligence organization to achieve those functions (such as convert data, or manage a project, or analyze trends, or publish results). The model also gives the relationships between the intelligence processes and the specific portion of the infrastructure tasked with that function (e.g., Intelink as the information services medium for the publishing of intelligence).

This model is particularly significant to the Intelligence Community as a whole because it contains a detailed description of the concept of an "integrated information space," and defines a vision for the future of electronic publishing based on World Wide Web technology. As we shall see later in this book, these concepts form the basis for information management improvements across the Intelligence Community.

The definition of the *information space* concept and an explanation of its relationship to the Functional Reference Model were written by Ms. Bonnie C. Blades, a senior engineer with the Washington, D.C. Division of the MITRE Corporation, a federally-funded research center with extensive involvement with the U.S. Intelligence Community. As explained by Ms. Blades, this notion embodies a set of integrated information "objects." Once a set of these information objects (e.g., reports, video/audio clips, maps, logs, databases, even traditional documents) is generated, the objects can be accessed, reused, and combined by other intelligence analysts and customers in the production of other intelligence in any context, format, or media that is required. She further defines a new environment where intelligence production is shifting from the traditional hardcopy products to the Intelink-like, Web-based electronic environment. In this new Intelink environment, as production and publishing tools as well as collaborative capabilities continue to improve, she envisions that "the traditional boundaries between authoring, production, publishing, and dissemination [will] begin to blur; one person's finished product [will become] another's source material."

The "Functional Reference Model for Intelligence" recognizes several guiding principles that foster an electronic production and publishing environment. These principles are extremely important to the Intelligence Community as it approaches the 21st century because they constitute many of the primary ingredients that will allow improved management of intelligence information. According to Ms. Blades, these principles include:

1) Allowing intelligence reports to be prepared and published quickly, without post editing

2) Supporting collaboration in intelligence production by allowing users to interact, including the ability to use *all* available information on a 24-hour basis

3) Using standards-based tools for common viewing by all users

4) Providing visualization and other tools to allow users to tailor the information space to meet their own individual need

5) Providing for a common metadata structure to improve search and retrieval capabilities within the information space

6) Providing a multiple security level structure to handle information at all security clearance levels rather than publishing products on multiple servers

7) Supporting a wide range of information such as text, maps and other graphics, audio, imagery, digital video, metadata, hyperlinks, finished intelligence products, recorded broadcasts and other unevaluated material

8) Ensuring that users with limited communications (low bandwidth) capability are accommodated

9) Providing the ability to store information indefinitely, in a non-proprietary form, and in multiple media (electronic, CD-ROM, hard copy)

Indeed, an organization with a common set of collaborative processes (such as the Intelligence Community), interconnected over a common telecommunications infrastructure (such as Intelink), and using the concept of an information space, would have the ability to become "agile" and better manage its information—the goal of the 21st century intelligence enterprise. The Joint Intelligence Center, Pacific (JICPAC) is just such an organization, and its success story is detailed in Chapter 8. JICPAC is a prototype of the future of intelligence production, as we shall discuss in Part 3 of this book.

3.2.2 Unified Cryptologic Architecture 2010

An initiative from within the Intelligence Community that embodies the approach, concept, and lessons learned from the JTA and the DII COE, is the architectural equivalent within the cryptologic world of General Shalikashvili's *Joint Vision 2010*. Known as the *Unified Cryptologic Architecture 2010*, this is the vision and legacy of General Kenneth A. Minihan, Director of the National Security Agency, for a single, overarching architecture across the entire U.S. cryptologic community between now and the year 2010. This unified architecture will improve management by allowing budgetary and other programmatic decisions to be made across the entire spectrum of cryptologic programs in the most cost-effective manner. In addition, it will facilitate the goal of information system interoperability across the diverse cryptologic infrastructure.

After an intensive period of several months, with national experts and many of the brightest information technology professionals detailed to this special effort from across NSA, the Unified Cryptologic Architecture (UCA) 2010 was unveiled in September 1997. The UCA 2010 plan, patterned after the same three basic architectures (operational, systems, and technical) of the JTA, addresses the total cryptologic process, from requirements to the delivery of products and services. It includes specific common technical standards, security mechanisms for the protection of "Signals Intelligence," and metrics for evaluating cost/benefit studies. The UCA Technical Architecture contains six components related specifically to cryptology:

1) **Security**

Architecture, policy, integration, and services including authentication, access control, encryption, and auditing

2) **Systems and Process Management**

Naming and directory services, time services, and event services, prioritization and resource allocation, and control/feedback

3) **Common Object Services**

Extensions to common services such as performance accounting and metrics, including intelligence modeling

4) Common Facilities

Human interface, browsers, collaboration tools, display formats, and presentation tools from the DII COE

5) Applications

Specific cryptologic applications that are common to all users, analytical and intelligence reporting services, and cryptologic research services

6) Networking

Physical and logical connectivity, protocols, network management, metrics, and accounting

   The UCA Technical Architecture framework addresses the integration of all legacy applications as well as new systems development, including necessary training. The UCA transition plan also discusses partnerships and organizational implications for the near term (1998-99), mid-term (2000-03), and long-term (2004-10).
   Under the leadership of Paul Newland, and with support from NSA and all cryptologic-related agencies, the UCA 2010 effort is now in the process of being implemented across the Intelligence Community. It represents an important standards-based initiative with the potential to significantly reduce costs while also contributing to the long-term goal of Intelligence Community information systems interoperability.

3.3 INTELINK STANDARDS

How do these standards efforts relate to Intelink? Why are standards an "issue" in this book? It was realized early on that in order for the Intelink concept to realize its full potential, adherence to standards was absolutely paramount. This included, of course, the Intelligence Community commitment for implementation of a true commercial off-the-shelf environment wherever possible. As a result, Intelink development went down a path of standards-based, COTS software environment, with an understanding that the security concerns and other shortcomings of this approach would have to be "risk managed" as opposed to the previous mantra of total risk avoidance.

Mr. Ronald D. Elliott, the second Director of the *Intelligence Systems Secretariat* of the Intelligence Community Management Staff, believes strongly in the need for standards. He served as the first "Corporate Information Officer" (CIO) of the U.S. Intelligence Community, a role that was defined in legislation passed in August 1996 known as the *Information Technology Management Reform Act.* Mr. Elliott summarizes, "We must put in place a set of integrated information systems tools and services that can be managed with an integrated security management infrastructure. However, even with the tools and services, we must also produce the policies and accreditation by which to integrate these across command, function, domain, and discipline boundaries."

The U.S. Intelligence Community is beginning to do just that. In addition to the COTS-based software environment, specific architectural standards are being used extensively in Intelink. The operational portions of Intelink are compliant with the Department of Defense Joint Technical Architecture (JTA), and the Defense Information Infrastructure Common Operating Environment (DII COE). Intelink will use or be integrated with other relevant ongoing DoD programs, including the development of the Defense Message System (DMS)—discussed below—and the Multilevel Information Systems Security Initiative (MISSI) of the National Security Agency which we will discuss in Chapter 5.

The bottom line is that government standards efforts have had a profound impact on Intelligence Community activities. The mandated use of SGML in the JTA for example, as well as the consensus gathering activities that preceded this mandate, had a significant impact on the development of electronic publishing improvement strategies within the Intelligence Community. In 1994, these efforts convinced CIA management to establish the *SGML Resource Center.* The Resource Center provided technical assistance and training to other intelligence agencies and organizations that were beginning their SGML efforts. In other examples, the Intelink requirement for SGML was quickly reiterated by the Intelligence Systems Secretariat, and the Intelligence Community *Electronic Publishing Board* was established. The *Electronic Publishing Board* [13] is a forum that addresses many electronic publishing issues,

---

[13] Chaired by David Miller, the Electronic Publishing Board is currently referred to as the Electronic Publishing *Group.*

including the use of SGML. In addition, the National Security Agency formed its own *SGML Executive Steering Group* in 1996. With the support of NSA's standards implementation organization, the Group addresses agency-wide SGML implementation issues. Similar forums were established in other Intelligence Community organizations.

3.4 RELATED INITIATIVE: DEFENSE MESSAGE SYSTEM (DMS)

It is useful at this time to acknowledge the development of a large-scale Department of Defense project related to Intelink that adheres to the standards activities outlined in this chapter: The Defense Message System (DMS). DMS, in development since 1988, will provide military and defense related personnel with a modern messaging and e-mail capability into the next millennium. DMS is important to Intelink because when fully implemented, it will provide a viable alternative to the many legacy e-mail applications currently in use across the DoD. E-mail is usually considered the primary collaboration tool available on intranets in general, and Intelink in particular.

The Defense Message System incorporates all the hardware, software, procedures, personnel, and facilities required for electronic exchange of messages among organizations and individuals within the U.S. Department of Defense. Thus, DMS will provide secure, reliable messaging for strategic, and tactical national intelligence, as well as various business applications, across multiple commercial vendor platforms. The DMS components are derived from commercial off-the-shelf products. Consequently, users can expect to see products with which they are probably already quite familiar, such as Microsoft Exchange or Lotus Mail.

The implementation of DMS also will allow the phasing out of DoD's previous messaging system, the antiquated and costly Automatic Digital Network (AUTODIN). AUTODIN was based on late 1950's proprietary architecture, and although it had undergone numerous enhancements over the last three decades, it could not easily be upgraded to support today's information requirements.

A primary goal of the DMS is to reduce overall costs and personnel staffing while improving the elements of messaging service and security. DMS uses the newest commercial e-mail technology to increase speed, reliability, and security of messaging and provide a worldwide directory that has applicability to the many other information systems that support the warfighter. As one of the first, and certainly the most visible implementation of secure messaging, it provides joint and interoperable messaging between strategic and tactical environments across U.S. military departmental boundaries, and across international borders to our Allies in combined military operations. It is interesting to note that in the early days beginning with World War II, only organizational (message) traffic was exchanged; personal messages or messages between two individuals did not exist. Accommodating this contemporary need, DMS will allow the user to send and receive both organizational (referred to as *message traffic*) and e-mail (referred to as *personal traffic*).

DMS provides a fully integrated, supportable, secure, accountable, and completely COTS capability for individual and organizational messaging for the Defense Department, thus ensuring that the capability keeps pace with technology for many years to come. The DMS system consists essentially of four main components:

1) Message Handling System

Compose, submit, format, transfer, translate, deliver, store, and display both organizational and individual (e-mail) messages

2) Directory Services

Enter, store, and retrieve user addresses, security credentials, and routing information

3) Systems Management

Monitor, report, and track overall system performance

4) Security Services

Create, store, and process cryptographic and other codes to ensure user safeguards

The security components in DMS are based on the FORTEZZA "Crypto Card" that was developed by the National Security Agency as part of its

Multilevel Information Systems Security Initiative (MISSI). The FORTEZZA card contains specific information that gives the card its authentication and part of the keys that are used to encrypt and decrypt messages as well as generate a digital signature. In turn, the digital signature validates the originator of a message and ensures that the message has not been tampered with during its delivery. A description of the NSA MISSI program and its relationship to Intelink is contained in Chapter 5.

In remarks presented to the Intelink community at a special conference held in San Diego in June 1996, Emmett Paige Jr., stressed the importance of DMS and the effective security regime that it would bring:

I know that Intelink is working to be DMS-compliant, and I want to emphasize that I consider that extremely important. Intelink, as the secure analog to the Internet, will serve as the bridge connecting the information systems of the many organizations and functions that participate in the intelligence process as collectors, producers and users. It is therefore critical that the development and management of Intelink reflect our most advanced thinking and the most innovative capabilities offered to us by the commercial sector.

The U.S. Intelligence Community plans to utilize DMS. They recently established an office to implement DMS within the Intelligence Community. Located at NSA and headed by Dr. James A. Donnelly, this office will ensure that Intelligence Community interests are addressed.

3.5 How Does this Relate to Business?

Taken as a whole, the broad-based *Technical Architecture Framework for Information Management* (TAFIM), the specific *Joint Technical Architecture* (JTA), along with the related software infrastructure and components of the *DII Common Operating Environment* (DII COE) offer a formidable architectural framework with specific methodologies and actual standards and products. Clearly, the efforts of the U.S. Department of Defense, spending literally billions of dollars on its goal of seamless interoperability, are a lesson to all organizations involved in information systems.

Time and time again, the federal government as a whole and the Intelligence Community in particular, have found themselves locked into the proprietary solution of a single vendor or a single set of vendors. The individuals who are responsible for providing information technology and solutions within a company must recognize the critical nature of decisions involving the use of standards. They must guard against "locking" the company into a single vendor or proprietary standard without extensive discussions with the people affected by such a decision.

Businesses today, as well as the U.S. Intelligence Community, face some very turbulent times and challenges as we prepare for and enter the third millennium. In order to meet these challenges, we must be better positioned to exchange our information with our customers. The use of information technology standards, and commercial products that are compliant with these standards, provides us with the most promise by eliminating system redundancies and incompatibilities.

In Chapter 2, we mentioned that the Intelink Management Office has wisely chosen to follow the standards lead of the World Wide Web Consortium (W3C)—it even became a member of the W3C. Following the lead of the standards bodies, and adhering to those standards are undisputed goals of the federal government and the Intelligence Community in particular. Given the resource savings that following standards will provide, it should be the goal of every business enterprise.

Chapter 4

Defining Security

Security and privacy are all the rage these days. Intelligence agencies like the National Reconnaissance Office and the National Security Agency are becoming more open about their respective roles. Television shows like the *X-Files* and Hollywood movies like the 1992 Universal Pictures *Sneakers*, starring Robert Redford, are stirring up images of how the United States Government is supposedly controlling and interfering with people's lives (not unlike the "Big Brother" concept from George Orwell's classic novel *1984*). Privacy in this digital age concerns many, as companies like Arkansas based *Acxiom Corporation* gather and sort information on nearly 200 million Americans ranging from credit card transactions to telephone numbers, car registrations, and real estate transactions. Debates are ongoing about the extent to which we should have limits on the exportation of strong encryption techniques. But what really *is* security?

Webster's *New Universal Unabridged Dictionary* states that security is "the state or feeling of being free from fear, care, danger," it is "safety or a sense of safety." As general a statement as that may seem, it actually is quite appropriate in the application of computer networks, since security in this context is expressly concerned with providing a safe environment for the users of the network. For example, no user should have to worry about other people interfering with their data. The network should be sufficiently secure such that when a user logs in to his computer each morning, that person should be able to count on their e-mail being untouched by others, and their report for the Big Boss (the one upon which the next promotion hinges) being intact.

This chapter will describe the basic framework for applying security to networks. We will define the concept and importance of network security, and explain how it applies to intranets such as Intelink. Next, we will discuss the psychology of the people who attack networks, because developing an understanding of "the enemy" can enable one to implement the most appropriate and effective protections. We then consider three basic components of network security: authentication, access control, and auditing/accountability. This will lead us into a discussion of encryption, a way of transforming information on your network to make it much harder for unintended users to read, including the most common techniques for applying encryption over a network. Also as part of access control, we will discuss "firewalls" and their use today in providing network security. The chapter will contain a discussion of physical security measures, such as how to protect the components of the network from being damaged. Finally, we will touch briefly upon the use of policy to address the security issues that cannot be solved by physical measures and encryption alone. With this background, we then can discuss in Chapter 5 specifically how security is applied to intranets, as exemplified by Intelink.

4.1 WHY IS SECURITY IMPORTANT?

In Chapter 1, we said that a network is an *interconnected group of computers*. When DARPA originally created ARPANET—the forebear of the Internet—in 1969, the fundamentals of computer networks were still being developed and security was not the highest of priorities. After all, with the constituent machines on the network all being either military oriented or related to academic research, it was not unreasonable to assume that everyone could be trusted. Plus, given the relative small number of computers that were initially connected to ARPANET, it was not too difficult to police the network and keep problems in check. However, with the number of nodes growing exponentially on the now-global Internet, with computer viruses running amok and unscrupulous hackers and criminals lurking to steal personal and financial information, it obviously is not safe to assume that one can simply trust the Internet to provide the necessary security. Arguably, the same case could be made for any corporate intranet; and for those that allow access to the global Internet, the fact is undeniable.

Consider the extreme cases for a moment. What is the *ultimate* in security, in terms of providing the most protection? The answer would be complete and total separation of a computer from the entire network. In this way, there is absolutely no way that an unintended user lurking somewhere could adversely affect that machine. This may seem ideal at first glance, the "Holy Grail" of all security-minded people. Yet, clearly such an approach is also fundamentally flawed, since as soon as one cuts off a computer from the network, the usefulness of the network as a tool to make information easily accessible is lost. On the opposite end of the spectrum, consider the arrangement where that same computer is connected to the network in such a way that it can be accessed by anyone, from anywhere, and at any time—the ultimate in flexibility. Such blind faith in human nature, in which a person simply *trusts* others not to disturb his or her computer, is sheer folly. Indeed, such a computer would most likely turn out to be the "Holy Grail" for an unethical hacker or criminal. Neither of these extreme cases is desirable, so the challenge is to find a reasonable point in between. And therein lies the difficulty: how do you design a network that will provide flexible access to all legitimate users, while at the same time denying access to unauthorized users?

4.2 DEFINITION OF SECURITY

For the purposes of this book, we shall define *security* as *"protecting information from unintended access."* As simple perhaps as that definition may sound, those five short words belie the complexity behind attaining a secure network. Indeed, it is important for us to realize how general these words really are. In Chapter 1, *"information"* was defined as any computer data that exists on the network; for example, reports, e-mail, sound, and video files. The definition was purposely made broad so that it could cover any future types of information as well.

"Access" is a similarly general word. In the simplest of terms, information can be accessed in one of two ways: either a user can *read* a particular file or he can *write* to that file. The permission that one may set for one particular piece of data might be different than that set on another. For example, the community README file that contains the office's monthly activity reports probably should be both readable and "writable" by everyone, while the company policy on drugs and alcohol should more than likely be kept as read-only. Additionally, since information may reside on the network in many different forms—as a file in a directory on some server's internal hard drive, as "live" packets being transmitted through the network cables, or as data on portable media such as a floppy disk—the word "access" also has the connotation of how one might go about getting to that information. Developing a defense against unwanted network attacks and intrusions requires an understanding of all of the implications of "access."

The word *"unintended"* has wide implications as well. A major factor in providing good security is determining who has the rights to the information on the network, and who should be restricted. The situation may seem clear-cut when the two sides are the Legitimate User versus the Horrible Hacker, but what about when the issue is between two users on the same network in the same office? There is definitely a case for wanting to protect one's data from coworkers. A primary example in the Intelligence Community is the "need-to-know" policy discussed earlier, in which access to information is only given to those people whose job directly depends on such knowledge. Therefore, it is important to make sure that people who are supposed to access specific information can do so, while at the same time preventing others—despite the fact that they might have security clearances as well and can use other parts of the network—from accessing that same information.

Finally, it must be stressed that the word *"protecting"* was chosen for this definition over something more powerful like "preventing" because security is not absolute. Interestingly, Webster's dictionary lists an archaic definition for security that has an intriguing implication: "overconfidence; carelessness." In the world of intranets, extranets, and particularly Intelink, becoming overconfident or careless in the measures one takes to achieve a secure environment is almost as bad as not taking any action at all. After all, overconfidence implies that one has placed complete trust in the network, that it is invincible to infiltration and exploitation. Simply stated, no network is 100% secure—to think otherwise can only lead to disaster. Consider network attacks as a testament to our ability as humans to innovate and conquer challenges, or merely accept them as annoying facts of life in keeping a network up and running, but the bottom line is that there is no simple solution that will solve all security problems.

4.3 PSYCHOLOGY OF NETWORK ATTACKERS

Why would someone be interested in attacking a network in the first place? Human psychology is fickle, and motives will certainly vary among different people, but the most common are money, revenge, and terrorism, whether it be good old-fashioned curiosity with perhaps a twinge of publicity seeking, or full-fledged *information warfare* attacks on a country.

- **Money**

The financial rewards that one may gain by exploiting a network can be considerable. Consider, for example, the customer database that a company has painstakingly developed over the past five years. *Corporate espionage*: It would be extremely valuable to a competing firm, and all that might be necessary to acquire it is for someone to break into the network and make off with a copy of it on a floppy disk or two. *Theft*: In fact, with access to a corporate database, a criminal can create an invisible flow of money directly into their own bank account. Black marketers with access to purchase authorization data can traffic in stolen goods while having the intended retailer still foot the bill.

- **Revenge**

Revenge is another common motive. With computers and networks as important as they are today, a person could do considerable damage to an organization if he were to bring the computer assets down out of retribution for some perceived wrong, genuine or not. Even worse, the damage can be set to occur long after the departure of the assailant, occasionally frustrating attempts to identify the culprit.

• Terrorism

Frequent attacks are by hackers who want simply to *do* it: some of the protection schemes that are put onto computers present a very challenging task. To some people, the sense of satisfaction gained from defeating a security mechanism is all the reward that is necessary to prompt them to engage in such network attacks. Fanatics seeking publicity on CNN dream of penetrating Wall Street computers and bringing the New York Stock Exchange to a standstill. Or worse yet, consider an *information warfare* attack specifically designed to cause massive electric blackouts or communication satellite outages in support of a hostile military operation.

4.3.1 Who Would Attack a Network?

We next consider the type of person that is likely to develop these kinds of motives. For those that enjoy the sport of breaking into networks, the stereotypical profile is of the young computer hacker, probably a college student—or even younger—whose school offers free use of the computers. With perhaps financial support from his family, he would likely have plenty of free time to roam around and explore all the intricacies of computer networks. To an extent, curiosity is innocent enough; one can hardly blame a person for seeking knowledge. However, the problem starts when they put aside their ethics in order to get inside a network. Such a disregard for the property of others is analogous to a public park in a crowded city: When the population reaches a certain point there will always be those who do not care about the scenery and who will instead litter or vandalize it. Admittedly, not all hackers are interested in infiltrating and damaging networks, yet there are enough of them that network security must be considered.

Although curiosity implies intellectual pursuit and suggests the image of a student or other academic, when it comes to money as a driving force, all bets are off as to the type of person involved. The power of money is considerable. Consider, for example, the spy cases of recent history. From the Walker family in 1985, to CIA mole Aldrich Hazen Ames in 1994, the motivation has almost always been *greed*. The Walker family provided the Soviets with information on encryption devices; Ames and his Colombian-born wife provided counterintelligence information to the Soviets that resulted in the executions of at least 10 U.S. and allied agents over a nine-year period. In both cases, it was done for monetary gain. The Ames case caused a significant backlash, causing many observers to question not only the counterintelligence proficiency of the Intelligence Community, but also the very "fabric" or "culture" that allowed a traitor to be retained for so many years.

Occasionally there have been exceptions. In 1960, for example, two infamous traitors in the history of the NSA were William H. Martin and Bernon F. Mitchell. These two mathematicians decided to turn their backs on their country and defect to the then-Soviet Union, with reasons that were supposedly based on deep-seated beliefs that communism was the better ideology compared to capitalism. In 1976, Edwin G. Moore II was so disgruntled with the CIA, over lack of a promotion and other issues, that he regularly provided the Soviets with classified documents. Just recently (April 1998) a disgruntled former CIA operative, Donald F. Groat,. was charged with espionage. He apparently was seeking revenge for not being given the assignments he believed he deserved. And in 1996, Robert C. Kim, a native of Korea who had access to classified information since 1979, passed dozens of Top Secret documents to the Korean Embassy out of loyalty to his country of birth. Yet in most cases, such tragically noble issues do not typically trouble the minds of the modern spy: Robert Lipka (NSA), Harold Nicholson (CIA), and Earl Edwin Pitts (FBI), were all tempted by dollar signs rather than philosophy. So if the right amount of money can cause a person to jeopardize their freedoms and become a traitor to their country and fellow citizens, it certainly can prompt someone to break into a network.

Lastly, the most common example of a person that would be driven by revenge would have to be the disgruntled employee. Like CIA spy Edwin Moore II, this kind of person is particularly insidious from a security point of view, because it is likely that they would be familiar with all of the internal workings of an organization. They probably would know, for example, the security guards at the door, could be familiar with the company policies (and possibly with any loopholes that exist), and might even still have their computer account if the company is not quick enough to remove them from the access list. From a risk standpoint, these *insiders* pose the greatest threat of all potential attackers. However, according to the FBI's *Computer Emergency Response Team*, these incidents frequently go unreported, and represent the least number of referrals to law enforcement. In the case of Aldrich H. Ames, it took a very long time—nine years—to discover that he was selling secrets. Why? One of the reasons was his knowledge of the system, as well as the fact that one tends not to suspect a familiar face.

The situation is worse than intrusion incidents simply not always being referred to law enforcement authorities. Indeed, companies have not yet recognized the severity of this problem and are spending very little to protect themselves. According to a February 1998 study by a leading research firm, the *Forrester Group*, "Companies are holding back on fortifying their networks, with more than 40% of Fortune 1000 companies spending less than $1 million a year on this task." The security area of greatest common concern today, according to Forrester, is mainframe applications.

The relevance of the psychology of network attackers to Intelink and corporate intranets is clear: Many of today's corporate intranets, and certainly Intelink, have "outside" access to the global Internet, and every business, including the Intelligence Community, has its share of employees who would be willing to sell out for the right amount of money or other motivation.

4.3.2 How Are Networks Attacked?

There are two fundamental kinds of attacks that can be carried out on computer systems:

• Passive (Reading/Intercepting)

The network assailant is merely interested in viewing or copying particular data that exist on the infiltrated computer system. Financial records, lists of customers, or (in the case of Intelink) classified national intelligence are all example of files that contain sensitive information meant only for legitimate users. Despite the fact that no overt damage is done, any leak in the system could have drastic repercussions for the owners of the network.

The *passive* attack may not be purely "read-only." An assailant could, for example, hack into a system the hard way the first time around, and then install a "trapdoor" so that he could get in much more easily during subsequent visits. Usually, the key motivation behind this type of attack is not to damage the network, but rather to keep a low profile. From the unscrupulous hacker's point of view, it is a good thing to get into a system once and make off with valuable data, but it is much, much better to be able to enter a system at will and download such data at any time. The important lesson to remember here is that anything is possible.

• **Active (Modifying)**

Akin to "electronic vandalizing," this type of attack is far more malicious than simply reading data: the network assailant has willfully altered, and probably done serious damage to the computer system he has infiltrated. The notion of "modification" includes altering the contents of data, as well as the outright deletion of it.

In most cases, the *active* attack is the most dangerous since corrupting the data on the network generally implies that productivity will grind to a halt. Given the potential severity of the problem that they pose, some additional notes should be made. The computer virus was named as such because it is programmed to "infect" computer systems by attaching itself to legitimate files, modifying or even deleting data contained by those files, and then replicating itself to wreak further havoc, just like a biological virus. Viruses typically are seemingly harmless programs, or programs that actually contain some useful function, and only reveal their true destructive nature when they are run (for this they are frequently nicknamed "Trojan Horses," from Greek mythology). Another similar, yet subtly different type of data corruption attack is the "logic bomb," a resident computer program so-called because it only goes off when a certain condition has been met, such as a particular calendar date or the 1000th mail message has been sent. When the bomb has been triggered, a special section of code (unused prior to then) is run, causing the system to crash, certain data to be erased, or perhaps even a virus-like program to execute. This is a particularly insidious attack because its instigator can arrange to be absent from the scene of the crime, thus providing him an excellent alibi.

In November 1988, Cornell University student hacker Robert Morris engineered an attack on the global Internet. The virus rapidly infected an estimated six thousand computers around the country, creating a media scare and launching the era of public concern. Even though the virus caused little damage to data, an attack need not destroy data directly in order to harm the system. The Morris "worm" (a "worm" is a special type of virus that replicates itself without being attached to a program file) worked by replicating itself so many times that it invariably overloaded the system it was attacking, making that system inaccessible to its users. The harmful potential of this kind of "denial of service" attack should be clear: if intended users cannot access their stores of information, they cannot do their jobs.

To further underscore the importance of access, consider the following: A classic network attack scenario involves an intruder taking advantage of little-known weaknesses in a computer operating system (e.g., Windows NT or UNIX) to get unrestricted, or "root" access, to the whole network. Or perhaps the would-be network assailant knows of a way to coerce the network to give him access to critical user information files, from which he may be able to deduce a way to pretend to be a legitimate user of the network. Once the attacker has gained access, he is then free to cause more serious damage on the network.

The underlying theme of all of these modification attacks is that they function maliciously, generally catching the user completely unaware. Viruses and their ilk generally work by attacking the computer with low-level system calls, which are unfortunately the same kinds of calls that legitimate programs use to perform their own functions. The *Java* language from Sun Microsystems was created with this very concern in mind, and so the individual programs (called Java "applets") cannot execute with the conventional "full privileges." This works well in theory, but in practice does not quite live up to expectations. Overall at this time, the best that one can do to guard against potential viruses is to have specific software in place that continually inspects files for viruses and other malicious programs. Many "virus checker" program work by scanning executable code for certain "signatures"—strings of bytes that uniquely identify a known virus. This type of software is discussed further in Chapter 6, where Intelink tools are described.

What about Intelink or corporate intranets in general? Sure, it might not be smart to trust something as big and seemingly untamed as the global Internet, but surely internal intranets such as Intelink need not worry about viruses and hackers, right? Unfortunately, this is not the case. Any network is subject to attack, and all possible means of penetration must be considered. In fact, would-be cyber bandits constantly probe and attempt to enter Intelligence Community networks, and regularly "surf the Internet" looking for prey.

4.4 APPLYING SECURITY TO NETWORKS

What are the countermeasures available to us to prevent the exploitation of our computer networks? The fundamental issue for providing good network security, as implied by our working definition, is having a good mechanism for determining who the *intended* users of the network actually are. Simply stated, easy-to-use and reliable *authentication* should always be the primary objective of any network security approach. Then, provided that the identities of its users have been established, it becomes much more straightforward to implement the other functions that are important to running a secure network. These other functions include *access control* (ensuring that only specific users can access data files and other resources on the network) and *auditing* (which addresses the need to keep a record of all network activity in order to maintain secure operation of the network).

There are many techniques available to authenticate users, varying in their ease of use and reliability. Two of the major ones—*passwords* and *certificates*—will be considered in this section, setting the stage for a discussion of how security is being applied to Intelink itself in Chapter 5. And, of course, no talk of security would be complete without an explanation of *encryption* and how it can be applied to networks.

4.4.1 Authentication: Passwords

If security is protecting information from unintended access, then a core issue of security is devising a reliable way to tell the difference between the *intended* users of the network and the *unintended* ones. This is no trivial task. While it may be relatively easy for a human to recognize a colleague or a friend, a computer network has no intelligence to guide it in making decisions about its legitimate users. Instead, determining whether a user is intended or not—that is, *authentication*—must be done through other means.

One of the most basic forms of network authentication is the use of a password. This is simply a word that is supposedly only known by its user. Even those who have never used a computer before are probably familiar with the concept of a password. For example, in order to access a bank account via an automated teller machine (ATM), one must generally provide a *personal identification number* (PIN); this is basically a numeric password. Passwords are a worthwhile security technique in that they do provide a way to limit access to the network in a way that is somewhat convenient to the user. They are also straightforward to implement: normally the user types in their name, and then their password. Based on the user name, the computer looks up in a table what the associated password should be, and if a match is found, the user is given access to the account. In the event that the password given by the user does not match what is in the table—perhaps the wrong key was pressed by accident—typically the user is given a couple of extra chances to try again. To make it harder for an outsider to guess the password for a particular user, though, after a certain number of tries the password authentication procedure might be set up to deny access altogether for that specific user until after a certain amount of time has elapsed.

The data file that contains the passwords for a given set of users is generally a prime target for a network intruder. This is because if the password file can be read, then the assailant will be able to masquerade as a legitimate user of that network. Fortunately, if security through passwords has been implemented well, the contents of the password file will be scrambled so that a human cannot read it by merely looking at it. On the other hand, many of the standard encoding schemes are relatively weak, given the computing power of current low-cost computers, and can be circumvented with a certain amount of effort. Thus it is important to not only use common sense in choosing passwords, but extra care must be taken in implementing system critical resources like password files.

Passwords, in spite of their ease of use, have drawbacks in addition to their vulnerability of exploitation by computer. First of all, authentication through passwords relies solely on the fact that each user is linked to a specific password. This can not always be possible, since sometimes passwords are shared among multiple users. This may be a legitimate arrangement; for example there is only one license for an entire office to use a specific piece of software. More often then not, however, password sharing has been done purely out of convenience: an employee calls in sick the day that the boss is to be briefed, so in order to allow a coworker to have access to computerized notes and slides, the person reveals their password. Ideally, passwords should be changed whenever their secrecy has been compromised; yet people have a tendency to cling to their old passwords in order to keep from having to memorize something new.

This last fact encapsulates another problem of passwords, that of "memory overload" on the part of the user. Given the number of software programs in existence today, and the fact that there usually is not a single password table to service all programs simultaneously, it is not unusual for a person to have multiple accounts and passwords. Ideally, each account should have its own unique password. This helps to prevent the scenario where an unintended user has somehow discovered a password for one account, and then tries to use it to gain access to other accounts. Each password should also be difficult for an adversary to guess (i.e., it should contain a mixture of upper case and lower case letters, numbers and punctuation marks), and should be changed often enough that even if someone does happen to compromise it, access will be possible only for a short amount of time (i.e., only until the password is changed). Unfortunately, it is the rare person that actually follows through on this practice. For ease of use, many people use the same password for all accounts. And, more times than not, the password is something that has significant meaning to that person. For example, if the user is a big fan of military aircraft, that person might tend to use the names of fighter planes for his passwords. Even worse than this practice, however, is the person who is so overwhelmed by having multiple accounts that they simply write down all of their passwords on a sheet of paper and then post that paper right next to their computer monitor! Relying on passwords to secure a network only works as long as the passwords themselves remain uncompromised.

4.4.2 Encryption

Many in the U.S. Intelligence Community consider William F. Friedman (Figure 4-1) to be the dean of modern cryptology. Born in Kishinev, Russia in 1891, he was brought to the United States when he was one year old. Although he trained as a geneticist, graduating from Cornell University in 1914, his interests

Figure 4-1 William F. Friedman—Dean of American Cryptology.

were in codes and ciphers. During his career with the U.S. Government, he pioneered the application of scientific principles to cryptology, and is largely considered to be the major catalyst for U.S. cryptologic successes during World War II. Friedman retired from the National Security Agency after 35 years of service in 1955, and died in Washington, D.C., in 1969. The main auditorium at

NSA is named in honor of both Friedman and his wife of 52 years, Elizabeth Friedman, a prominent cryptologist in her own right.

Friedman explained the difference between code and cipher in his writings:

> *In code systems, the units or symbols to be translated can be of different lengths: a letter, a syllable, a word, a sentence, or just a string of letters or numbers is agreed to stand for a particular word or a whole phrase in the message. In contrast, the units in cipher systems are of uniform length and bear a uniform relationship to the units of plaintext. Usually one letter in the cipher corresponds to one letter in the message.*

A critical component of overall computer security is *encryption*. Today, with the advent of the modern digital computer, we can think of encryption according to the Friedman definition, except it is now in terms of binary digits, or "bits," of cipher corresponding to bits of plaintext. But in addition to the use of encryption as an overall means to protect data, it is also becoming a cornerstone of user identification. For our purposes, encryption can be thought of as a mathematical function that encodes information so that it becomes unreadable until someone reverses the process by decrypting it. The algorithm used in an encryption scheme is written so that, in theory, only the intended receiver can properly read messages sent by the sender. This obviously has tremendous implications. Not only does encryption allow a way to significantly hinder unintended access of all types of information, but, as we will explain, it also serves as a vehicle to provide secure identification of users. It is, therefore, applicable to not only authentication, but to access control, and auditing as well.

Figure 4-2 is a simplified block diagram of how encryption works in a general sense.

The information to be encrypted is called *plaintext*. It is fed to either a software program or a hardware device that contains a mathematical algorithm; this algorithm then performs the actual encoding. Since an encryption algorithm must be reversible in order for the intended receiver to use the data, the set of operations that it employs must be known on both ends of the communication path (i.e., the network in this case). However, to hinder an unintended user from intercepting and analyzing encrypted communications so that he can then read

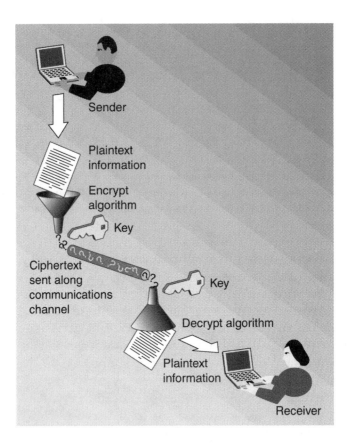

Figure 4-2 Encryption Process.

the data himself, encryption schemes are a function of not only the information to be sent but also of another variable called a *key*. Thus, even if the adversary knows the algorithm—for example, perhaps it is an industry standard algorithm like the ones used in the popular Web browsers—he must still somehow guess the key before he can decrypt the information. To make proper use of this security feature, the key must also be changed with each use of the algorithm, such that information sent during one session would be encrypted using a different key than that sent in a subsequent session. Once the information has been encrypted, now called *ciphertext*, it is sent over the network. On the receive side, the intended recipient then applies the algorithm with the corresponding key in order to decrypt the ciphertext and thereby recover the original information.

In general, the strength of an encryption algorithm can be derived from the length of its key. This is not an absolute truth, since a poor encryption scheme is doomed to fail no matter what size key is used. However, assuming a sound algorithm, the longer the key that is used, the more difficult it is for an outsider to read a message so enciphered. The relationship of the strength of the encryption to the length of the key has to do with the nature of the methods that are commonly used to "break" a particular algorithm. In order to remove the encryption that protects a particular piece of data, the most logical approach is to intercept many examples of encrypted communication sessions and then analyze them for common patterns. Invariably, this process will involve a significant amount of trial-and-error, in which the unintended receiver will apply, in "brute force" fashion, an incredibly large set of keys to the intercepted information in order to find the one true key.

Thus, the length of the key used in an encryption scheme determines how large the space is that someone must search in order for him to be able to break that particular instance of the encryption. For example, if an algorithm uses 32 bit long keys, then generally the total number of keys that it can have—that is, its key "space" —is 2^{32} or 4,294,967,296. As such, a person wishing to read a message encrypted with a 32 bit key must search through as many as nearly 4.3 billion possible keys before he chances upon the correct one. And even then, he will have found the key *only* for that particular message. To further put the relationship of the key length to the strength of encryption in perspective, note that a 33 bit long key would entail a key space twice as large as that implied by a 32 bit key. Correspondingly, it would take twice as long to find the one true key through a brute force search.

4.4.2.1 DES: Data Encryption Standard

There are many encryption schemes in existence today. One of the most popular is the Data Encryption Standard, or *DES* for short. Originally developed by IBM (International Business Machines), DES was accepted by the U.S. Government as a standard in 1976, and later on by the International Standards Organization as an International Standard. The key used by DES is effectively 56 bits long (so its key space is 72,057,594,037,927,936 or over 72 quadrillion), and although quite powerful, is beginning to show its age. For example, in June of 1997, the *Deschall* effort showed that DES could be broken if one is given access to sufficient computing power. The Deschall effort was a private cooperative effort organized in response to a monetary challenge contest offered by RSA Data Security, Inc. Their method was to use the "spare" time on tens of thousands of computers, linked together across the United States and Canada by the Internet, to brute force its way through all 2^{56} possible DES keys. Over the span of four months, they were able to discover the right key and decrypt the message.

This effort exposes two important points. First, while DES has been successfully attacked, it must be said that no algorithm is completely unbreakable, given sufficient resources. DES was a target because it is a standard used by, among others, the financial community, which uses it to protect sensitive electronic transactions. Yet if a group like Deschall had not attacked DES, it would have happened to another algorithm by someone else. Indeed, the seemingly unbreakable 128 bit key-based algorithms of today may in time fall by the wayside as computing power increases and techniques are honed. To put it simply, no encryption is invincible, and one must never put blind faith in the abilities of a particular algorithm.

Second, while it is true that DES has been broken, consider the resources that were required to do so: the Deschall effort took four months of time using tens of thousands of computers in a somewhat sophisticated parallel arrangement in order to break a single message. (By "sophisticated," it is meant that someone had to divide the DES key space into discrete parts and write the program to process those pieces of data on multiple computers. The skills, as well as the necessary hardware configuration, are currently unavailable to the average person.) Admittedly, the length of time could have been shortened if the Deschall team had been able to use the full computing capability of its constituent machines, rather than just the spare time in which those computers were otherwise not engaged. However, since the key that was found by the Deschall group was applicable only to that particular message, the fact remains that this was a significant effort to crack just a *single* instance of DES. True, the algorithm is obviously not 100% defensible against attack, but other than the national governments of the world who have legitimate military and law enforcement needs, there are few that will be willing to go to all this trouble—unless there is some significant financial gain to be had by doing so.

The bottom line to this second point is that a person or business seeking to secure a particular item of information must consider what constitutes *sufficient* security for that information relative to the cost of protection. A Fortune 500 company with billions of dollars vested in its information should place a high value on its encryption and security practices in general. The Intelligence Community, of course, also falls into this same category. On the other hand, someone who wants to keep an outsider from reading their e-mail will not need to devote quite the same level of attention to their encryption schemes. Since there is always some kind of cost associated with security—whether an actual dollar value or simply the fact that a person has to spend the time to use it—determining the proper level that is needed is an important consideration. Of course, the Deschall effort proves that DES can be broken in a certain amount of time, and this kind of awareness of the nature of a particular algorithm's limitations is a crucial part of the process to determine sufficient security. An algorithm like DES might not be acceptable for encrypting customer databases that will be around for the life of the company. However, there are many cases where the information to be encrypted is perishable, i.e., the information is worthless to adversaries after a relatively short period of time has elapsed. For example, a reporter in the field would need to protect a story sent to his newspaper only so that no one could read it *before* the newspaper itself publishes it. In cases such as these, it is worthwhile to consider using DES since it does provide reasonable security.

4.4.2.2 Symmetric Key versus Public Key Cryptography

DES is an example of an algorithm that relies on what are known as *private* or *symmetric* keys. This means that security with DES is attained by ensuring that the sender encrypts a piece of information with a specific key that is known only by the receiver, who then uses that same key to decrypt what was sent. This approach is referred to as *symmetric (or private) key cryptography*.

Clearly, the importance of maintaining the secrecy of the key is paramount. If an outsider was able to get a copy of the encrypted data and was able to determine the key, then the encryption would be broken and the underlying information would be laid bare. This raises the question of *key distribution*: how does the intended receiver obtain his copy of the key?

Presumably, the receiver would get his key through an alternative secure channel, perhaps by a trusted courier. Unfortunately, while this might work in some cases, it limits the effectiveness of encryption when applied to a network environment. With networks, communication sessions tend to be set up spontaneously, such that there is not really any opportunity for the sender to give the receiver a copy of the key.

Also, symmetric algorithms require a unique key for each sender/receiver pair, such that as the number of users on the network grows, the number of keys that must be administered grows exponentially to the point of becoming unwieldy. This is especially a problem in a Web-based environment where there is a single Web server but multiple clients: with a symmetric encryption scheme, each user would have to have his own key in order to talk to the server. Otherwise, if there were only one key used to talk to the server, there is little chance of it remaining secret—and therefore, secure—for long.

In 1976, Whitfield Diffie and Martin Hellman published a paper that described a variation on this theme: instead of using the same key for both encryption and decryption, why not use a scheme in which there were two separate, yet related keys for those functions? Then, it would not matter if the key used to encrypt were to be discovered, since only the corresponding decryption key could be used to recover the underlying information. This is the essence of *public* (or *asymmetric*) *key cryptography*. Compare Figure 4-2 to Figure 4-3.

Since the encryption key can be known by anyone, it is sometimes referred to as the *public key*. Likewise, since the decryption key is known only by the receiver himself, it is called the *private key*. (Beware of confusing the private key in a public key cryptographic system with the concept of a private cryptographic system—indeed, it is better to refer to private key cryptography as "*symmetric*" instead.) One of the major benefits of public key cryptography is that, unlike the symmetric approach, it eliminates the need for every pair of users to have its own unique key. Instead, whenever *any* sender wants to transmit some data, all he needs to do is obtain the public key for the intended receiver and then use it to encrypt. There is also no need to establish communication in advance, in order to ensure that both parties are using the same key, since the encrypting key is publicly known.

Clearly, public key cryptography addresses some of the major problems that symmetric algorithms have in a network environment. In fact, one of the

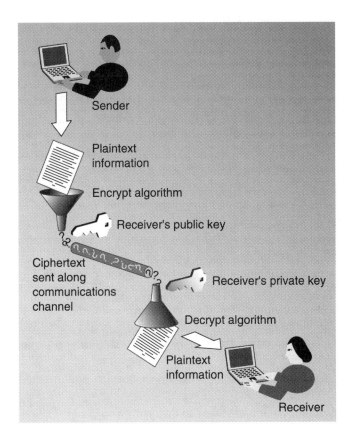

Sender

Plaintext
information

Encrypt algorithm

Receiver's public key

Ciphertext
sent along
communications
channel

Receiver's private key

Decrypt algorithm

Plaintext
information

Receiver

Figure 4-3 Public Key Cryptography Process.

most popular public key algorithms, RSA,[14] is the basis for the encryption used in most popular Web browsers, such as Netscape Navigator. Unfortunately, public key cryptography is not without its drawbacks. The most notable is the length of time that it takes to actually use this type of encryption. Barring the use of specialized hardware to accelerate the execution time, public key cryptography can be on the order of a thousand times slower than a comparable symmetric algorithm. For example, RSA Laboratories' own website states that a software implementation of the DES algorithm generally executes 100 times

---

[14] RSA is an acronym of the last names of its inventors; Ronald Rivest, Adi Shamir, and Leonard Adelman.

faster than RSA, while in hardware DES is 1000 to 10,000 times faster than RSA.

One reasonable way around this problem is to use a combination of both asymmetric and symmetric approaches. To do this, the sender could generate a random number to be used as the *session key,* so-called because it will be thrown away when the sender is finished communicating with the receiver. After this, the sender can encrypt the data message by using the session key with a symmetric algorithm, and then encrypt the session key itself with the receiver's public key. Since the message has indirectly been secured by the public key, it can be said that public key cryptography provides a *digital envelope* for the message. In so doing, the receiver can take advantage of the conveniences of public key cryptography in order to recover the session key, at the same time that he enjoys the speed advantage of symmetric algorithms when decrypting the data message (which could presumably be quite long).

One more important point should be made concerning encryption in general: if the length of the key is directly related to the strength of an encryption algorithm, than why not pull out all of the stops and use extremely long keys? For example, one might think that DES could have easily been made more secure if instead of 56 bit long keys, it used 56,000 bit long keys. True, this would make DES extremely strong, but keep in mind that as the key length is increased, so too is the execution time necessary to process the data in order to decrypt it. At some point, the level of security attained by a specific-length key does not merit how long it takes to decrypt it.

Unfortunately, there is no clear-cut formula for determining the best length for a key. There are two reasons for this. First, it is not a straightforward process to determine how much security is really needed for a given application. While one can approximate how long it might take to break an encrypted message based on the key length used, it is still not always easy to map that knowledge to one's security needs. Say, for example, that you at first assume that you only need a month's worth of protection for your data, so you opt for a shorter-length key; later, you realize that the information you thought was perishable within a few weeks has hung around a lot longer than expected.

Second, whether the algorithm is a software program that is run on a computer, or is actually embedded in a hardware device (such as a *smartcard*), the execution time needed to decrypt a message ultimately depends on the speed of the hardware being used. Gordon Moore, one of the co-founders on the *Intel Corporation*, observed how the density of transistors in a silicon integrated circuit has doubled every 1 to 2 years since the technology was first invented. Although conceding that the laws of physics are closing in, he continues to predict that this increase (popularly referred to as *Moore's Law*) will continue into the next century. Since transistor density can be roughly equated to computational power in silicon chips, and since silicon integrated circuits form the basis for the most popular types of computers that are available today, this observation suggests that the key lengths and algorithms that are unbreakable today might soon become trivial. In spite of these ambiguous factors, though, encryption is critical in providing security in any network environment, whether it is a corporate intranet, Intelink, or the global Internet.

4.4.3 Authentication: Digital Signatures and Certificates

Encryption provides a critical security function in that it can generally protect information from being seen by unintended eyes. Once data has been scrambled it can be sent through an "untrusted," publicly accessible network like the global Internet. Also, public key cryptography provides a mechanism to address the dynamic communication needs of a network in which users do not typically have the luxury of determining in advance when they want to speak to each other. By effectively splitting the encryption key into two parts, with one kept private and the other freely shared, a person can send encrypted data without having to worry about exchanging the key prior to the communication. Still, there is a danger here: how can you be sure that the person on the other end of the network can be trusted, just because he has your public key? Say, for example, that the receiver gets a particular message that requests his credit card number. Certainly, by using public key cryptography, one can make sure that both the request for the number and its reply are encrypted, thus securing the transaction itself from unauthorized eyes. But, since the sender of the message is by definition using a public key, verification of the true identity of the sender becomes a significant issue. In a small corporate intranet, one in which everyone knows each other, this is not much of an issue. However, as intranets grow larger—like Intelink and certainly the global Internet—reliable authentication of a user becomes paramount.

Fortunately, public key cryptography offers a way to verify that what a particular user says about himself is true. As already discussed, in order to provide secure communications, the sender encrypts a message with the receiver's public key, such that the receiver can then decrypt the message with his private key. However, the two keys are related such that one could also reverse the process; that is, the sender could encrypt a message using his own private key, and then have the receiver decrypt it using the sender's presumably known public key. By doing this such that the sender gives some kind of preliminary identification message first before any real data is communicated, the receiver knows that only the bearer of the sender's private key could be the one sending the message. No private key is ever explicitly exchanged, and thereby never compromised. Yet, by doing this, each pair of users can readily authenticate each other. This "reversal" of public key cryptography is what is known as a *digital signature*. To better illustrate how it can be used to authenticate users, consider the following approach to establishing a secure communications path:

1) Sender has a message to give to the receiver, so he obtains the receiver's public key.
2) Sender sends two messages, encrypting them as stated below;
   a) a short message that identifies the sender, encrypted with the sender's private key and thereby forming the digital signature;
   b) the actual data message intended for the receiver, encrypted with the receiver's public key.
3) Receiver takes the identification message and decrypts it using the sender's public key.
4) Assuming the identification message is in the format that the receiver expects, the receiver can now trust the sender to be the person he said he was.
5) Receiver can now confidently decrypt the message from the sender using the receiver's private key, and then follow through with a response to the message (such as sending back a credit card number).

One important caveat to this approach to authentication is that the identification (ID) message must be something that cannot be reused; otherwise, it would be possible for someone to intercept the ID message, replay it, and thereby pretend to be the original legitimate sender. There would still be the issue of how such a "pretender" would be able to decrypt any messages that might be sent back to him, since presumably the receiver would use the original sender's public key to respond; yet the important point here is that the authentication would have failed. To avoid this, however, the ID message simply has to have some component that makes it unique in time. For example, the ID message could include the date and time that it was sent, or it could include a message counter value that would increase by one for each and every new ID message. By looking at this extra information, the receiver would then be able to determine whether the ID message was actually just a previous one that was being replayed.

One other useful application of cryptography related to this idea of "replaying" data is the *message digest (or hash) function*, which is basically a one-way encryption scheme. Such a scheme is important in that it provides a way for the receiver to reliably verify the integrity of the data that has been transmitted by the sender. Essentially, a hash function works by using encryption to condense a message of an arbitrary length into a single word of a fixed, and definitely smaller length. For example, one popular hash function is MD5 (Message Digest 5) from *RSA Data Security, Inc.* which condenses data down into 128 bit long words. Every bit in the original message is used to determine the final output of the hash, yet the hash result cannot be decrypted to provide the original data. Instead, the sender is meant to provide the hash result to the receiver, along with the original message. In this way, the receiver can then calculate their own copy of the hash result and compare it to the one that the sender gave: if they are the same, then the message can be assumed to be genuine. If they are not the same, then the original message has been altered in some way, perhaps due to a transmission error or possibly due to someone willfully altering the message. In any case, not matching the hash result implies that the message cannot be trusted.

Perhaps more significant than the concept of replaying ID messages, this method of authentication hinges on one other important fact: somehow, the sender must get a copy of the receiver's public key. This may at first sound like the same problem for which symmetric algorithms became less favored for networked applications than public key cryptography. After all, the fact that each user must have the public key of the intended receiver sounds very similar to networks where communication security is based on a symmetric algorithm. The fundamental difference between public key and symmetric key cryptography, however, is that symmetric key cryptography has only one shared (private) key for each pair of users, while public key cryptography splits its key into two parts: a public (shared) key and a private key. As a result, there exists a way to have each user only remember a small number of public keys, rather than all the public keys of every user on the network.

The mechanism by which this is possible is a *Certifying (or Certificate) Authority* (CA), a trusted third party that will allow the receiver to verify the identity of the sender. In order for this to work, the sender has to first register himself with a CA that is recognized by the receiver. This registration involves the sender giving the CA his public key, and then the CA verifying the identity of the sender. Once the CA is satisfied that the sender's identity has been properly established, the CA will use its own private key to digitally sign a copy of both the sender's identifying information and his public key, thus forming a *certificate* for the sender. Now, whenever the sender wishes to communicate with someone, that receiver can first request a copy of the sender's certificate. Since presumably the sender is using a CA that is accepted by the receiver, the receiver will have the public key of the CA and can thereby decrypt the certificate. Once this has been done, the receiver can verify the sender's identity and then use the public key contained in the certificate with confidence. Thus, rather than be forced to keep track of every possible sender's public key, all the receiver needs to do is maintain a relatively much shorter list of public keys for the CA's that he trusts.

Clearly, the use of a *Certificate Authority* depends on the ability to trust that particular CA. Also, since commercial CAs may offer several different levels of scrutiny when verifying a user's identity, the reliability of a CA can likewise be called into question. However, the usefulness of a CA in a network environment in terms of allowing dynamic secure communications to take place should be evident. It forms an integral part of the infrastructure necessary for network security.[15]

The basic function of the CA is to manage the distribution of certificates. One aspect of that management is maintaining the *Certificate Revocation List* (CRL), which contains a database list of all certificates that are invalid and thus can no longer be trusted. Certificates can be invalidated for several reasons, as shown on the top of the next page.

---

[15] Intelink's infrastructure will be further discussed in Chapter 5.

• The part of the certificate that identifies its user may become outdated (e.g., the user's name or address changes).

• The validity period for which the certificate could be used may have expired.

• The private key contained within the certificate (or worse, the CA's own private key) may have become compromised.

At best, such conditions imply that the certificate does not reflect the most current information, and at worst, the certificate may no longer be safe to keep around since it could be used to gain access to the network by an unauthorized person. In any event, the network must be told of the fact that the certificate is invalid by updating the CRL database. In this way, all parties relying on certificates to set up their communication can first query the CA to see if everything checks out with the CRL. If so, the session can continue on as normal; if not, there could be a problem and network management should be notified.

One final point about certificates should be made. Just as giving out passwords harms their usefulness, and compromising the keys used in an encryption scheme allows information so encrypted to be read, if a certificate falls into the wrong hands, the ability to use it as a reliable method of authentication is lost. There are ways to help protect certificate information from being stolen. One method is to store it in a separate location away from the network, placing the responsibility on the user to physically protect their certificate. PCMCIA cards, or "PC cards" as they are now known, provide one storage alternative for networks that use personal computers. In Chapter 5, we will discuss the *Multilevel Information Systems Security Initiative* (MISSI), an NSA-developed approach to network security that involves PC cards—and the approach that Intelink itself plans to use in the future. Chapter 5 will also touch upon the *smartcard*, an even more likely candidate for storing certificates, given its convenient credit card-size, inherent security and relative low cost.

4.4.4 Access Control and Auditing

Whether one relies on simple password protection or decides to go the more complicated (though potentially much more secure) route of using certificates, there are still other network security needs that must be met in addition to authentication. First, there must be some way to provide selective *access control* to the data and other resources that are available on the network. Despite the similarity to authentication, this function addresses a different need. Whereas the former strives to authenticate the identity of authorized "insiders" (e.g., company employees) and thereby separate them from the "outsiders" (e.g., unethical hackers), the latter instead attempts to control which particular "insiders" have access to specific aspects of the network. Access control would thus provide a way for legitimate users to use the same network for separate tasks without interfering with the other. It could, for example, guard against accidental deletion of one user's data by another, or it might protect data from being read by a user without the necessary permissions (even though he is authorized to use the network in some other capacity). Access control as described here is very much the network equivalent of the "need to know" principle of the Intelligence Community discussed in Chapter 2.

Intelligent use of access control can also provide a means to further protect the network in the event that authentication fails to filter out unauthorized users. To illustrate this, say that an unintended user has discovered the login password for a specific user—suddenly, that unintended user has all of the rights and privileges that the original, legitimate user had. However, with access control in place, the unintended user would also be *limited* to only those data files or resources that the original user could access, thus protecting everything else that was available on the network. This is why a hacker with ill-intent will aim to figure out the primary "root user" password for a particular network, since this will effectively give him carte blanche to do just about anything he so desires. To be truly effective, of course, access control must be implemented wisely: giving every user equal and unrestricted access completely nullifies its whole intent. However, a judicious use of access control does provide an additional line of defense for the network.

A second important function that is enabled by authentication is *auditing*. Even with good authentication and access control techniques in place, there is still a need to keep records of all network activity. These records are useful not only to track illicit activity, but also to assist in maintaining network operations. For example, if a user complained that a specific program did not work, the systems administrator could use an audit log to see where things might be breaking down. In addition, auditing is important because even seemingly legitimate users may attempt to do something that they are not supposed to do.

For example, Intelink users may place an incorrect security classification on a document and post it to an unauthorized—perhaps even publicly accessible—area. It is important to know who that person was so that action can be taken to correct the mistake.

4.5 OTHER ELEMENTS OF NETWORK SECURITY: PHYSICAL SECURITY AND SECURITY POLICY

In this Information Age, it is easy for a user sitting in their isolated office and using their seemingly isolated computer to lose sight of the implications of being on a network. After all, the machine with which one works day after day is the tangible object; therefore, it is easy to forget that all of the information that can be accessed via that machine does not exist solely on it. Consider Microsoft's new *Windows 98* operating system for personal computers. This product is intended to create a seamless environment in which there would be no apparent distinction between accessing information stored locally on the user's own machine, and that which is stored elsewhere on the network (other than, perhaps, the unavoidable time delay that would occur when data was being accessed from some distant part of the network). While this might make accessing remote information more straightforward, it does also tend to cloud one's perception of what is actually going on in the network: while a single computer might have its own store of information contained within it, more importantly it is its user's window to all the information that exists on the other computers in the network. This is an important notion, for having an awareness and understanding of the network as a whole is essential to being able to secure it properly. In the spirit of increasing network awareness, we will now discuss two less obvious components involved in securing networks: *physical security* and *security policy*.

4.5.1 Physical Security

Falling into the trap of viewing one's own computer as the only machine in the network as described above might easily lead one to forget about the most basic form of security: *physical security*. This refers specifically to protecting the physical components of the network—from the main server computers to the individual client machines, and all the physical interconnecting infrastructure in between—from being stolen or damaged in some way. After all, a network can function only so long as its constituent pieces are present and intact, and since a network may extend over a building, an entire campus, or an even wider area, good physical security presents its own set of challenges.

In order to secure a network from a physical point of view, one must consider all of the available access points, and then put some kind of appropriate protection in place for each of them. Chances are that a would-be assailant will approach a network from its most weakly guarded point, unless there is some unusual, overriding factor to not do so. For example, the computer terminal that is located just inside the front door of the main office is most likely not going to be a primary target since it would be difficult for an attacker to work unnoticed with the presumably large number of people that would be coming and going. On the other hand, any network access point that seems unguarded—such as that seemingly harmless workstation down in the corner of the basement, the no one likes to use anymore because it is old and slow—is potentially a prime target. Dial-up connections in which a user may remotely access the network with a modem are especially difficult to deal with since they provide a way to get into the network without being physically present. However, for those access points that can be addressed, it is a necessity to put an appropriate level of protection in place (such as posting a guard or installing locks on the doors).

Another not-so-obvious physical aspect of the network is embodied by the discs, tapes and other portable data storage devices that are used to contain the software necessary to run the network. For example, making periodic backup copies of important network data is critical to avoid losing that information when the inevitable system crash occurs. Yet, it is conceivable that someone might try to take one of those backups in order to either recover the information that it contains or simply prevent the rightful owners from using it. This same principle would also apply to the various commercial products, whether software or hardware, that the company might have purchased. Protecting such items from being stolen not only helps keep unscrupulous employees from walking off with company property, it also ensures that an outside assailant would be less capable of committing an alternative form of "denial of service" attack, say by stealing the RAM chips from the primary network server computer or the company's only copy of its database management software. Thus, it is important to keep in mind that locking up critical network components—and keeping reliable records as to their exact location—is also critical to protect against a physical network attack.

4.5.2 Security Policy

Physical security is primarily intended to keep the bad guys out, but how do you deal with the supposedly good guys that are on the inside? This is where a good *security policy* comes into play. A policy in this context is simply a list of rules and procedures that should be followed in order to keep the network up and running at an optimal level of performance. A well-written and easily accessible policy should make users sensitive to the network security issues of concern, instilling a sense of responsibility into them to do what they can to take care of their network. For example, given the widespread use of passwords as a means to authenticate users, a good security policy would address the fact that giving out passwords to others creates the potential for unauthorized access to the network, which in turn could cause significant loss of important data. Of course, a policy is only effective if the users themselves choose to enforce it (consider how many people give out their passwords). Hopefully, the policy can be made important enough that users will go out of their way to follow it; at the very least, there needs to be some administration aspect involved to keep people in check. Regardless, a good security policy will force people to stop and think about what they are doing when they use the network.

The following are some *general* guidelines to illustrate the areas of security policy. This listing is *not* comprehensive, and is not meant to be an absolute guide for policy:

1) **Basic understanding of the network:**

• Cover not only what functions the network performs, but also what information the network holds in order to make the users want to protect their network from being infiltrated. For example, most networks contain sensitive personal information about their users, such as social security numbers or financial information, which would be undesirable to disseminate publicly.

• Stress that passwords and other authentication mechanisms such as *smartcards* are not meant to be shared. They are used only to identify users, so unauthorized disclosure would disrupt the system's ability to perform access control and auditing.

• Since passwords can be guessed, be creative about how passwords are chosen; be sure to use different passwords for different systems (otherwise, once *one* password has been broken, they *all* are broken), and change passwords periodically.

• If applicable, discuss the fact that networks with outside connections (e.g., to the Internet) are especially vulnerable to attack; downloading untested software before checking for viruses could have disastrous consequences for the network when that software is run.

2) Guidelines to follow in the case of a network attack:

• If a break-in or any suspicious activity has been detected, the act must be reported immediately so that the damage can be assessed and (hopefully) controlled.

• Attempt to resolve the issue quickly and with minimal disruption.

3) Set of security related maintenance procedures to keep the network running smoothly:

• Backup copies of all critical software must be made on a regular basis; backups should be kept in a secure location.

• Old, outdated, or superceded documents should be filed away or disposed of properly. It is important to keep tabs on *all* information, as losing track of even an *outdated* copy of a document could be very damaging.

4.6 LESSONS LEARNED

No matter how strong the physical security, the security policy, or the identification and authentication algorithms, no security is going to be 100%

effective. Perhaps this sounds unacceptable, but we should keep in mind that the tools presented here can potentially provide, if used wisely, a *sufficient* amount of protection. Consider the two extremes outlined in the beginning of this chapter: complete isolation or unhindered accessibility. Neither one works, so the network designer must find the appropriate solution that balances these two extremes. We do not need round-the-clock surveillance and guard dogs for something trivial, but the server with the company financial records should be backed up several times a day. We do not need to have a password policy that requires changing passwords every day. We do not need an encryption algorithm that is completely unbreakable, but rather one that will protect the data for the length of time necessary, based on how perishable the data is. For example, a report on troop movements is only valid during the battle, but a report that reveals a company's research and development plan for the next five years has significantly more longevity.

With the concept of a balanced approach to attaining a sufficient amount of security, adherence to the following key principles is recommended:

- **Use products that are based on industry standards**:

Proprietary solutions could very well provide a higher level of security than what might be available through products based on standards. But care must be taken to prevent committing resources to something that will not be around in a year.

- **No security is 100% effective:**

Given time, anything can be overcome. Always assume the worst case scenario: that an adversary can intercept your data and break your encryption algorithm. Thus, you must choose an encryption scheme that provides the appropriate amount of security that, for example, cannot be broken in one day, one month, or one year

- **Security is only as effective as the sum of its parts:**

We must always remember that the weakest part of a security scheme is likely to be the primary target of an attack.

• Awareness is critical! Software is not foolproof:

Desire for profits has driven development cycle times down and increased the acceptability of software that has not been thoroughly tested. For example, flaws in the security of Web browsers were big news just recently. It is vital to be knowledgeable about all of the computer products that we use in a network. If a particular product is found to be vulnerable, corrective action must be taken quickly.

• Bells and Whistles:

Do you really need them? It is best to install the minimum configuration possible that still maintains all of the functionality that is desired. The idea behind this is to keep things "lean and mean," i.e., 100% functional yet still easily manageable. The moment the system gets out of hand, the network begins to be vulnerable to attacks that really could have been avoided.

Chapter 5

Security in Practice

*I*n Chapter 4 we have looked at the basic building blocks for good security. We have seen how encryption and certificates allow one to address the authentication, access control, and auditing concerns of an intranet. We have also touched upon the need for good physical security and a comprehensive, enforced policy in order to round out any network security plan. All networks should be built with these issues in mind, and Intelink is no exception. Given the sensitivity of the information that it contains, security has long been a major priority of Intelink management. Indeed, as we will see, the security used in Intelink is continually evolving in order to better address the stringent security concerns imposed by it.

5.1 OVERVIEW OF INTELINK SECURITY STRATEGY

The purpose of an intranet is to provide a set of tools and services to its users. However, to do so without concern for security would not only open up the network to the potential for unauthorized use, but it would also cause its administration to be much more difficult. Ultimately, poor security practices would likely cause the network to become less reliable and certainly less useful. This statement is true for all intranets, but for Intelink, where lack of such protection could very easily jeopardize national security itself, it is essential. Security services truly form the foundation of the network, upon which the "real" tools and services—those most obvious to the users of the network—can be built. For Intelink, the critical security services include:

- **Strong Authentication (Two-Way Challenge/Response)**

As discussed in Chapter 4, reliable authentication is the cornerstone of a secure network, for it establishes the identities of the network users. Authentication provides the mechanism by which access control can be implemented on network data, as well as by which auditing and network monitoring are made easier. Intelink was specifically looking for an authentication approach that used "two-way challenge/response," that is, both the network server and the client (i.e., the user) would have to authenticate themselves to each other by properly responding to the other's challenge.

- **End-to-End Confidentiality (Integrity of Data During the Transmission)**

Despite the fact that Intelink is an Intelligence Community network, not all people have equivalent access. Therefore, like most intranets, there is a strong need to ensure that the confidentiality and integrity of the data being transmitted is maintained. Confidentiality means keeping the data private so that only the legitimate recipient can see its contents, while integrity refers to ensuring that the data has not been modified en route to its intended recipient. Not surprisingly, encryption is the method of choice for this, and Intelink has sought a similar solution.

• Enhanced Access Control

Certainly, in support of the basic "need-to-know" principle, there is a need to control access in general to the information available on Intelink. More specifically, however, one important feature of Intelink is that it is meant to provide forums for discussion on particular topics that are only accessible to those users belonging to the respective "Community of Interest" (or COI). Protecting these forums from unauthorized access can potentially be even more important than some "normal" data since COIs typically have access to the most recent—and therefore most sensitive—information. Seamless control of COIs ensures that the right users can access the proper data whenever necessary. More will be said about COIs in Chapter 6.

• Network Auditing and Monitoring (Logging, Analysis, and Reporting)

An important secondary objective in meeting all of the security needs listed above, is that each of the solutions must be easily managed and administered. Fortunately, reliable authentication allows a way to provide good control over the intended users of the network. Other tools can be put in place to address the need to monitor the network for unauthorized use as well.

In addition to the above primary security services used by Intelink, the following additional considerations are important in many intranet applications:

• Single Sign-On

Ease of use from the user's perspective can be vital: no security is going to work if the user himself refuses to use it. *Single sign-on* refers to the convenient ability of an intranet user to obtain total network access by using one convention. For example, it is common to type in a single password in order to gain access to a network. *Single sign-on* extends the use of that one password to allow the user access to all of the network resources to which he has rights (particular databases, specific Web sites, etc.), as opposed to having to type in a separate password for each resource. The objective of *single sign-on* is that security should be transparent to the user, providing control over the network environment without intruding into the user's perception of the network. Very difficult to achieve in a heterogeneous environment, the best examples of *single sign-on* occur in monolithic systems with strong central control.

• Secure Collaboration

Secure collaboration is usually considered to be an *information service* rather than a *security function*. Nevertheless, Intelink must also provide tools that will allow its users to interact. Specifically, the group authoring of intelligence reports and electronic group discussions are two important examples of this kind of network collaboration. More will be said about these tools in Chapter 6; however, this chapter will focus on the security concerns imposed by them.

The one limiting factor in striving for a high level of security is that the cost of the network—both the initial investment and the continual operating expenses—must be kept as low as possible. This is true for all intranets, and it is certainly true for Intelink. Jack Torok, the CIA security expert who heads up Intelink's *Security Policy and Plans Directorate* (SPPD), has long been a proponent of using either publicly-available software from the global Internet or commercial off-the-shelf software and hardware to address network security requirements. Torok, who has the overall responsibility for security on Intelink, states, "Since every intranet has its own idiosyncrasies, security products in their original form would not be capable of precisely addressing all security requirements." "Therefore," he continues, "there is a clear need for network security products that are easily customizable." With the relative newness of the World Wide Web concept and the security resources to control it, deciding in which products to invest can be especially daunting. Although each intranet must be considered individually, we will discuss the major security products that Intelink currently uses.

5.2 SECURITY BUILDING BLOCKS

In order to provide the security services outlined above, Intelink management—like its counterparts in private industry—is developing its own *Security Management Infrastructure* (SMI) for the Intelink network.

From Intelink management's perspective, the SMI must, at a minimum, support the four security services outlined above:

1) Strong Authentication
2) End-to-End Confidentiality
3) Enhanced Access Control
4) Network Auditing and Monitoring

To accomplish this, the SMI must include:

• **Encryption (which includes Key Management)**

Directly addresses the *privacy* security service; it is also used in most of the other services as well.

• **Certificate Management**

Provides an excellent means with which to *authenticate* users and *control access* to information resources, in addition to being important for the other security services.

• **Communities of Interest**

The Intelink SMI includes a Web-based service for establishing and maintaining access control lists, i.e., membership information for specific "Communities of Interest" (COIs). This capability is known as the Intelink *COI Registration Service* (CRS). The overall concept of COIs is further explained in Chapter 6.

It is important to note that the management functions mentioned above must occur on a community-wide basis. To perform these functions piecemeal, say by controlling different parts of Intelink independently, is counter-intuitive considering that a network is meant to unify. Such division of management may lead to incompatibility, or at the very least inefficiency, as individual components pursue different approaches. Without community-wide synchronization of the encryption and certificates used on the network, its overall management becomes much more difficult.

The remainder of this section will describe SMIs in more detail. Before we begin, however, it is important to keep in mind two points: First, SMIs are not unique to Intelink. In fact, they are rapidly evolving in the private sector, being led by such industry leaders as *VeriSign*, *AT&T*, and *GTE*. Financial services companies—such as *MasterCard*, *Visa* and *Wells Fargo*—are particularly interested in SMIs as a way to securely reach potential customers, and thereby safely take advantage of the business opportunities represented by the global Internet. Other areas of the U.S. Government are also investigating and developing SMIs, including the National Institute of Standards and Technology (NIST) and the Internal Revenue Service (IRS). The *Multilevel Information Systems Security Initiative* at the National Security Agency, also has an SMI effort. Secondly, although much progress has been made in the implementation of Intelink's SMI, several components have not yet been formally implemented. Thus, in the following discussion, keep in mind that Intelink's SMI is still in the process of evolution.

5.2.1 Certificate Authority

As we discussed in Chapter 4, the goal of network security is to protect against unintended access, while simultaneously allowing the legitimate user easy entry. Reliable authentication is the primary means by which this is accomplished. Through the application of public key cryptography, the Certificate Authority (CA) provides a centralized mechanism by which certificates can be issued to all of the users as well as the individual servers out on the network. It is through these certificates that secure, encrypted channels can be established and easily administered on the network. Thus for Intelink, and for many corporate intranets as well, the CA concept forms the basis of network security and is clearly a key component of the SMI.

The CA must of course handle all the normal certificate management functions described in Chapter 4. This includes the issuing of certificates and the control of the network's *Certificate Revocation List* (CRL), the database which denotes when certificates are invalid and therefore no longer trustworthy. One important aspect of the CA that might not be readily apparent is that, in addition to providing certificates to every user on the network, the CA must similarly provide certificates for every computer server that the users *might* want to access as well. Keep in mind that the procedure mentioned in Chapter 4 for using certificates must be applied in *both* directions in order to handle two-way secure communications. Therefore, just as the receiver must establish the identity of the sender by verifying the sender's certificate via a CA, so must the sender establish the receiver's identity. With the many users and information servers that exist on Intelink, there is a correspondingly large number of certificates that must be managed, further evidence that centralized certificate management is key to providing reliable network security.

The CA provides two other fundamental components that relate to security for Intelink: the Secure Sockets Layer (SSL) protocol and the internationally accepted X.509 standard. The SSL protocol acts as a bridge between an application (such as a Web browser program) and the lower levels of the network (in particular, the *Transport Level* of the OSI network model mentioned in Chapter 1), protecting data from unintended access through encryption. The X.509 standard, on the other hand, contains a formal definition for how the certificates used by the CA must be structured. Nevertheless, certificates currently issued by different CAs may or may not be interoperable and will probably contain proprietary extensions. Although the X.509 standard is a specification that has been agreed upon by industry leaders and formalized into an International Telecommunication Union (ITU) standard, each vendor's implementation frequently contains proprietary extensions, to the bane of users and implementers alike. Each of these fundamental building blocks will be discussed in more detail below.

5.2.2 X.509v3 Certificates

The X.509 standard contains a definition for the format of certificates, specifying what information must be included in the certificate and how that information is formatted. As it turns out, X.509 is actually only one part of the overarching X.500 standard proposed by ITU. X.500 itself puts forth the idea of a "directory service," which is essentially a means to organize the access of in-

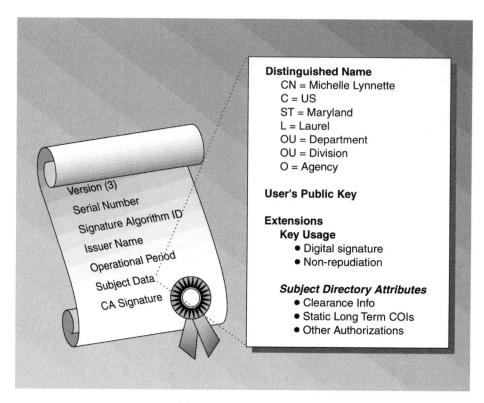

Figure 5-1 X.509v3 Certificate.

formation over a network. X.509 covers the authentication aspect of the information access, one part of which involves certificates. These standards are still evolving, with Version 3 being the most current iteration of X.509 that has gained industry support. Certificates using this version of X.509 are referred to as being X.509v3-compliant (Figure 5-1).

Note that the most important information fields are:

Version: Denotes the version of the X.509 specification that the certificate follows.

Serial Number: Identifier for the certificate.

Issuer Data: Includes the name and identifying information of the CA that issued the certificate.

Validity Per.:   Time period for which the certificate is valid.

Subject Data: Includes the name of the person for which the certificate was created, as well as his public key and any extensions that might be used (such as specific access privileges that the person might have).

CA Signature: Proves that certificate was legitimately issued by a trusted CA.

Although the use of certificates has not yet been completely integrated into Intelink's SMI, Torok's *Security Plans and Policy Directorate* is striving to incorporate them to provide protection for Intelink's COI concept. One key aspect that has been prototyped, but not implemented on a full scale at the present time, is how certificates will be obtained. To give an idea of how the process should work once certificates have become a fully integrated security feature, consider the following:

The Certificate Authority, of course, is in charge of distributing the certificates. For Intelink, the CA process will actually consist of two parts: a Web front-end, which provides a graphical HTML-based interface through which certificate requests may be made, and the actual CA hardware itself. The CA process is considered to be an infrastructure service and therefore has been located in the Intelink Service Management Center *operating under their direct control.*

Torok envisions a CA process that is divided into two different parts for how initial requests for certificates will be made. In the first part, an Intelink user would apply directly to the CA to obtain their certificate. Using their browser to access the Web front-end, the user would provide their identification information to the CA and apply for the appropriate access privileges. Intelink management could then properly verify the identity of the user with security personnel and thereby determine the appropriate level of access to bestow on that person. Once this is complete, the CA could then place a signed certificate on the Web front-end that the user could then retrieve with their browser.

The second part of the process that Intelink plans to support is one in which the user requesting a certificate has their organizational security officer send their clearances, through official channels, to the CA. This "out of band" part of the process validates the identity of the requesting person.

5.2.3 Secure Sockets Layer (SSL)

The other major component that works in conjunction with the Certificate Authority and rounds out Intelink's *Security Management Infrastructure* is the *Secure Sockets Layer* (SSL) protocol. SSL was originally developed by Netscape Communications Corporation for use in its *Navigator* Web browser software. It has since become a primary *de facto* standard for encrypting network traffic, superseding such security protocols as S-HTTP (Secure HTTP) and Microsoft Corporation's own PCT (Private Communications Technology) protocol which was initially written for its *Internet Explorer* Web browser. First and foremost, SSL supports the use of X.509v3 certificates during the authentication process. And not surprisingly, the core security of SSL is based on encryption. In fact, SSL supports a variety of encryption schemes for each of its important functions:

- **Initial Authentication**

Either RSA public keys or Diffie-Hellman key exchange can be used.

- **Message Privacy**

One or more of these symmetric algorithms are used: DES, Triple-DES, RC2, or RC4 (the latter two of which are from RSA; Triple-DES is an extra strong version of DES which uses 112 bit long keys).

Another prominent symmetric algorithm is the *International Data Encryption Algorithm* (IDEA), originally proposed by James Massey and Xuejia Lai in 1990. IDEA is now an algorithm patented by *Ascom Tech AG*, a Swiss telecommunications and service automation company, and is used by the popular e-mail encryption software known as *Pretty Good Privacy* (PGP).

• Ensuring Data Integrity

One of these hash functions is used: MD5 from RSA or the Secure Hash Algorithm (SHA).

Even more importantly, as we will discuss later, some implementations of SSL fully support all of the encryption algorithms used in *Fortezza*, providing future compatibility with the *Multilevel Information Systems Security Initiative* as needed.

Figure 5-2 presents a very simplified view of how an SSL communications channel is established.

It should be evident that the combination of a Certificate Authority and the use of X.509v3 certificates with the Secure Sockets Layer protocol provides a significant amount of security for a network. However, it must be emphasized that SSL is a transitory standard, and will be superceded in the near future by *Transport Layer Security* (TLS). The TLS effort is focused on providing security features specifically at the Transport Layer of the OSI Model,[16] rather than applying general-purpose security and key management mechanisms.

Nevertheless, these are all key aspects of the *Security Management Infrastructure* used by Intelink, which in turn directly lays the groundwork for all Intelink security services. There are other security services as well, either in place on Intelink today or intended for inclusion at some point in the near future. We will go over these other major security services in the following section.

5.3 INTELINK SECURITY SERVICES

According to Torok, Mike Zajdek, a computer security expert assigned to Intelink's *Security Policy and Plans Directorate*, and Susanne Rosewell, the Intelink Information Systems Security Officer (ISSO), the basic security building blocks cited earlier are most important for Intelink. These additional security services include strong authentication, the concept of end-to-end confidentiality, enhanced access control, and network auditing and monitoring.

---

[16] See Chapter 1 for additional details of the OSI Model.

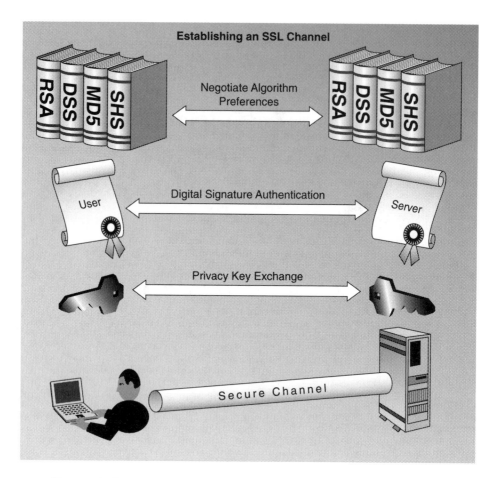

Figure 5-2 Establishment of an SSL Channel.

5.3.1 Strong Authentication

This service is perhaps the most critical to Intelink, which explains their reluctance to employ a single sign-on capability. Indeed, single sign-on implemented by using a password does not, by itself, provide the best solution for an intranet such as Intelink. In particular, the large number of users and decentralized structure do not facilitate the use of a single large password database. Just the thought of having to manage the password needs for all of the users in the entire Intelink Community is daunting. There is a question of whether this approach is even feasible, or at least whether it would be cost-effective.

Instead, a better solution would be to make use of X.509v3 certificates. In this way, a user would be able to log into Intelink with their password as they would normally. However, after the authentication process, an Intelink Certificate Authority will issue a certificate to the user which will then be managed by their Web browser (alternatively, the certificate could be stored in a local Private Key Database). The certificate will be transmitted securely using SSL. Thereafter, whenever the user wishes to access, for example, a particular intelligence database on Intelink, the browser simply needs to present the respective database server with the user's certificate. The database server can then grant or deny access accordingly, based on whether the user's certificate reflects the required security clearance.

In spite of the convenience that single sign-on could one day bring to Intelink users, it concerns many to think that the wealth of classified data that exists on Intelink might eventually be protected by only one password. After all, a password is like a key to a particular locked door, such that using a single sign-on approach to protect the information of all of the various organizations on Intelink would be akin to having the same key for all of those locked doors. This concern has been addressed with the concept of a security *token*. A token is merely a piece of hardware, such as a PC (PCMCIA) card or a *smartcard*, credit card-sized devices that can act as a repository for the certificate. The security advantage is that, in addition to the password for a particular user, an adversary must also have that user's token. This approach combines the convenience of an individualized password with the added security of certificates. It does raise the new issue of forcing users to be watchful of their tokens, for without them they would not be able to access Intelink. However, this may not be so difficult if the token was a *smartcard* that could also double as the user's identification badge. More will be said about tokens in Section 5.5, when we discuss MISSI and *Fortezza*.

In any case, although several pilot projects are underway that use X.509v3 certificates for authentication, their widespread use on Intelink as a whole has not yet been established. Currently, users must be content with using multiple authentication passwords in order to gain initial entry into Intelink and then subsequently use its information resources. The *bottom line* for Intelink—or anyone in a network environment—is that reusable passwords, even if they are encrypted, offer no value-added from a security standpoint since they are so vulnerable.

5.3.2 Enhanced Access Control

Another service that directly follows from the use of certificates is that of an enhanced access control capability (Figure 5-3). Currently, the intelligence products that are available on Intelink fall under the category of "general access" data. Intelink does provide services at different security classification levels, but this is done on separate instantiations of Intelink. Within each instantiation, there is no real distinction among users. Thus, the information available at each classification level, i.e., within each instantiation, must be capable of being viewed by its general population with no special caveats. Within each instantiation of Intelink, intelligence products with a limited distribution are made available through what the SPPD refers to as the *COI Program*, a more formal arrangement for protecting sensitive information.

The Intelink COI Program takes advantage of the fact that certificates do provide a reasonable solution to the problem of identification. Once a user has been authenticated onto Intelink, his browser will have access to his certificate. All that must be done, then, is to make sure that the user's certificate contains the user identity information necessary to access the restricted COI. This, of course, would be verified by an appropriate "out-of-band" security officer to ensure the legitimacy of the clearance. Specifically, data fields must be defined within the certificate which contain a sufficient amount of uniquely identifying information. Examples of possible data fields include:

- Name of Person
- Organizational Identifier
- Role or title of the user
- Nationality
- Government Employee/Contractor

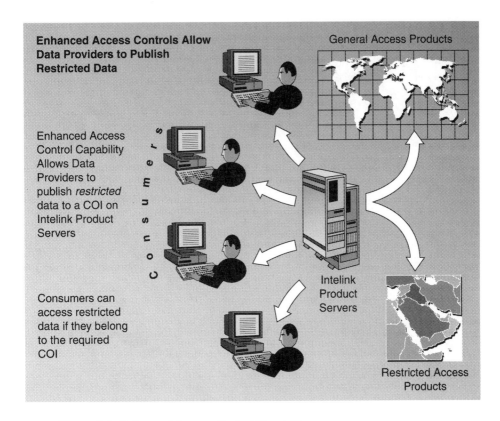

Enhanced Access Controls Allow Data Providers to Publish Restricted Data

General Access Products

Enhanced Access Control Capability Allows Data Providers to publish *restricted* data to a COI on Intelink Product Servers

Consumers

Consumers can access restricted data if they belong to the required COI

Intelink Product Servers

Restricted Access Products

Figure 5-3 Enhanced Access Control Capability.

Several fields are still being developed. Nationality, for example, is a relatively recent distinction that will provide direct support for instantiations of Intelink such as *Intelink-Commonwealth*.

COIs can be defined and updated by "COI Managers" using a registration service hosted at the ISMC (see Figure 5-4, top of the next page). This arrangement allows a certain degree of flexibility in the management of COIs and is therefore an important factor in their successful implementation. The key characteristic of this certificate-based approach, though, is that it enables access to be controlled by the original producers of the data. Should new requirements arise, such as allowing additional COIs to have the ability to access the information originating from a particular data provider, the data providers merely

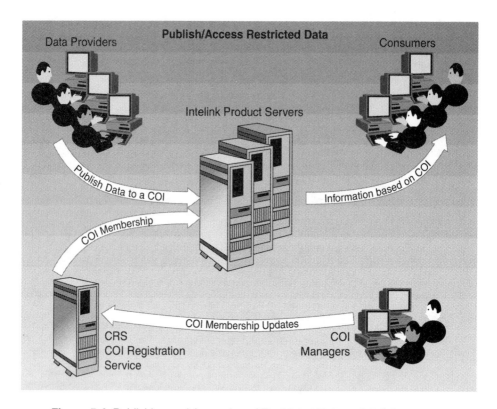

Figure 5-4 Publishing and Accessing of Restricted Data on Intelink.

need to update the respective product server. More will be said about the concept of COIs in Chapter 6.

5.3.3 Network Auditing and Monitoring

The purpose of network auditing and monitoring is not to make the lives of Intelink users simpler, as the previously mentioned security services have done, but is instead targeted at making overall management of the network much easier to perform. For a network as large as Intelink, its administration is a monumental task. Thus, no security approach would be complete or reliable without considering how to monitor the network. Auditing network traffic provides a window into the operation of that network that can then be logged for future reference. This in turn provides, for example, the ability to monitor the overall flow of the network in order to better pinpoint areas where it might not be functioning properly. An even more critical function of auditing is that it provides a mechanism by which network intrusion may be detected, as well as providing evidence of whether the server access control scheme is working as intended. The fact that Intelink's Security Management Infrastructure uses SSL and X.509v3 certificates facilitates the generation of the audit log, which can then provide reliable, precise information about the users that are accessing a given set of servers. Other information that can be included in the audit log includes: protocol (e.g., SSL version number), encryption key size, and browser identification. Figure 5-5 shows a sample audit report that might be generated with this security service.

5.3.4 Security Services Summary

We now summarize our discussion of the various security services that Intelink either currently provides or will soon be able to provide in the near future. Strong authentication and end-to-end confidentiality are implicitly provided by the Secure Sockets Layer protocol and X.509v3 certificates, while the application of these two security building blocks provides a way to support single sign-on authentication, enhanced access control and Communities of Interest, secure collaboration, and network auditing.

The SPPD explains that the set of commercial products that is being used by Intelink is being continually updated. Some of the major products that Intelink has evaluated, or is currently using in order to provide security include:

Software Configuration:

- SSL Server:
  Open Market WebServer

- SSL Browser:
  Netscape Navigator and Internet Explorer

- Certificate Authority:
  GTE CyberTrust, Open Market Web Front-End, ORACLE, ICS Motif

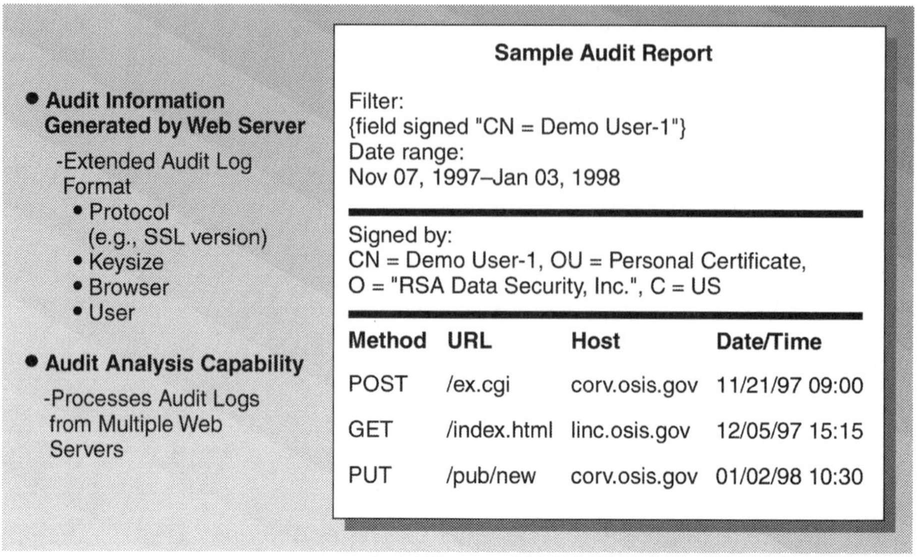

Sample Audit Report

- **Audit Information Generated by Web Server**
  - -Extended Audit Log Format
    - Protocol (e.g., SSL version)
    - Keysize
    - Browser
    - User
- **Audit Analysis Capability**
  - -Processes Audit Logs from Multiple Web Servers

Filter:
{field signed "CN = Demo User-1"}
Date range:
Nov 07, 1997–Jan 03, 1998

Signed by:
CN = Demo User-1, OU = Personal Certificate,
O = "RSA Data Security, Inc.", C = US

Method	URL	Host	Date/Time
POST	/ex.cgi	corv.osis.gov	11/21/97 09:00
GET	/index.html	linc.osis.gov	12/05/97 15:15
PUT	/pub/new	corv.osis.gov	01/02/98 10:30

Figure 5-5 Sample Audit Report.

- Audit Analysis Tool:
    Open Market WebReporter

- COI Registration Service (CRS):
    Web/Database Interface Software, Web-Oracle-Web (WOW), ORACLE, Custom HTML Forms from MITRE, Scripts

In short, Intelink has adopted a COI approach and solution set which provides the security services necessary for COI data exchange and collaboration. Operated from the ISMC, this *COI Program* is based on *trust* between the various Web servers containing intelligence information and the specific COI users. The *trust* is based on public key certificates, employing software using the X.509v3 certificate standard, which have been "signed" by a common Certificate Authority.

5.4 MINIMIZING THE COST OF SECURITY

Cost is always an issue, with government and private industry alike. Yet, protecting an intranet with security products—or more specifically, protecting the investment that an organization has made in information technology—is of critical importance. The question, then, is how to develop a strong, comprehensive security solution for our intranet while simultaneously keeping the cost of such efforts to a minimum.

5.4.1 The Need for Standards

The most significant implication of this attitude of striving towards the best possible security implementation while still keeping an eye on cost is that standards must be used wherever possible. Chapter 3 discussed the importance of commercial off-the-shelf products, in terms of being capable of providing readily available solutions to information management problems. Proprietary products, on the other hand, although desirable from the standpoint of offering the most customized version for an organization, tend to cost more and have a greater potential for becoming obsolete over time. Given the critical need for good network security, obsolescence is unacceptable: standards must be followed.

The use of standards is very much a part of the strategy that is used by Intelink management. Referring again to the list of software products given at the end of Section 5.3.5 above, we see that these products are primarily COTS. In addition, most of the categories contain multiple products. This reflects the desire of Intelink's *Security Plans and Policy Directorate* to investigate multiple solutions to a particular aspect of network security. This will help ensure that that the best overall product is selected in order to meet the security needs required by Intelink. More will be said about this approach in the next section.

5.4.2 Pilot Projects: NPC and ADNET

Choosing security products based on standards is crucial in order to provide cost-effective solutions that are not only easy to use in an immediate-term sense but also maintain the long-term viability of the intranet in general (in the sense of being capable of upgrading the network in the future). Yet, deciding to go the route of COTS products is only the beginning. With security being such an important issue across government and the private sector alike, there are many products available in the market today from which to choose. The next step, then, is to analyze the available products, comparing and contrasting them in order to find the best security solution.

Clearly, the best way to verify how well a security product works is to actually install it into a real operating environment. However, to implement that product across all of Intelink at once has the potential for disaster. For example, Intelink's SPPD frequently participates in programs to test and evaluate preliminary versions of security products, such that widespread installation of a particular so-called "beta test version" product might have an unpredictable and decidedly undesirable impact on operations. A better plan is to select a specific subset of the Intelink community, and then limit the evaluation of security products to that isolated area only. After such potential candidates from the Intelink Community have been identified, then the real process of pilot testing new security products can begin.

Two candidates in particular with which ISMC has worked on security pilot projects in the past are the Non-Proliferation Center (NPC) and the Anti-Drug Network (ADNET), both of which represent specific *Communities of Interest* on Intelink. The NPC, organizationally contained within the Central Intelligence Agency, is concerned with analyzing the global proliferation of nuclear and other weapons of mass-destruction such as the chemical weapons used by Saddam Hussein against the Kurdish people earlier this decade. This COI includes the Defense Intelligence Agency (DIA), the Department of Energy (DOE), the National Air Intelligence Center (NAIC), the National Ground Intelligence Center (NGIC), the National Security Agency (NSA), and the Special Operations Command (SOCOM) among its users. ADNET is a secure data network that supports U.S. national detection and monitoring of drug trafficking. Among the organizations that it services are the Drug Enforcement Administration (DEA), the Federal Bureau of Investigation (FBI), both the East and West divisions of the Joint Interagency Task Force (JIATF-East and JIATF-West), the El Paso Intelligence Center (EPIC), and the Defense Information Systems Agency (DISA).

By working with NPC and ADNET to develop the security of their respective networks in a pilot project mode, Intelink's SPPD was able to begin gaining experience with the various security products available, establishing a baseline of understanding for their widespread use across all of Intelink. The SPPD was especially interested in all of the issues implicit in deploying a *Security Management Infrastructure.* Although they realized how useful certificates were in terms of providing strong authentication, they still had many questions about how to actually go about using them. For example, they wanted to know what process is involved in the creation and distribution of certificates, how difficult it is to manage those certificates with a *Certificate Revocation List*, and what such an approach costs from the perspective of operation and management. The NPC and ADNET pilot projects went a long way to allow Intelink to develop a comprehensive understanding of the security products that it tested.

The test environment provided by the NPC and ADNET pilot projects also helped to address other issues as well. For example, being the global intranet that it is, one major concern for Intelink is *interoperability.* Specifically, the *Intelink Management Office* must ensure that an SMI that seems to work well within a local and limited context, can also work on a global level with others elsewhere in the U.S. Government, or with those used by American allies and coalition partners. Along these same lines, another major issue to consider is *scalability*, that is, how easily the products used in an SMI architecture can be upgraded or changed in the future as networking technology advances. Without ensuring interoperability and scalability, the cost of maintaining individual security solutions across Intelink would be prohibitively expensive.

Overall, the NPC and ADNET pilot projects were extremely useful to Intelink. The pilot projects helped to confirm that the chosen commercial products could be applied to all of Intelink and properly satisfy its requirements for network security. The feedback received from system administrators, information system security officers, as well as individual users involved in the pilot projects also aided in assessing the functionality and ease of use of the many security products. Additionally, the *Intelink Management Office* was able to forge ties with the vendors of those products, making it easier to obtain technical support and providing a channel through which vendors could make improvements to their products in order to better serve their customers.

Thus, through the use of commercial off-the-shelf products that follow the standards set by industry, and by testing those products initially in a pilot project environment, Intelink was able to establish a much more cost-effective security solution than it otherwise would have.

5.5 U.S. GOVERNMENT NETWORK SECURITY EFFORTS

Although commercial off-the-shelf products are certainly important to Intelink, it is important to note that there is also a need for it to be compatible with the information security standards that are being developed internally by the U.S. Government. In particular, one of the stated goals of Intelink security management is to ensure that Intelink remains compatible with the *Multilevel Information Systems Security Initiative* (MISSI), a network security effort being developed by the National Security Agency. By keeping Intelink open to new approaches—that is, not just commercial products, but to U.S. Government approaches like MISSI as well—helps to ensure that the network will be sufficiently flexible to handle future network security requirements.

5.5.1 Multilevel Information Systems Security Initiative (MISSI)

The *Multilevel Information Systems Security Initiative* actually refers to a broad set of products that are intended to become the basis for a government standard for network security. For example, MISSI specifies a particular *Security Management Infrastructure* that involves commercial "Certificate Authority" workstations running trusted, government-certified operating system software. The core component of this SMI is reliance on the use of user-specific hardware *tokens* to contain user certificate information. The cards are also programmed with a set of approved cryptographic algorithms, which in turn are the mechanism by which they can provide such critical security services as authentication and end-to-end confidentiality of data. The two primary versions of these hardware tokens are known as *Fortezza*, and more recently *Rosetta*, cryptographic cards.

5.5.2 Fortezza and Rosetta

Fortezza is the name of the original hardware card used by MISSI for providing cryptographic functions and certificate storage capability for users

Figure 5-6 NSA MISSI Icon.

in a secure network environment (Figure 5-6). It comes in the form of a PC (PCMCIA) card, and is designed to protect both the information and the system of its user. The main element of *Fortezza* is the "CAPSTONE/KEYSTONE" integrated circuit. This hardware chip houses four cryptographic functions that are based on *Federal Information Processing Standards*, as established by the National Institute of Standards and Technology. These algorithms include:

- Secure Hash Algorithm (SHA-1)

- Digital Signature Standard (DSS)

- *Skipjack* Encryption Standard

- Key Exchange Algorithm

The card is accessible through a 12-digit *Personal Identification Number* that its user must provide in order to activate the card. It is intended to be used in conjunction with the Certificate Authority workstation of the MISSI-specified SMI. Specifically, the user's certificate is loaded onto their Fortezza card, providing portable storage of their certificate information. Whenever needed, the user merely enters in their PIN in order to access their certificate. The encryption algorithms used in Fortezza are strong enough to protect information classified as high as the Secret level. In addition, a stronger version of Fortezza, called *Fortezza Plus*, is being developed to handle higher classification levels.

In spite of its usefulness as a security tool, Fortezza does have one significant limitation: cost. The price of a Fortezza card alone has been estimated at around $100. There is also the issue that many networks do not use PC cards, and therefore cannot directly support the use of Fortezza. For these cases, there is also a cost involved in adding PC card compatibility. To address this issue, there is a new MISSI project being developed that intends to provide a low-cost alternative to Fortezza: the *Rosetta* smartcard. Although the relatively small integrated circuit space provided by a smartcard means Rosetta will not be able to provide the functionality of a full Fortezza card, the estimated $3 cost per card will be very attractive to many users.

5.5.3 Outlook for MISSI

The *Multilevel Information Systems Security Initiative* is on-going. It is too early to tell whether MISSI will become as ubiquitous as the Data Encryption Standard (DES) or the TCP/IP networking protocol suite, both of which have become major forces in shaping the modern network. The approach being taken by Intelink, that is, following a dual path of commercial security solutions and maintaining compatibility with the U.S. Government solution, will serve them well. As long as cost can be kept tolerably low, following this approach certainly provides architectural flexibility for Intelink in the future. Indeed, this same concept is equally applicable to commercial networks as well.

5.6 ACCESS CONTROL ISSUES

As we have already mentioned in Chapter 4, as well as in our discussion on COIs in Section 5.3.2, controlled access of the information contained on Intelink, or for any other network for that matter, is a major concern. Certainly, authentication is critical to help ensure that only the legitimate users of the network are able to access it. Indeed, the core purpose of network security is to protect against unauthorized users intruding into the network. Yet, the ability to effectively partition the network into specified sections for select users truly extends the overall usefulness of the network, because it allows the network to mimic the natural hierarchy found in any business or government entity. Essentially, by doing this, the same network can be used to service multiple groups of users without fear of one group interfering (whether by accident or intentionally) with another.

The "need-to-know" policy so common in the Intelligence Community is a perfect example of a government requirement for access control. Although each employee has been granted a security clearance and is thereby deemed trustworthy to handle classified information, the best way to keep the circulation of classified information under control is to limit its distribution at the start. The same is true in many parts of private industry, in particular where a company has developed proprietary information that forms the basis for the products that it offers. For example, a file clerk or other junior member of the administrative staff at an engineering firm simply does not need to know the inner workings of that company's next-generation computer architecture. A manager at that same company, however, may be entitled to know such details, if it will aid him in his management of other, similar projects (and therefore help his company in general). Thus, so long as it does not prevent an employee from doing his appointed job, restriction of information is very important in order to ensure its protection. This is true in both the private sector as well as the government.

5.6.1 Access Control through the Instantiations of Intelink

Every network, regardless of whether it is commercial or governmental, will have its own, potentially unique configuration for handling the access control of the information that it contains. For Intelink, one of the most important forms of access control is based on the security classification of the information itself. In a general sense, this approach is very fitting. The policy infrastructure for assigning a classification level to specific information is already well established in the government, and it maps easily to a network environment: unclassified data has the least restrictions placed upon it, while information at the highest classification level obviously would have the most restrictions.

The primary way that Intelink enforces this form of access control is to physically separate itself into multiple different networks, or instantiations. These have already been described in some detail in Chapter 1, but what may not be so clear is how these individual networks fit together to form Intelink as a whole. Each of the telecommunications networks has evolved on its own and pre-dates the inception of Intelink. What is now referred to as Intelink-SCI uses the DoD "Joint Worldwide Intelligence Communications System" (JWICS) network, which is capable of carrying data that is classified at the "Top Secret/Special Compartmented Information" level. Similarly, Intelink-S uses the "Secret Internet Protocol Router Network," or "SIPRnet," operated by the Defense Information Systems Agency. This network is capable of distributing information at the "Secret" level. These two different networks addressed two separate needs: JWICS allowed producers of intelligence to generate and distribute the most detailed versions of reports, while SIPRnet frequently could be used to distribute that same basic information (although with the most sensitive details removed) to the wider audience that existed at the lower classification level. Now, both of these networks, are vital components of an overall Intelink architecture, each addressing the varied needs of individual users.

5.6.2 Problems with the Instantiation Approach

In spite of the seeming simplicity of this approach, it does pose several significant problems. First and foremost, by dividing Intelink into several instantiations, each with its own network, interaction among users of different instantiations is not easily done. For example, it is not uncommon to see Web pages on Intelink in which a person gives three different sets of contact information, one each for Intelink-SCI, Intelink-S, and Intelink-U (arguably, the three major instantiations of Intelink). In order for an Intelink-U user to contact that person, he must use a different network address than what an Intelink-S or Intelink-SCI user would use. If there was some way to interconnect all three networks in a secure manner acceptable by all members of the Intelligence Community, then it would be possible for the entire Intelink user community to communicate with each other in a much more straightforward manner. Unfortunately, the partitioned nature of Intelink does not facilitate communication among instantiations. Indeed, it seems to go against one of the fundamental purposes of intranets, i.e., that of unifying individual employees into a cohesive unit.

Not only do the different instantiations of Intelink make communication among their users relatively difficult, they also make management of the available information relatively more difficult. This is because each instantiation must have its own copy of the information in order for its users to access it. Consider again the Web page example from above. Although it may seem to an Intelink-U user that he is able to access the same information that an Intelink-SCI or even an Intelink-S user can access, this appearance is merely an illusion. Rather, the information on the page has been portrayed with the same common "look and feel" on the other instantiations. Thus, if the creator of that Web page wanted to update the information on one page, he would have to make sure that it was updated on all three instantiations in order to keep them consistent. The bottom line is that the Intelligence Community is paying a very large price for security. While the instantiation approach is presently "by design," a clear solution to the "multilevel security problem" that was acceptable to all elements of the Intelligence Community would significantly improve their ability to become a more "Agile Intelligence Enterprise."

Another major stumbling block for the instantiation approach has more to do with how intelligence data is actually classified. Over the years, each agency within the Intelligence Community has developed its own security classification guides that are designed to *consistently* interpret the U.S. Government security guides. In practice, however, these differing approaches have the potential to result in the same piece of intelligence being classified at different levels by different agencies. The origin for these potential discrepancies is generally related to the "sources or methods" used by one agency to generate a particular piece of intelligence. Given the high investment cost that is generally made in developing unique intelligence sources and methods, it is not surprising that a particular agency would be sensitive to all aspects of its security. Thus, what is thought to be extremely sensitive or "compartmented" information by one intelligence organization may instead be erroneously considered as "only" Secret by another. The differences in handling sensitive information among the various national intelligence agencies has led some agencies, such as the CIA, to isolate their version of Intelink, further frustrating the sense of "jointness" that Intelink strives to engender.

One final problem with access control based on classification level has to do with those people who are meant to have only limited exposure to intelligence data. Specifically, in addition to the U.S. military and civilian employees who work for Intelink Community members, there are also a large number of private industry employees working under contract for the government. These so-called "contractors" may be fully cleared to access a certain level of information, but because they have only been hired to handle a specific project, they seldom are given unrestricted access to all of Intelink. Although arguably a separate issue, a similar situation exists for U.S. allies and coalition partners on Intelink-C.

All of these problems prove that a better approach is needed than just the simple breaking apart of Intelink into separate instantiations. A more flexible solution must be found that provides straightforward, secure communication among all Intelink users and easy management of Intelink data, while simultaneously addressing the possibly unique classification requirements of the various intelligence agencies.

5.6.3 Multilevel Security versus Multiple Security Levels

Mike Zajdek succinctly summarized the instantiation approach to Intelink security. Zajdek said, "Intelink has *multiple security levels* rather than *multilevel security*." The wording may be deceptively similar, but the distinction is definitely significant. The current instantiation approach that Intelink follows is very much like providing multiple—and very separate—security levels. As we discussed above, such isolation does not promote interaction among the different instantiations and tends to complicate the management of data contained within Intelink. What is needed instead, then, is a single *multilevel* security solution.

The key characteristic of such an approach would be a single, unified network shared by all Intelink users. To provide secure access control under this scenario, only communication from a higher classification level to a lower one would be allowable, while the opposite direction would not be permitted. Authentication could be provided by certificates, and an encryption protocol similar to SSL will no doubt be involved as well.

An example of high level to lower level access would be an Intelink-SCI user who needed to get copies of unclassified, open-source material from Intelink-U. Hopefully unauthorized requests for sensitive information would only occur by accident, say because some user thought that he was allowed to access some data when in reality he was not, or perhaps his request for access was still pending. Certainly, if an unauthorized user were consciously and willfully attempting to access classified information, such action would be documented, and resolved.

Unfortunately, there are still many challenges to overcome before a true multilevel security solution can be implemented on Intelink. One of the most notable challenges would be convincing the various member organizations of the Intelink community that such a configuration is sufficiently secure. The danger of an unauthorized intruder being able to access intelligence data, particularly at the highest level of classification, is serious. There are many people who remain unconvinced of the ability of current network security technology to successfully defend against all possible threats. For example, one possible scenario would be a cyberterrorist successfully attacking Intelink just as war breaks out against the United States or one of its allies. The potential for such disaster is too great for some Intelink community members to be persuaded to change from their decades-old attitude of relative isolation. Still, the benefits of a multilevel security solution for Intelink are compelling, and perhaps eventually such an approach will be achieved.

5.7 PERSONNEL/PHYSICAL SECURITY AND SECURITY POLICY

We have discussed the application of security to the networked environment of Intelink in this chapter. We have attempted to provide an overview of the strategies, approaches, and specific products as well as issues and concerns that constitute the application of security to an intranet. However, according to Jack Torok, we cannot overemphasize the importance of overall *personnel/physical* security and security policy. Although there may be variations in how each component of the Intelligence Community may implement them, personnel security, physical security, and security policy have always been of paramount concern.

The *Joint Security Commission*, a joint panel under the Director of Central Intelligence and the Secretary of Defense, has identified four principles that should guide the formulation, evaluation and oversight of U.S. security policy:

• Security policies and services must realistically match the threats we face and must be sufficiently flexible to facilitate change as the threats evolve.

• Security policies and practices must be consistent and enable us to allocate scarce resources effectively.

• Security standards and procedures must result in the fair and equitable treatment of all Americans upon whom we rely to guard our nation's security.

• Security policies, practices, and procedures must provide the security we need at a price we can afford.

These four principles guide the set of specific security policies used by the Intelligence Community. Policies exist specific to computer security and all aspects of physical security for each national intelligence agency.

Personnel and physical security are readily apparent. Generally speaking, only fully "cleared" employees have the ability to enter a secure building unescorted. At the National Security Agency, for example, prior to gaining employment each person must pass a rigorous background investigation and polygraph or "lie detector" test in order to ensure their integrity. Such investigations originally occurred only when a person was first hired, though now each employee is re-investigated approximately every five years. Employees are then provided a badge containing their picture, as well as an associated PIN, which denotes that they have been properly cleared. In order to gain access to the building, an employee must first pass through a perimeter fence and barricade by showing their badge to the guards that are posted there. Then to actually enter the building, the employee must pass their badge through an electronic reader and enter the PIN in order to authenticate their identity. Since there are circumstances in which "uncleared" personnel are allowed inside secure buildings (e.g., cafeteria and construction workers, as well as certain visitors), all employees must prominently show their badge while inside. Additionally, many individual rooms that contain more restricted information also have a combination lock or badge reader to provide further physical security. The procedures at other national intelligence agencies and other intelligence facilities are similar, and badge reciprocity among many intelligence units is a reality.

Information transferred between locations over the various intelligence networks is also treated with the same types of precautions. Although commercial telephone lines are leased whenever possible in order to save money, the seeming security flaw of using these publicly accessible communication paths is well taken care of by the fact that the information flowing across those lines is scrambled using extremely high-grade encryption.

Security policy is also extremely important. Although the basic tenets of security policy remain the same, each component of the Intelligence Community may implement it slightly differently. At the NSA, one simple example that is closely related to the physical security discussed above is the fact that employees are encouraged to confront anyone that does not prominently display their badge inside a secure building. Similarly, if an employee sees another wearing their badge outside of the secure area, the employee is also supposed to remind that person to remove it. Exit signs at the CIA remind employees to remove their badges. Such vigilance may perhaps seem overbearing, but it definitely helps to maintain a high level of security awareness in the minds of the employees. Another example of policy, more directly related to networks, involves the use of passwords. At the NSA, passwords are still the primary means used to provide authentication on its own, highly classified, internal intranet. Stringent physical security and the fact that there are no direct physical connections between the NSA's most sensitive computers and the outside world make up for the shortcomings of this approach. Nevertheless, it is always very important to have a good policy in place to handle how passwords are chosen, how often they must be changed, and what to do to remove a network account when an employee no longer needs access to that particular area.

The establishment of a clear set of security policies and strong physical security are critical to the implementation of an intranet. Without them, the intranet will likely become a totally unorganized repository of largely unusable information.

5.8 ADDITIONAL CONCERNS

Security and privacy concerns in this digital age are on the minds of everyone these days, and the security professionals in Intelink's *Security Plans and Policy Directorate* are no exception. Indeed, it has not been possible to provide a comprehensive look at *all* of the issues that are being examined as Intelink continues to grow. However, it is useful to point out a few additional concerns that are currently under study by the Intelink ISSO, Susanne Rosewell. She points out that these are examples of Intelink security issues that also apply to the private sector. They include:

- **Data Labeling**

  A good example of data labeling concerns for the Intelligence Community is the issue of properly "labeling" or identifying the specific security classification of a particular document or set of data. Access control only works if the proper permissions have been placed on classified information. Say, for example, that someone writes a document and improperly marks the classification to be Secret when it should have been Top Secret. Then, even if the security system that has been put in place can be trusted to only provide classified documents to those with the appropriate clearance level, all users that are at the Secret level will now have unrestricted access to Top Secret information. This is not a new problem. Classification mistakes will happen occasionally as policy changes. However, what has changed with the advent of Intelink is the speed at which documents can be transferred. Intelink provides a path of virtually instantaneous access that is, of course, ideal from the legitimate user's point of view. However, we must keep in mind that the "checks and balances" of the old, manual system did have one advantage, in spite of its slowness. Since requests for information had to pass through a whole chain of command, there was more opportunity for the security level of a particular document, as well as for the requester's "need-to-know" status, to be verified. The sheer speed of information transfer that an intranet like Intelink can provide is, from this perspective, actually a negative side effect.

The most important aspect of data labeling, however, relates to the overall concept of multilevel security (MLS). Without a valid integrity mechanism, no *automated* method of data labeling can be accomplished. And, of course, the absence of an automated method of data labeling means that no acceptable construct for MLS can be developed.

• Copyright Infractions / Nonapproved Software Distribution

Another negative side effect that comes along with implementing a mechanism that can easily transport information, like Intelink, is that it can be difficult to control distribution of unofficial data, proprietary data, and software. Data is data from the intranet's point of view, so it doesn't matter if it is a legitimate report that is being transferred or a cartoon that someone scanned in to send to his friends. Even worse than misusing government equipment, such as scanners and printers, is to send copyrighted material over the network. How does one keep someone from making copies of a software product, for which no legitimate licenses exist for using them? A good security policy helps to thwart this by making users aware of their responsibilities. Also, by having good auditing techniques in place, it is possible to pinpoint those users who have broken the rules. Yet, there currently is no comprehensive solution for this problem.

• Chat Channels

The concept of Chat channels as a collaborative tool will be discussed in Chapter 6. Essentially, they allow real-time interaction between two or more parties over the network. Chat channels bring to light two important security-related issues: the identification of users, and the classification of the information discussed over the channel. User identification is critical since other users must know with whom they are talking to in order to ensure that the "need to know" principle has been met. If the identity of the users cannot be reliably determined, then there is the potential that the information discussed is inappropriate for some of the people that are using the chat channel. This first problem is dealt with by implementing a good user authentication scheme. The second problem, however, is much more difficult to deal with. Certainly, there always exists the potential that someone will let slip a detail that is classified at a higher level than what the chat channel is cleared to carry. This is actually a long-standing problem, akin to the classification marking issue that has already been discussed above. More insidious than this, however, is the possibility that during the length of a conversation, a group of users will discuss enough details of a particular problem that, although any one particular part of the conversation maintains the classification level of the chat channel, the aggregate classification of the conversation as a whole exceeds the "rating" for the channel. If this were to happen in a static document, the solution is simple: mark the individual paragraphs with their appropriate classification levels, then mark the entire document as being at an appropriately higher classification level. In the dynamic environment provided by a chat channel, however, classification issues are clearly a major concern.

All three additional issues are not unique to an intranet environment, and have existed for decades on their own. However, intranet technology has clearly exacerbated these problems that now require specialized solutions.

5.9 How Does this Relate to Business?

In this chapter we have seen how network security has been directly applied to Intelink. The major security services that it offers are: strong authentication for its users, end-to-end confidentiality of transmitted data, enhanced access control, and network auditing and monitoring. Support for single sign-on is coming but has not been fully implemented. All of these services are provided on Intelink through the use of several key security building blocks, including Certificate Authorities, X.509v3 certificates and the encryption-based Secure

Sockets Layer protocol. Commercial off-the-shelf products form the basis for Intelink's security, though maintaining flexibility in order to accommodate future U.S. Government security standards such as MISSI and Fortezza is also a high priority.

In spite of the many security services that Intelink provides, there is still much room to improve the network. For example, the implementation of a unified multilevel security approach, instead of the separate instantiations that exist today, would go far to create a more versatile environment for Intelink users, facilitating the sharing of data and managing information across the enterprise. Other issues, such as better control over data labeling and chat channels, as well as a better solution to prevent copyright infractions, must also be worked out.

To the business leader, there are three primary lessons to keep in mind:

• Security Is Critical

As we have seen in both Chapters 4 and 5, security is *critical* in order to maintain the functionality and reliability of any network, government and private alike.

• No Single Solution

Unfortunately, there is no single comprehensive security solution that will satisfy all of the requirements, for all networks. This means that it is not yet possible to simply purchase a standard product that will meet the security needs of all intranets. Each individual network must be analyzed, and a specific solution generated to respond to the specific and unique needs of that network.

• Costs Must Be Balanced

The desire for a high level of network security must be tempered by the reality that costs must be kept to a minimum. However, as we discussed in Chapter 4, studies indicate that too *little* is being spent on network security.

However, by judiciously following industry standards for network security, and using proof-of-concept pilot projects prior to full-scale implementation, the long-term effectiveness of an intranet can be assured.

Chapter 6

User Tools and Services

*T*oday Intelink users can view the most recent satellite photos on their computers, as well as any number of literally thousands of pages of classified reports from various intelligence agencies. White House aids using Intelink to monitor the recent build-up in the Middle East as the world prepared for additional hostilities with Iraq were able to receive daily CIA updates on the crisis. State Department analysts, the Pentagon, and the warfighter in the field all have instant access to the bulk of the Intelligence Community's classified information on their computers. The information available on Intelink is enormous, and very easy to exploit and manipulate. What makes Intelink—and any well designed intranet—so powerful, and its information so easy to manipulate, is the set of tools used to perform its various user and security services, as well as collaboration, intelligence dissemination, training and other functions.

The very genesis of Intelink came about after a series of conversations between Steve Schanzer, considered to be the "father" of Intelink, and James Woolsey, the Director of Central Intelligence at the time. Woolsey and then Deputy Secretary of Defense John Deutch (Deutch himself became Director of Central Intelligence in 1995) were concerned about system interoperability among the intelligence agencies and their customers, and wanted to improve the automated tools used to accomplish intelligence functions. Schanzer, noticing what was going on at CERN, and who also had been to see Marc Andreessen (who later co-founded Netscape Communications) at the University of Illinois, asked himself, "Why not build a 'CompuServe' for the Intelligence Community?"

Popular, nationally available, "internet content providers" such as *CompuServe*, *America On-Line* (AOL), and Microsoft are successful because they collectively offer a variety of proprietary browsers and tools as well as business related and other services to their users. AOL offers internet access, updates on weather, email, news, sports, and stocks, multimedia entertainment, and their own proprietary search engine. Successful intranets, like Intelink, must have at their disposal a similar vast array of mission relevant tools.

Admittedly, trying to choose appropriate and cost-effective tools for an intranet can be a difficult task. This chapter will describe the complete set of *user-specific* tools that operate on Intelink, including search, collaboration, and reference tools. Non user-specific tools are covered elsewhere in this book. For example, the various security implementation tools are described in Chapter 5, and examples of intelligence producing tools, including electronic publishing and dissemination tools, are cited in Chapter 8. This chapter will conclude with a brief look at a few "future tools," providing example areas of research currently being explored to extend the capabilities of intelligence networks.

6.1 THREE CATEGORIES OF USER TOOLS AND SERVICES

The user-specific tools and services currently available on Intelink can be classified into a general framework containing three categories: search, collaboration, and reference. As we shall see, a robust array of intelligence analyst support tools, listings, collateral news services, and other topics are available as *hypermedia*. Of course the entire concept of hypermedia—the genesis of which can be attributed to former MIT president Vannevar Bush who described a similar concept as early as 1945—is perhaps the most powerful intranet tool of all. References to hypermedia links can be depicted as text, icons, or even as related images, and are frequently duplicated. This duplication, albeit redundant, is actually a useful tool in itself. We will observe this duplication as we proceed linearly through the "Intelink Central" homepage (Figure 6-1). For example, in the figure below—a snapshot of the actual "Intelink Central" homepage that users see initially upon logging on to Intelink—a hyperlink to the *Intelink Service Management Center* currently appears in three locations: as a "hot link" under the main map of the World, as an organizational listing under "Intelink Directorate," and under the category "Support." It is hoped that by examining the approach taken by Intelink, one can gather insight into the automation and streamlining of the flow of documents, data, and other mission-critical information on an intranet.

6.1.1 Search Tools

The ability to quickly find information related to a particular topic is one of the most critical components of any intranet, and certainly of Intelink. Indeed, perhaps the single most frequently asked question within the Intelink environment is how to find a particular reference to imagery or a piece of fragmentary data, intelligence report, or other item of interest. On a typical corporate intranet, for example, if you submitted the keyword "employee benefits," you would receive back a number of items to which you could then hyperlink, perhaps including:

- Health insurance brochures

- Wage and pay chart

- Employee benefits handbook

- Human resources information system

- News article on new exercise equipment

Unfortunately, finding the information or data that you are looking for is not always this easy. Indeed, search engines on the global Internet are notorious for returning *too much* information—a simple query will often return tens of thousands of webpages to the frustrated searcher. And, it gets worse. According

Figure 6-1 Screen Shot of Intelink Homepage.

to a study published in the April 3, 1998 issue of *Science* journal, published by the *American Association for the Advancement of Science*, the most efficient search engines are able to locate less than 34% of the pages on the World Wide Web. According to NEC Corporation researchers Dr. C. Lee Giles and Dr. Steve Lawrence, who wrote the article based on extensive research, some popular search engines can locate less than 10% of the available pages. As more and more pages are added each month, the situation continues to worsen. The study concludes that unless search tools are improved, many users may simply give up out of frustration, jeopardizing the value of the Internet or the large intranet application.

Recognizing the basic search requirement, as well as the known problems associated with this technology, Intelink has invested considerable resources and effort in providing its customers with a variety of effective techniques to perform searches for information. There are three primary approaches to finding information on Intelink:

1) View the Intelink Server Directories

The "Intelink Central" website or homepage contains hyperlinks to all of the servers currently available on a particular instantiation of Intelink, such as *Intelink-S*. This means that a user can hyperlink to the homepage of the "information space" of any Intelink organization. The directory listings are available by using either an icon or text representing the desired organization. For additional convenience, a user can also enter the name of the organization into a special query box that will then return a listing of links to homepages matching the search query. For example, on *Intelink-SCI*, the search string "NSA" will produce a set of links to all NSA affiliated entities with existing servers and valid homepages at the time of the query. This technique allows you to easily access the server that you believe contains the information you want, but requires prior knowledge about what is located on that particular server.

2) Use Subject/Category Indices

Another method of locating information on Intelink is to use a categorized list of links to specific organizations, products, and other sites. On Intelink, there is an area called *Wer'zit!?* (as in "Where is it?"), analogous to the popular global Internet search tool *Yahoo*. Wer'zit!? is a categorized listing of intelligence products, normally registered by the various intelligence producers themselves.

3) Use Search Engines

The third method of locating information on Intelink is to use one of several available "search engines" (or even multiple engines simultaneously, as we shall see), allowing you to search for various words or phrases (keywords) of interest within Intelink. The basic idea behind a search engine is to enter one or more keywords at a prompt, and then the search engine will respond with a list of links to documents on Intelink that contain those keywords. There are currently four different types of search engines available on most of the Intelink networks, including both commercial products and modified, handcrafted versions specifically designed for Intelink.

6.1.1.1 Server Directories

Server directories list all intelligence agencies, commands, offices, centers, and other organizations, including their subordinate units, that have information spaces accessible through Intelink. Each listing, whether a textual description or an icon of the organization's symbol, is actually a hyperlink to the homepage of the information space of that organization, set up by the ISMC as a service to its users. Each individual organization is responsible for ensuring that it has not been overlooked by the ISMC, and that it has been listed in the most effective manner. Figure 6-2 shows sample server directories listed by name in a textual format, as well as by an icon representing the organization.

6.1.1.2 Category Indices: Wer'zit!?

Similar to the server directories is the list of links provided by Wer'zit!? (Figure 6-3). What differentiates it from the previous service, though, is that Wer'zit!? specializes in finding links to specific sites on Intelink for which one does not know the formal organizational designation. Like the popular *Yahoo on*

Figure 6-2 Screen Shot Showing Directories as Organizational Icons.

on the global Internet, each site must be registered and approved—in this case by the Intelink Management Office. Upon entering the area called Wer'zit!?, the Intelink user is invited to find the data he or she is looking for using any one of four generalized search categories: geography, product type, intelligence subject, and service. These are described in more detail below:

• Geography

If the country or region related to the information is known, this listing by geographic location can be most useful.

• Product Type

This listing actually refers in turn to six general types of intelligence "product" available on Intelink:
- Administrative
- Documents/Reports
- News
- Databases
- Imagery
- Reference

• Intelligence Subject

Similarly, Wer'zit!? currently contains nine general intelligence subject areas:
- Business and Economics
- Energy, Resources, and Physical Environment
- Military
- Science and Technology
- Transportation
- Commodities
- Intelligence and Security
- Political, Government and Society
- Terrorism, Proliferation and Narcotics

• Service Categories

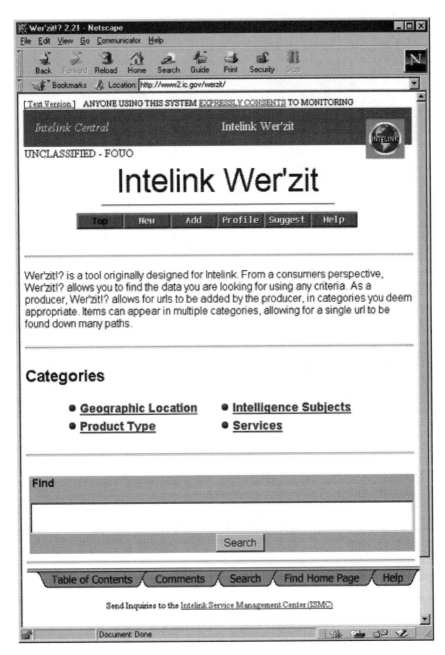

Figure 6-3 Screen Shot of Intelink Search Tool *Wer'zit?.*

Finally, there are currently ten specific categories of service:
- ♦ Announcements
- ♦ Development
- ♦ Organization
- ♦ Security
- ♦ Tools
- ♦ Collaboration
- ♦ Feedback
- ♦ Regulations
- ♦ System Information
- ♦ Training

As the Intelink user progresses down each subsequent level of the Wer'zit!? hierarchy, he encounters more options, eventually narrowing the path down to the specific area or homepage of interest. Items can appear in multiple categories, allowing a single location to be found by multiple paths or approaches. In a fashion analogous to *Yahoo*, these topics and sub-topics, as well as the actual products available, are subjected to a rigorous "registration" procedure. This registration procedure, which can be done on-line, is important as it facilitates and enhances the search process for the user. As the user navigates through the hierarchy, he receives a good overview of the information available on Intelink. This navigation process can be particularly helpful to an Intelink novice, and the results of their search will very likely be, or be very close to, their subject of interest.

6.1.1.3 Intelink Search Engines

There is no doubt that the most widely used method of finding information on Intelink is also the same approach used by most people to find information on the global Internet: the "search engine." One problem with search engines, as highlighted by the Giles and Lawrence study cited earlier, is that each one behaves a little differently, potentially producing varied results. Fortunately, there are five major search engines available on Intelink, including the ability to automatically use all engines concurrently, as well as several new approaches to search that are on the horizon. We will start out by briefly describing each of the current and planned Intelink search engines. We will then discuss the basic approaches that are used by search engines in general, relating them back to the Intelink examples. The five basic Intelink search engines are:

- **AltaVista, a commercial product from the *Digital Equipment Corporation***

AltaVista search software is considered by many to be the fastest on the market. The version of AltaVista available on the global Internet, using powerful *Digital Alpha* processor-based computers, frequently can respond to a search query into its database in two seconds or less. Not surprisingly, it is much quicker on a relatively smaller intranet application. AltaVista offers both a *Simple Search*, still containing the full power and scope, and an *Advanced Search*, where users can search by date, or perform detailed searches that process various combinations of words or phrases. Digital offers customized versions of its product for enterprises.

- ***Harvest*, originally developed by the University of Colorado**

Harvest is a set of tools that lets you retrieve, organize, search, cache, and replicate information that is gathered from across the global Internet or an intranet. A product of the Internet Research Task Force on Resource Discovery (IRTF-RD) and supported by the Advanced Research Projects Agency (ARPA), Harvest is based on *Glimpse*, originally a freeware product developed at the University of Arizona that provided index and searching facilities for UNIX systems only. Although funded as recently as 1996, it is likely to be phased out as newer, more sophisticated tools emerge.

- ***SLICK*, a specialized engine developed by Intelink**

Slick is an acronym for *Strategic Locator of Intelligence Community Knowledge*, and was developed in-house by the ISMC. It was designed specifically to optimize search operations by taking advantage of certain unique features of Intelink, such as its directory structures and locations of particular files.

- **Webinator, a commercial product from Thunderstone, an independent research and development company**

Webinator is a powerful and sophisticated index and retrieval package that allows the website administrator to provide a high quality retrieval interface to collections of Web documents, no matter where they reside on the network (Figure 6-4). One of its special features is "Concept Searching," which refers to the ability to automatically and selectively expand a search keyword to become an entire "concept set" of keywords. The new "concept set" is based on a special equivalence list that is maintained in the thesaurus for that word.

- *Hydra*, an "All-in-One" product developed by Intelink

Since all search engines have their own independent strengths and weaknesses, many Intelink users tended to send queries to several engines and compare the results. *Hydra*, another ISMC-developed application, responds to this need (Figure 6-5). *Hydra* allows users to perform a "multifaceted," search of Intelink with a single query. Essentially, *Hydra* provides a single prompt in which to enter the keywords and then simultaneously searches across all available indices (as we explain below), returning a set of interleaved results. The primary disadvantage of *Hydra*—or similar engines on the global Internet—is that they are unable to take advantage of the most advanced features found on the different engines. For example, special formatting used to customize a search on *AltaVista* will not be recognized by *Webinator*, so it must be filtered out.

As one might expect, currently the two most often used search engines on Intelink are the commercial products *AltaVista* and *Webinator*. However, *SLICK*—the ISMC developed and therefore easily adaptable search tool—is being enhanced by the use of metadata (data about data), and metadata tags, which we will discuss in Chapter 7. Metadata has the potential to significantly improve the ability to retrieve information by providing greater insight into its content and structure. In addition, several new commercial products with high potential are being evaluated by the ISMC. Two of the most promising "knowledge-based" search and retrieval products are shown on page 166.

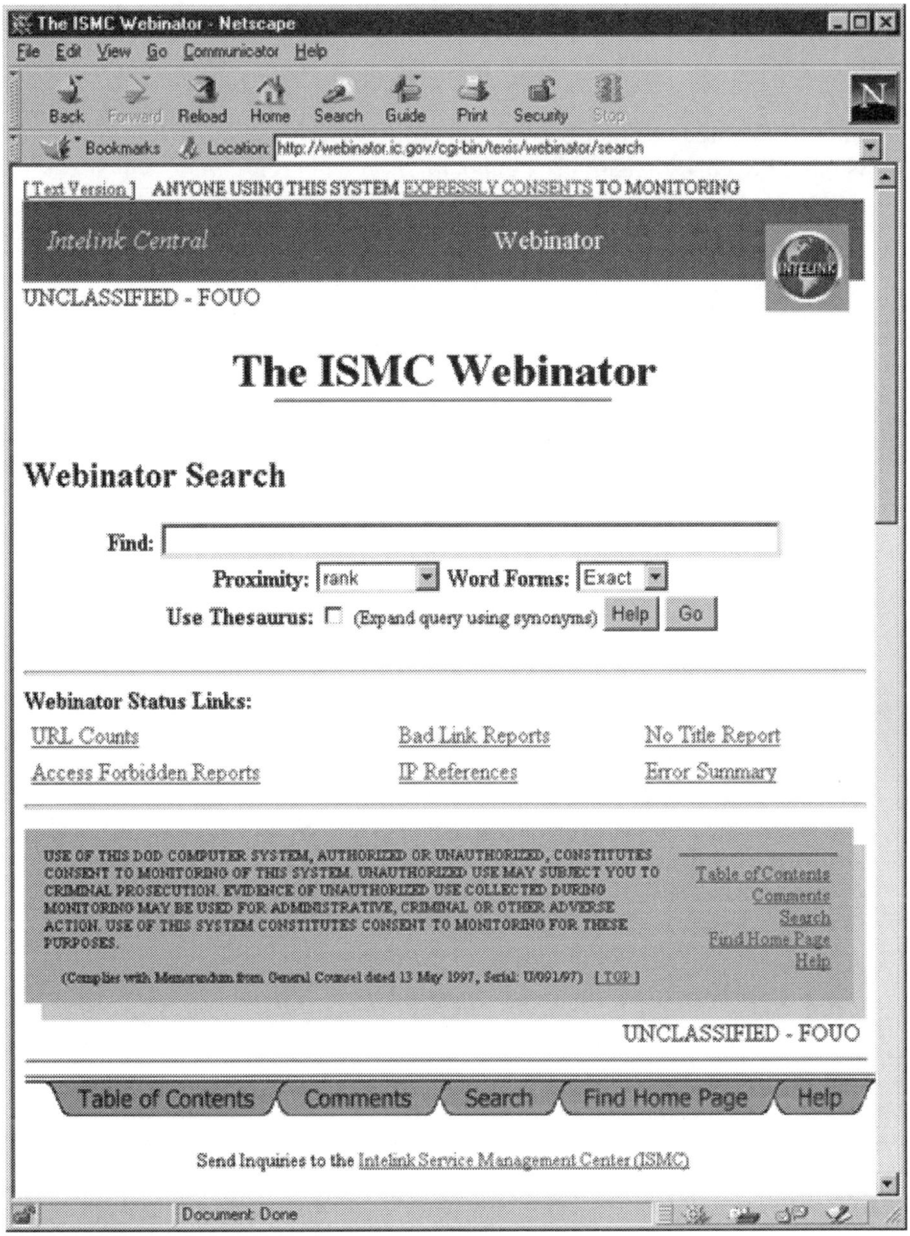

Figure 6-4 Screen Shot of Intelink Search Tool Webinator.

• *SEARCH'97*, **a product from the** *Verity Corporation*

The *Verity Corporation* has been around since 1988, and was one of
the early companies that played a major role in the development of the
National Security Agency's *Center for Applied Technology*, which we
will discuss in Chapter 8. Their early work within the Intelligence
Community in the late 1980's led to the development of a sophisticated
knowledge-based categorization product known as *Topic*. *Topic* has
since matured into a robust, scalable, and cross-platform product family
known as the *SEARCH'97* product suite. The *SEARCH'97* suite
contains tools for disseminating data across the enterprise, with
automated routing of information to individuals or workgroups based
on unique user "profiles" that are developed.

• *Excalibur RetrievalWare*, **a product from** *Excalibur Technologies*

RetrievalWare is a set of automation tools that facilitates the
development of mission-critical information from multimedia,
including unstructured text, database fields, images, video, and audio.
This innovative product is designed specifically to work with a
person's intuitive, native senses and natural language abilities. Using
proprietary algorithms, and built-in "knowledge databases,"
RetrievalWare is able to search for specific word meanings that can be
augmented by related terms and concepts. The ease of use and natural
language capabilities of this product contribute to its high potential in
the Intelink environment.

6.1.1.4 Search Engines—How They Work

In the use of any search engine, whether it is on the global Internet or an
intranet such as Intelink, the user enters specific keywords into a prescribed
area on a webpage. This information is then evaluated by the engine, which
then returns a list of links to pages that contain the specified keywords. In order
to accomplish this, the engine must evaluate each request against an index that
it has previously prepared to determine if anything matches the given search
criteria. The format of these indices will vary from search engine to search engine,

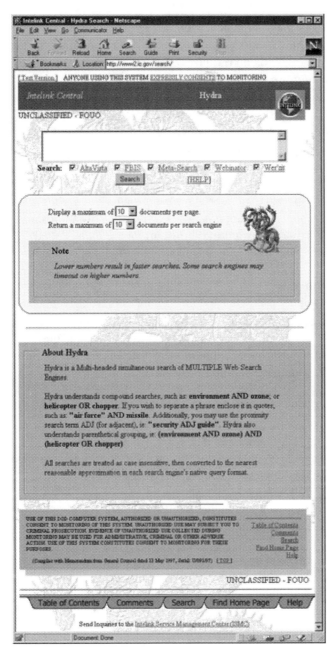

Figure 6-5 Screen Shot of Intelink Search Engine *Hydra.*

but essentially they represent an abbreviated version of all available information from the intranet. Any word determined to be superfluous is eliminated, and by focusing on only the most important information, the search process is much more efficient.

To see how this applies to Intelink, we turn to Randy Marks, one of the original members of the ISMC and now known as *"Dr. Surf"* to Intelink users around the world. Marks, who has been intimately involved in the development and implementation of Intelink's various search strategies since its inception, explains that there are three different approaches used in the creation of search engine indices. The three methods are: a Web "walker" (also known as a Web "crawler" or "spider"), a Web "broker/gatherer," or the "directed index." Understanding how these approaches work will allow the user to create better searches, and provides insight into how current the data is at any given time.

• Web Walkers

This type of search engine examines the Web and builds its index in no particular prescribed order. It starts its walk through the intranet from some central location—in the case of Intelink, it would be within the *Intelink Text Directory*—and travels to the next available site or page. Upon arrival, it begins to build its index by taking note of much, but not necessarily all, of the text, graphics, and especially any hyperlinks that appear on that page. Once the Web walker finishes documenting the most salient features of that page, it will then move on to the next available site by following another hyperlink. If the hyperlinks on that page have been exhausted, then a link from the next possible page is used. The Web walker may make several visits to the same site over the course of its traversal through the intranet, and as a result, can require a considerable amount of time to complete its entire walk. AltaVista, which uses a Web walker to build its index, currently takes a day or so to walk through Intelink. Thus, information in its index could be over 24 hours old. Whether or not this would pose a problem for the intelligence analyst, requiring him to use alternative search tools, would depend on the situation at hand.

The *Strategic Locator of Intelligence Community Knowledge* (SLICK) is another Web walker, but it has the added advantage of being able to interrogate an additional program to determine any changes that have been made on the server since it was last visited. Server administrators at the various individual Intelink sites run this additional program, known as *New Stuff*, and SLICK is then able to immediately identify changes without having to re-index the server itself. With this approach, SLICK provides users with the ability to search material with an index that has been updated on a consistent 24-hour basis.

It is interesting to note how quickly the advantages of one search engine change relative to the others. At its inception, SLICK provided a clear advantage over AltaVista in that it could re-index Intelink far faster than the latter engine. More recently, the performance of AltaVista has been improved and its indexing speed is now comparable to SLICK. However, with the use of metadata as described above, SLICK may once again prove to be have a clear advantage in that it will be able to provide more precise answers to search queries.

• Web Broker/Gatherers

This type of search engine, which is used by *Harvest*, takes a two step approach to improve response times by building a special composite index. In the first step, a software program known as a Web "gatherer" locally indexes all of the pages on an individual Web information server. Since this is a local process, it can be scheduled at any desired time of the day (for example, during a period of known low use), and takes very little time to accomplish its task since it does not have to actually go out on the network to perform its indexing as a crawler does. In the second step, a software program known as a Web "broker" is then run from some central location (the ISMC, in the case of Intelink). The broker, which contains the locations of all of the gatherers and the times that they are scheduled to complete their task, then queries the gatherers for their indices and builds the composite index. This new composite index is used at the broker's site to respond to all user search queries. Theoretically, this technique allows the information to be updated as frequently as desired. Unfortunately, primarily due to its complexity, *Harvest* is running on less than half of the Intelink servers.

• Directed Index Engines

Randy Marks refers to this type of search engine, which forms the basis for Intelink's popular Webinator product, as a directed search. Although it creates its index by processing one server at a time, multiple processes or programs are run simultaneously, significantly reducing the amount of time it takes to build the overall index. On Intelink, the Webinator index is updated approximately every day or so.

Intelligence analysts with search needs on information that must be indexed more frequently than approximately every 24 hours must resort to their own private intranets within their own agencies. Various portions of the internal NSA intranet, for example, are updated as frequently as every two hours. In most cases with daily indexing, satisfactory results can be obtained nearly every time as a user gains familiarity with the very powerful search and retrieval capabilities of Intelink (Figure 6-6). Indeed, improved use of the search prompt can be obtained through judicious use of the rules, syntax, and other available features. Particularly on AltaVista and Webinator, these features allow the user to be as creative as they are willing to take the time to learn them. The most common examples include:

• Boolean operators such as and, or, and not

• Use of a "+" sign prior to a keyword
   This informs the search engine that it is mandatory that the keyword be present in the returned information.

• Use of a "-" sign prior to a keyword
   This instructs the search engine to exclude references to that keyword.

• The wildcard symbol "*"
   The wildcard symbol can be used to match just the prefix or suffix of a keyword, or to ignore the middle of a term.

• Use of double quotes " "
   This tells the search engine that the quoted keyword must appear exactly as stated.

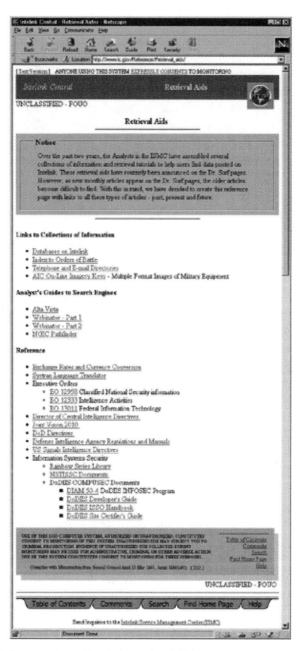

Figure 6-6 Screen Shot of Intelink Retrieval Aids.

6.1.2 Collaboration Tools

As the Intelink Community continues to grow, and the U.S. Intelligence Community itself becomes an organizationally decentralized and geographically distributed "virtual enterprise," the *need* for effective collaboration, as well as the *difficulties* associated with effective collaboration, also continue to grow. Indeed, the success of such a "virtual enterprise" is dependent upon its ability to bring its various dispersed assets together to bear on a particular intelligence problem. As we will discuss in Chapter 10, the future success of U.S. intelligence operations will be greatly dependent upon our ability to enhance speed, flexibility, and capacity through collaborative operations.

The importance of the concept of collaboration continues to gain recognition within the private sector and the media. Michael Schrage, collaborative design consultant for MIT and a fellow of the Merrill Lynch Forum, has authored *No More Teams!: Mastering the Dynamics of Creative Collaboration* (1995). This book was an updated version of his *Shared Minds: The New Technologies of Collaboration* (1990), which in turn was among the first books to explore both the tools and dynamics of successful collaborations in business, science, and the arts. In these books, he stresses that collaboration, which he defines as the "act of shared creation and/or shared discovery," is not the same as simple communication. Rather, it is the process of forming a solution to a critical problem by applying both information and expertise that has been gathered from several different sources. Schrage also points out that the quality and quantity of collaboration normally depend upon the tools that are used to provide it. According to Schrage, the issue is not automating the process of collaboration, but rather using the technological tools that are available to build and enhance the collaborative relationship.

The need for collaboration is also recognized within the Intelink Community, and within the U.S. Intelligence Community as a whole. As applied to Intelink, and to computing and information technology, the Intelligence Community narrows the Schrage definition. Robert Ferrone, a research scientist at the National Security Agency, defines *collaborative computing* as, "providing geographically dispersed networked computer users the simultaneous capability for audio, full action videoconferencing, whiteboarding, and document and applications sharing on a real time basis, almost as if they were in the same room together." In a special 1997 technology forecast prepared by NSA's Office of Research, Ferrone predicts that in five to seven years, real-time collaborative computing will encompass simultaneous group and desktop videoconferencing, applications sharing, sharing of computer screens, and meeting management, all in a seamless environment among two or more people.

Ferrone says, "With the corporate workforce becoming more geographically dispersed and specialized, collaborative and cooperative work will be absolutely essential." Many agree with this, and research funding by the federal government is continuing to play a key role in developing and promoting collaborative computing technology enablers. The Defense Advanced Research Projects Agency (DARPA), the original developers of the global Internet as we discussed in Chapter 1, is sponsoring numerous collaborative computing efforts and developmental alliances with academia, the private sector, and even military counterparts from our allies. DARPA is taking the lead in research that has the potential to revolutionize and accelerate systems that will allow the warfighter to see, feel, hear, and interact with time critical information.

At this time, the Intelink approach to collaboration is a standards-based strategy centered primarily on the expanding capabilities of Web browsers, rather than the implementation of a *specific* general purpose, proprietary "groupware" product such as *Lotus Notes* or *Microsoft Exchange*. To this end, the Intelink Service Management Center continues to explore, through rigorous testing and evaluation, a number of commercial products to enhance the collaboration capabilities of Intelink users, as we shall see below.

To facilitate our look at the efforts of Intelink, we define the ultimate in collaboration to be the *ability to electronically see, hear, and interact with a geographically disconnected person or group of people as though they were not separated.* Using this definition, it is then useful to visualize the following framework for the continual progression of Intelink collaboration tools (see Figure 6-7). Electronic mail is considered by many to be the most basic of collaborative tools. It provides convenient data transfer and is not restricted to text. However, there is no "physical presence," i.e., no real-time interaction. Newsgroups, and other "bulletin board" type mechanisms provide an improvement over simple e-mail in that they allow *focused* discussions, and include an array of tools to facilitate the process. "Communities of Interest"

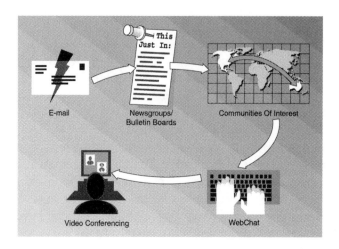

Figure 6-7 Intelink Collaboration Tools Framework.

take the concept of newsgroups yet another step further by exploiting the commonalities of groupings of people, organizations, business lines, and the like. The next stage includes a product called *WebChat*, which has a real-time presence, and begins to have a flavor of "physical" interaction. Within a few years, the capability for full video conferencing, sharing of whiteboards, and other advanced collaborative tools, will begin to be available across Intelink. For example, *Progressive Networks*, makers of *RealAudio* and *RealVideo*, plan to expand the capabilities of their product to stream any type of data. They recently announced the *RealMedia Architecture* technology, a next generation platform designed to stream any media type, such as audio, video, animation, three-dimensional images, as well as text. The *RealMedia* platform features a completely open architecture, and is among the first products delivered based on the *Real Time Streaming Protocol* (RTSP), a draft Internet standard supported by more than 40 companies. Real-time video teleconferencing is currently in limited use across the U.S. Intelligence Community among organizations that have the necessary bandwidth—clearly the limiting factor today—such as those with dedicated fiber-based networks. Always touted as the next "killer-application" for high performance desktop systems, this technology will someday allow a much higher quality—the next generation—of collaborative computing over Intelink.

In the three sections below we shall discuss the current status of the Intelink approach to enhancing collaboration capabilities, beyond the obvious e-mail tool. This discussion involves taking a closer look at several of the tools that are currently available, including the global Internet inspired *Newsgroups*, other *Bulletin Boards*, the concept of *"Communities of Interest,"* and a commercial product called *WebChat*.

6.1.2.1 Newsgroups

The concept of Intelink *Newsgroups* is directly analogous to the User Network (*Usenet*) Newsgroups that can be found on the global Internet. *Usenet* is a system estimated to encompass more than 10,000 different topic groups, to which people from all over the world can post messages and reply to other messages, including messages that they receive. Designed to facilitate discussions about specific topics of interest, these newsgroups are like a collection of thousands of individual bulletin boards with little notes on them, all posted in some public place. Other people can then comment on what has been written, in the same sense as if they had posted their response to the same public bulletin board, right next to the original article. Anyone with access to Intelink can "post" a specific message to be seen by everyone else on Intelink that has "subscribed" to that newsgroup.

To facilitate their use, individual "conversations" or bulletin boards are categorized by general subject area, and each newsgroup has a special title describing its particular topic. For example, on the global Internet, *misc.jobs.resumes* is the title of a newsgroup where people can post their resume in hopes of finding a new job. Similarly on Intelink, *misc.weapons.iraq* could be the title of a newsgroup devoted to weapons of mass destruction that are located in Iraq.

Interestingly, the use of newsgroups on Intelink has never met expectations. While this concept has become extremely popular on the global Internet, its use on Intelink is much less accepted. Although no studies have been done to determine the cause of this, many insiders believe that one of the underlying causes is the tendency to use the widely available Newsgroups on the intranet of an analyst's own agency. And, understandably, there are sometimes security classification issues that preclude some discussions being posted on Intelink. It must be reiterated once again that these roadblocks to collaboration and data sharing across the entire Intelligence Community enterprise will begin to fall as the Community evolves towards the concept of a more "agile" intelligence enterprise that we discuss in Chapters 8, 9, and 10.

6.1.2.2 Other Bulletin Boards

Fixed, electronic *Bulletin Boards*, functionally identical to the *Newsgroups* discussed above, have become a popular collaboration tool on Intelink. From a global perspective, these boards provide intelligence analysts with access to special products and services from Intelink headquarters or even their own "creations" within their organization's information space. From the "Intelink Central" homepage, users can access links to specific examples of fixed bulletin boards, or "click" on "*Other Bulletin Boards*" for hyperlinks to boards maintained at other locations within the U.S. Intelligence Community. Bulletin Boards maintained by Intelink Management include:

- **Intelink Management Office Director**

This is an opportunity to interact electronically with the Director of the Intelink Management Office, currently located at the National Security Agency. The incumbent, James P. Peak, devotes considerable time to responding to postings to this bulletin board, which generally is a forum to discuss his weekly column entitled, *A View from the Summit*. The column itself contains Peak's own honest examination of the multitude of challenges that are facing Intelink.

- **Dr. Surf**

This board is currently maintained by the technical leader of the ISMC, Mr. Randy Marks. In addition to responding to a myriad of problems and questions from Intelink users, Marks—in his guise as *Dr. Surf*—maintains a set of well-received Intelink Web page profiles. The profiles include his own unique "website reviews," which comment on the presence and effectiveness of a particular organization on Intelink. *Dr. Surf* also maintains a set of basic Intelink training materials that he has written.

Figure 6-8 Caricature of Intelink's Nooge.

• The Intelink "NOOGE"

In Yiddish slang, a "Noodge" is a nag or persistent critic. The ISMC version of this Yiddish slang is a "Nooge" (Figure 6-8). Indeed, a disclaimer from the ISMC management states, *"The Intelink NOOGE surfs Intelink looking for links that don't, information that isn't, and other stuff that frustrates users."* With an identity unknown to Intelink users, but suspected to be a composite voice of several Intelink management staff, the NOOGE represents the ultra-conservative side of Web operations. For example, he takes a dim view of fancy Java applets that have "razzle-dazzle," but do not add any real functionality or value to a website. The Nooge bulletin board hosts several areas including "The Nooge Reports," which contains the latest Nooge grumbles; "The Nooge's Clue-Mart," with various tips on how to better develop Web pages; and "The Nooge Tools," with links to recommended Web development tools.

• The BugBoard

The *BugBoard* was created in order to provide the Intelink Community with postings of critical, up-to-date information on computer viruses, program bugs, false information, and other real or perceived problems. Most of the information on the *BugBoard* is gathered from the global Internet on a weekly basis, with the source sites identified wherever appropriate. The *BugBoard* will soon have its own built-in search capability.

6.1.2.3 Communities of Interest

Microsoft Corporation, which continues to invest heavily in on-line services, still plans to seamlessly integrate the on-line publishing, electronic commerce, and other markets into a national network of consumer services. According to the *Wall Street Journal*, most of these commercial lines of business take the same basic approach that is at the very core of the *Microsoft* strategy—building online "communities of interest" that can be exploited for profit, i.e., transaction, advertising or perhaps subscription dollars. While the Microsoft strategy is still being debated and implemented, many websites today provide services including "virtual space" for communication and exchange on various issues. A good example is *Electric Minds*, a Web community for discussions about science, technology, and the future. Many analysts predict that this community building approach will have a significant impact in the business marketplace as well.

Intelink has implemented its own concept of "Communities of Interest" (COI). Indeed, a preliminary component of the "agile intelligence enterprise" that we discuss in Chapter 10, these communities revolve around, for example, selected regions of the world. They contain all new documents, archived documents, and a "bulletin board" for each of the selected regions/countries of interest. Another Intelink COI example is "Military Operations and Exercises" (Figure 6-9). This section contains hyperlinks to information about past, present, and future operations/exercises.

Communities of Interest are powerful mechanisms for collaboration and exchange of information on "bulletin boards" —sort of an automated e-mail exchange—on Intelink, and serve as a model for effective organizational knowledge sharing. Dr. Jennifer Stone Gonzalez, intranet consultant, host of on-line intranet discussions on her own "Community of Interest" known as the *Intranet Institute*, and author of the 1998 *Prentice-Hall* book entitled, *The 21st Century Intranet*, refers to this concept as "Communities of Practice." Citing examples of the use of this concept, she explains:

> *People can use* Communities of Practice *as discussion areas to communicate with their counterparts on a many-to-many basis and can*

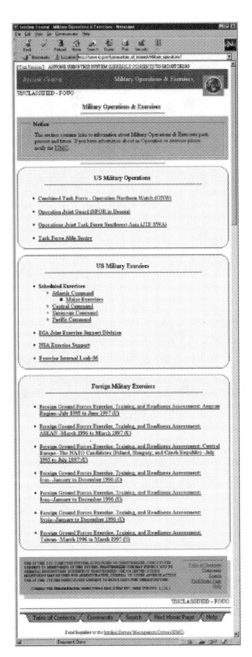

Figure 6-9 Intelink "Community of Interest" Example: Military Operations.

then communicate on a one-to-one basis via email with a simple click of a hyperlink, making this type of intranet [service] extremely attractive to people who are working together to solve problems. These kinds of intranets can be used to help employees learn and to increase their speed and proficiency. Research on teaching and learning shows that people do not learn new skills or ideas just by being exposed to them. Learners must be prepared to learn. Listening to networked discussions may help produce this 'absorptive capacity' in employees, both old-timers and new employees.

6.1.2.4 WebChat

One of the most popular features of commercial online services such as *CompuServe* and *America OnLine* (AOL) is their real-time chat groups, or chat forums. The ISMC viewed chat rooms as effectively being real-time newsgroups. They recognized that "chat" had significant potential as an analyst collaboration tool, so they looked for a tool that would be similar to the overburdened Internet Relay Chat (IRC) on the global Internet, but without the associated problems that have plagued this system. They found an answer in *WebChat*, a freeware chat program developed by Michael J. Fremont, co-founder of the Internet Roundtable Society, which allows moderated, synchronous, real-time, IRC-like chat to take place on Web sites. Essentially, anyone with a standard Web browser can talk in real-time with other people on the network at the same Web page. Since early 1995, the *WebChat Broadcasting System* (WBS), a service of *WebChat Communications* of Menlo Park, California, has offered this same multimedia chat mechanism on the global Internet. Its usage has become popular—their own website claims that 2.2 million users have registered, with an additional 4,000 members being added every day.

The *WebChat* software exists entirely on the server, eliminating any problems for the user from downloading or configuring the software. It also is better than some commercial on-line services and IRC in that it can incorporate some graphics and HTML links. It includes capabilities for setting up multiple chat "rooms," thus providing multiple forums to discuss many topics, with various levels of discussion moderation. Additionally, the software can easily be further customized, which the ISMC has done. As implemented on Intelink,

WebChat is an extremely popular collaboration tool, with a large number of active *WebChat* rooms (Figure 6-10). In the words of James P. Peak, the Director of Intelink's Management Office, "If you have the need to consult in real-time via keyboard chat with a peer anywhere in the world, WebChat is for you." Peak believes that WebChat is crucial to collaboration in the future, explaining, "WebChat is a laboratory for future collaborative work, sort of a distributed version of all of the work experiences that we have ever had."

For example, Intelink's *International Organized Crime* chat room is intended to support Intelligence Community members involved in the monitoring and reporting of international organized crime. These members can use *WebChat* as a mechanism to discuss ideas, bring attention to emerging activities or events, discuss common actions, or comment on Congressional or Executive policies. While the primary audience is comprised of those who are actually involved in this issue, *WebChat* can be very useful to introduce others to the primary topic of discussion. Other *WebChat* examples include the following categories.

- **Analyst Rooms**

Prevailing intelligence analyst issues can be discussed here, including a forum known as *Professional Intelligence Analyst Discussions*. General chatter is prohibited.

- **Office Rooms**

This room is intended to be a place where Intelligence Community members can briefly discuss general issues. The Office Room provides the opportunity to discuss areas of responsibility and develop professional relationships with other members of the Intelligence Community. In this way, Intelink has played a major role in relocating the traditional boundaries of an organization or office.

- **Geographical Regional Rooms**

The discussions contained here facilitate on-going analytical support discussions for selected regions of the world, for example the Middle East. These rooms are strictly controlled, and idle conversations are not permitted.

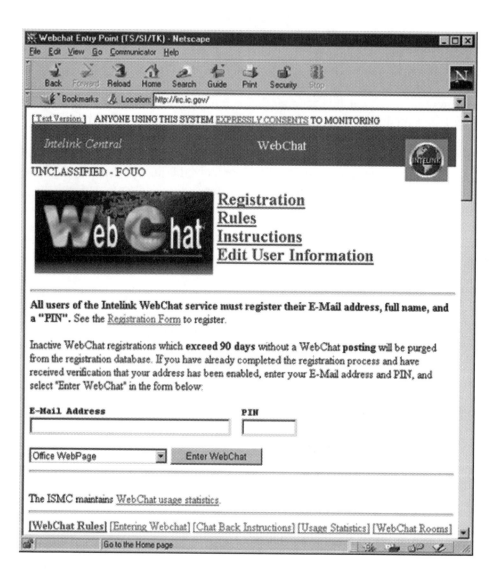

Figure 6-10 Screen Shot of Intelink's "WebChat."

- **Topical Rooms**

Also strictly controlled, these rooms are intended for members of the Intelligence Community who desire to solicit or exchange information on a particular topic in which they are interested or involved. The *International Organized Crime* room mentioned previously is a good example of this type of room.

- **Technical Questions & Answers**

The Technical Questions and Answers room is intended to be a place where analysts can ask questions concerning any technical problems that they may have encountered. This room is monitored by the ISMC itself whenever possible, and answers from them are always as complete as possible

Chat rooms on Intelink are used extensively around the clock and have created a number of problems for the Intelligence Community, ranging from boorish or even obscene behavior to potential copyright infringements. An example of the latter would be an inadvertent posting of the complete text of a *Reuters* news article. To date, no comprehensive study has been conducted to determine the cause of these problems, although it is generally believed that they may be more prevalent on Intelink than on comparably sized intranets in the private sector. As a result, chat usage is closely monitored by the ISMC/Intelink management, and a number of rules and corrective mechanisms have been put in place. Figure 6-11, taken from an actual on-line posting, describes and responds to many of the issues.

6.1.2.5 Microsoft NetMeeting

Intelink is also examining a number of standards-based collaboration products. Among the most promising is Microsoft's *NetMeeting 2.0*. This powerful tool includes a chat module for sending text among conference members, a whiteboard module for sharing ideas, an application-sharing module for displaying a specific program screen on multiple computers, and audio capabilities for sending voice over the global Internet. The chat tool is particularly useful when one or more meeting

Rules for use of WebChat on Intelink

1. WebChat is audited and logs of system activity are archived and subject to review. Anyone using this service expressly consents to monitoring.

2. WebChat users are expected to use this tool in a professional manner. The Intelink Service Management Center provides WebChat as a service to the Intelink community. WebChat runs on US Government networks and uses US Government resources and thus falls under the same laws and regulations regarding the use and abuse of any US Government system. Therefore, the following types of conduct will not be tolerated:

   - Sexual innuendo or the use of WebChat as a forum for "virtual dating"
   - Profanity, obscenity, name-calling or personal insults
   - Harassment of WebChat participants, or crude derogatory jokes that slander any person or group
   - Use of fantasy role-playng "personas" and postings describing imaginary activities

3. The ISMC reserves the right to limit WebChat. There is no requirement to issue any warning prior to ISMC action restricting (read-only) or banning a user from WebChat. The ISMC implements access control by individual e-mail address. If a manager of an organization desires a restricted (read-only) or ban mode for one or more individuals inthat organization, please contact us. WebChat access restrictions apply to all WebChat Channels. See the additional information section for more details.

4. Please do not post or discuss any ORCON ["originating agency controlled"] material, and be aware that another agency's document may not be posted here regardless of it's classification, if it is not already on Intelink. NATO data classified NATO SECRET or higher cannot be posted on Intelink. Check with your local security personnel for guidance regarding sanitization and dissemination of NATO classified data.

5. You may paraphrase or gist information taken from copyrighted sources, such as Reuters, but do not post entire articles onto WebChat.

6. If your chat qualifies as an official record under the Federal Records Act, you are responsible for saving such material and retaining it in your office's filing system. See the additional information section on how you can comply with this act.

7. The Analyst, Regional, and Topical pages are intended for discussion of specific issues. General issues should be directed to the Office page. We ask that conversations stick to the theme of the particular chat room. All pages are intended for official Government business.

8. Reports of violations of WebChat policy are taken seriously. Please feel free to report such violations to the ISMC.

Figure 6-11 Rules for Use of WebChat on Intelink.

participants is unable to use the audio features of *NetMeeting*. In essence, this software allows you to meet and work face-to-face with colleagues and friends, no matter how far apart you are, via the global Internet or your corporate intranet like Intelink.

Although *NetMeeting* is a separate Internet application available free for download from Microsoft—it does not require *Microsoft Internet Explorer* for proper operation—the ISMC has Microsoft's blessing to distribute this tool over Intelink from its "Software Archives," cited in Section 6.1.3 (see below). Downloading from the archives makes the process easier and more secure for Intelink users.

According to Jim Peak and *Dr. Surf*—Randy Marks, *NetMeeting* is the next step beyond the Intelligence Community's own classified, secure telephone system. Peak says, "We have routinely shared *Powerpoint* briefings complete with animation, while simultaneously discussing the slides in voice. We have clipped photos from various places in Intelink and annotated them with our own captions and handwritten notes using the whiteboard. We have jointly worked on [*Microsoft*] *Word* documents and then transferred the resulting joint product using the built-in file transfer utility. We have even used *NetMeeting* for video conferences on a one-to-one basis."

Peak suggests Intelink users try *NetMeeting*, saying that the only thing you do *not* get is the on-line community that exists on *WebChat*. While *NetMeeting* is currently only "peer-to-peer" as implemented on Intelink, they are working hard to change that.

6.1.3 Reference Aids

Reference aids constitute the third general category of Intelink user tools and services. For our purposes, consider a reference aid to be a tool or service that generally responds to a *single* Intelink user, as opposed to a collaboration tool that clearly involves *multiple* users. Using these reference aids, intelligence analysts can individually access a broad variety of mechanisms to facilitate the analysis, production, and dissemination of intelligence. On Intelink, all of these tools and services are accessible through a link from the *Intelink Central* homepage, and can be categorized into six areas, as described at the top of the next page.

1) Current Topics

This section includes links to various types of announcements (e.g., professional conference listings); imagery, intelligence, and weather reports for the current geographical areas of interest around the world; and "open source" information such as daily press reviews, and *CNN Headline News*.

2) Hot Spots

These links provide the latest classified and other information specifically categorized for world "trouble spots" that are likely to be of interest to intelligence analysts and other Intelink users, such as Iraq, Korea, and the Balkans.

3) Reference Databases

Databases include glossaries, dictionaries, and acronyms; "analyst working aids," ranging from telephone and e-mail directories to exchange rates and currency conversion tools; material from the *Foreign Broadcast Information Service* (FBIS) which is discussed in Chapter 8; and access to *Jane's Information Group. Jane's* is generally considered to be the leading provider of defense, aerospace, and transportation-related information to the governments, businesses, and universities of the world. *Jane's* was founded when Fred T. Jane published the first edition of *Jane's Fighting Ships* in 1898.

4) Special Support

This section includes links to provide needed support to Intelink operations, including the ISMC itself, security links, server requirements, and a special page that provides a time zone map, clock, and chart. The support section also contains access to the Intelink software archives, where Intelink users may download all available software subject, of course, to compliance with both commercial licensing agreements and local download policy. Software is provided in three forms—*Supported* (by the ISMC, such that ISMC will answer any technical question), *Provided* (on an "as-is" basis with no support), and *User Contributed* (containing useful in-house developed software, but also provided with no direct support from ISMC).

5) Help Index

This area contains hyperlinks to Intelink-related training material developed by Dr. Surf, graphics tips to develop better Web pages, a help section with "Frequently Asked Questions," and a comprehensive HTML Primer, which describes the language to first time or beginning users.

6) Other Services

Intelink users are able to access various usage statistics to see, for example, how often a particular page is accessed. In addition, users can convert Applix Word attachments to HTML, register a Java applet, and check on the status of a specific Intelink server in this area. This section also contains both a *Sun Clock* (a map of the passage of the Sun across the Earth) and a *Moon Phase* (a representation of the current moon phase including full data on the current phase) as well as the *Metadata Template Writer*, a tool for creating document metadata.

Clearly, the comprehensive set of tools and services discussed above is the *heart* of Intelink, providing its users with the means to access, navigate, and exploit the huge volume of diverse information that is available. These tools enable Intelink to support a full range of information dissemination, collaboration, and related services to the U.S. Intelligence Community.

6.2 FUTURE TOOLS

Tools change rapidly, and the tools of today are not necessarily the tools of tomorrow. Massive paradigm shifts will occur in a number of areas, as technology moves forward, user needs change, or intelligence requirements expand. Will the search engines of today be able to index the entire global Internet at the turn of the century? Will search engines even continue as the primary means to find information on an intranet or the global Internet? To begin to explore these possibilities, the U.S. Intelligence Community continually invests large amounts of energy, time, and money in an effort to predict the future direction of technology and to assess the impact that these technology changes will have on the Intelligence Community's ability to produce intelligence. One such mechanism for information technology collaboration among the agencies of the U.S. Intelligence Community is the *Advanced Information Processing and Analysis Steering Group* (AIPASG), which addresses the need for real-time collaborative analysis and decision making tools. The AIPASG, currently chaired by Dr. Joseph Kielman of the FBI, examines emerging applications within the private sector for their potential to achieve significant processing and analysis improvements within the Intelligence Community in the relatively near future. The following examples of future tools that are currently being evaluated by the U.S. Intelligence Community, which were presented at the 1998 AIPA Symposium, include:

- **Topic Clustering for Large Volume, Multilingual Text**

An operational prototype of a software tool that rapidly organizes large sets of documents into related groups that are easier to comprehend has been developed by *SRA, International, Inc.* SRA has been providing high-quality technology consulting and value-added systems integration to both government and commercial clients since 1978, with major corporate locations in Arlington and Fairfax, Virginia. This new tool partitions the documents according to language, allowing an analyst to quickly assess the overall document content for 15 different languages or other encodings (both alphabetic and non-alphabetic). The prototype contains a clustering tool that builds topic hierarchies for collections of documents. For each document, its "intelligence feature extraction algorithms" select the keywords that best represent the subject, or topic of that particular document. Fast clustering algorithms then automatically group documents with similar topics. This information can then be viewed graphically in a Java-based visualization interface. Instead of receiving a potentially large list of documents, users initially receive a handful of top-level topics that they can then selectively explore. The system is language independent, with the ability to cluster 100 one-page documents in under a second, and a gigabyte of information (up to 200,000 typical documents) in less than two hours. It contains an easy to use Java interface that provides a number of different browsing methods and visual cues. This tool has the potential to help alleviate the information overload typically facing the intelligence analyst today.

• **FALCON: A Machine Translation Support Tool**

The U.S. Army Research Lab continues to perform research on machine translation and information search and retrieval tools, developing a portable prototype called Forward Area Language Converter (FALCON). FALCON is a small, lightweight document reader and translator. It combines a laptop computer, scanner, and alternative power sources with special software for optical character recognition (OCR), text-to-text translation, and tailorable keyword search. In addition, these components are protected in a padded, rugged metal casing, with the entire contents weighing less than 30 pounds. FALCON is intended to help non-linguists in a forward area of the battlefield to assess the significance of captured foreign documents. The idea is to insert modified COTS packages for scanning, OCR, and translation. The refinements have been accomplished in cooperation with the U.S. Air Force and the Intelligence Community. FALCON prototypes have been used in Bosnia since May 1997 to assist U.S. Army intelligence troops to evaluate and transmit documents written in Serbian or Croatian.

• **Analysis and Visualization of Internet Data**

The MITRE Corporation, a federally-funded research center with extensive involvement with the U.S. Intelligence Community, has developed an approach to improve information retrieval from the global Internet. As we discussed earlier in this Chapter, locating information on the global Internet can be a very time-consuming operation since a user must sift through large volumes of data and frequently wait through network delays. In addition to these issues, the typical user simply does not have the time needed to evaluate large numbers of retrieval items on a one-to-one basis. MITRE has addressed these issues by developing a set of prototypes that has shifted much of the repetitive searching, monitoring, and pattern analysis functions from the user to a collection of tools with "intelligent agent" behavior. (In this context, according to MITRE, "Intelligent agents" are essentially goal-directed information management tools to support automatic generation of requests for information and to support efficient monitoring of the information available.) The new prototypes not only perform the typical notification or profiling of data, but also extract links, groupings, and other summaries through an off-line computation process. When the off-line analysis is completed, the user is notified and can then begin to submit ad hoc queries and other clustering techniques, including various filtering tools. Several visualization tools are also being assessed for use in these prototypes. The current focus is on an interactive 3-D tool to evaluate documents using multiple content terms, displaying the documents in 3-D space based on the frequency of the keywords in the document. With these tools, a much broader and complete search for a topic on the global Internet is possible with less user time expended to perform the search. These prototypes have significant potential in helping to alleviate the conventional problems associated with the use of search engines as the global Internet continues to grow exponentially.

• Automated User Interest Profiling for Intelink

Argon Engineering, under contract to *Rome Laboratories*, has developed a prototype of an automated tool to provide dynamic assignment of hypertext links for Intelink. Known as DALI (Dynamic Assignment of Links for Intelink), this prototype is a tool that is designed to integrate the concepts of interest profiles and hypertext links. DALI automatically searches Intelink for information that is customized by the analyst's own interests, and then dynamically creates hyperlinks within the documents as they are accessed by the analyst. DALI performs its search as the analyst performs other tasks, identifying and collecting lists of documents that contain relevant concepts. The document lists are then merged with previous concept lists (DALI actually "learns" over time), reading them and analyzing them for relevancy and currency, and then presents the list to the analyst for use. The new "concept profiles" can be shared, and modified, by other analysts so that profiles do not necessarily have to be reinvented. When the analyst opens documents from the search list, he or she is taken immediately to the relevant section, which is highlighted, of the document that matches the concept. In addition to keywords, paragraphs that contain information likely to be relevant to the research goals of the analyst will be highlighted. This "dynamic relinking" by DALI can direct the analyst to the best information available on Intelink.

These example tools have been evaluated by the Intelligence Community's *Advanced Information Processing and Analysis Steering Group* and were deemed to have significant potential to achieve improvements in the processing and analysis of information and thereby influence intelligence operations in the future. They represent a sampling of the multitude of research activities continually underway.

6.3 HOW DOES THIS RELATE TO BUSINESS?

Let's step back a moment as we assess the role of tools and services available on Intelink and discuss their relationship to the business leader of today. To accomplish this, we summarize a number of the basic lessons or conclusions relating to intranet tools and services that a business enterprise could apply to its own intranet application. For example:

- **Tools and Services are the Heart of the Corporate Intranet**

It is clear that, from the user's perspective, the corporate intranet is all about delivering information to its users. Tools and services are the *heart* of an intranet, giving users the ability to access, navigate, and exploit the huge volume of diverse information that is available. The tools provide the corporate intranet with the ability to support a full range of information dissemination, collaboration, and related services. Collaboration tools form the nucleus of intranet tool sets, progressing from basic electronic mail to the sophisticated seamlessly integrated set of tools that will allow "virtual" meetings in the near future.

• Intranet Tools Change Rapidly

Like the technology that drives them, intranet tools and related services, as well as the global Internet and World Wide Web, change rapidly. Solutions that seem right for today may not even apply to the new paradigms of tomorrow. A good example is the search engine, which is so critical to finding information on the global Internet today, yet may not be able to keep pace with the exponential growth of the World Wide Web by the end of this millennium. As a result of this constant change, it is not uncommon for COTS products to require modifications or customization to meet the ever-changing needs of individual business enterprises.

• Problem Sets Differ Among Organizations

Various organizations will encounter differing sets of problems, and therefore, will be required to respond with different mechanisms in order to cope. A good example to illustrate this point is the practice known as "spamming" of "junk" or otherwise unwanted or unsolicited e-mail. This is a real problem to almost anyone that has an e-mail address today on the global Internet, and is a serious concern to many companies. On the other hand, it has not been a problem at all for Intelink, or for the other intranets within the agencies of the Intelligence Community. The bottom line is that tool sets for corporate intranets need to tailored to the specific needs of that organization.

Chapter 7

Open Information Management Concerns

*I*n developing a technology-intensive application such as an intranet, particularly an intranet on the scale of Intelink, encountering unpredictable problems is always inevitable. As technology moves forward and the expectations of intranet users continue to increase, it becomes a difficult challenge to respond to those increasing expectations in a cost-effective manner. As the Intelligence Community quickly discovered, and as we have seen in Part 2 of this book, Intelink has become an information service that is *critical* to the intelligence mission of this nation. Recognizing the essential nature of Intelink, and the need to ensure that the continuing expectations of the Intelink user community are met, the *Intelligence Systems Board* (ISB) —the governing body of Intelink as we discussed in Chapter 1—established an overall management team known as the *Intelink Management*

Office (IMO). The purpose of this team, according to the February 1997 implementation memorandum signed by ISB co-chairs Richard S. Wilhelm and Joan A. Dempsey, was to "provide daily operational management and security support while addressing Intelink's two most significant challenges, information security and information management."

While the overall organization of the IMO was discussed in Chapter 2, and many of the Intelink information security concerns were addressed in Chapter 5, this chapter will focus on *open information management*. That is, how the IMO is addressing user requirements and responding to these needs in a comprehensive and realistic manner. It will focus on two areas that implementers of corporate intranets also face: standardizing operations, and improving open information management support to the users. These areas are essential because Intelink, like most corporate intranets today, was originally implemented on top of an existing information technology infrastructure. This means that Intelink, with its new Web-based technology, had to be integrated with the existing information systems within the Intelligence Community, which in turned created a certain level of chaos and uncertainty. An examination of how Intelink responded to the resulting challenges can be extremely useful to those with the task of building their own intranet.

Within the area of standardizing operations, Intelink was faced with several issues. These issues included how to gather consensus among users and promulgate standards decisions, how to use Web publishing and document management standards such as SGML and XML, how to improve search and retrieval capabilities, and finally, how to effectively distribute information to the user. In the area of improving support to users, the IMO has focused on the development of a new support infrastructure known as the *Site Intelink Information Manager* (SIIM) as well as an extensive training and education program. This chapter will discuss each of these concerns, and then conclude with a discussion of how Intelink plans to improve *Intelink-S*, the instantiation of Intelink used by the warfighter.

7.1 STANDARDIZATION OF OPERATIONS

One of the generally accepted differences between the types of information with which most corporations and business enterprises are concerned, and the types of information that are of interest to the Intelligence Community, is that industry tends to deal with *structured* data, while the Intelligence Community tends to deal with *unstructured* data. This distinction was recently articulated in an article written by Jay Finegan, a business and technology writer based in North Yarmouth, Maine. The article appeared in the March 15, 1998 issue of CIO Magazine, and was entitled, "Competitive Intelligence—License to Know." The article was based on an interview with John Dahms, currently the Associate Deputy Director for Administration/Information Services, and the *Corporate Information Officer* (CIO) of the Central Intelligence Agency. (In Chapter 9, we address the concept of a "CIO" as well as the legislation that mandated their creation within the government.) Finegan writes:

> *In the private sector, Dahms explains, most information is organized in relational tables. A bank card company, for example, works with transaction data—the store, the amount, the date, the cardholder. '[The data is] all very structured and operated on in a very structured way,' he says. 'The tools to manage and mine those sorts of databases are very well developed.'*
>
> *Intelligence processing of unstructured data is messier. The U.S. Intelligence Community deals daily with information that not only comes from a variety of media—texts, video, radio, journalism—but also arrives in a Babel of languages. At the CIA, information comes from a variety of sources, including reports filed by agents in the field, satellite photography, and reams of "open source" material— publications, studies, wire feeds, and documents pulled from the Internet. Somehow, all of that information has to be converted to knowledge by the Agency's many analysts, then sent up the chain to the CIA's ultimate customers—the President, the Cabinet, law enforcement agencies and warfighters at the Pentagon.*

This very concern, i.e., coping with the management challenges of unstructured data, led William H. Fleming, the head of IMO's Information Management Directorate, to focus on standardizing Intelink operations. This is extremely important to people involved with managing the information on intranets, because it is widely believed that the information that business enterprises will gather in the future *will become increasingly unstructured* as society copes with the global Internet and depends more and more on the use of Web technology.

Bill Fleming cites two important documents in his decision to concentrate on standardization. The first document—the real *driving force*—was the operational concept that was articulated on "information superiority" in *Joint Vision 2010*. This document defines information superiority as "the capability to collect, process, and disseminate an uninterrupted flow of information while exploiting or denying an adversary's ability to do the same." We discussed *Joint Vision 2010* in Chapter 3 as the template for a common direction to U.S. military services issued in July 1996 by the then Chairman of the Joint Chiefs of Staff, General John M. Shalikashvili. Another important document was the initial *Information Systems Strategic Plan*, issued in November 1997 by the *Intelligence Systems Board*. We will examine the strategic plan in more detail in Chapter 10, as we describe the future direction of information management in the U.S. Intelligence Community.

The Intelink Information Management Directorate (IMD) has focused its standardization efforts in four areas: the development of a Joint Standards Board, similar in mission to the MIT based World Wide Web Consortium (W3C); the development and implementation of metadata; addressing the use of Web publishing standards; and the concept of automated delivery of intelligence, including the issue of "push" and "pull" technologies. These four areas will be discussed in further detail below:

7.1.1 Joint Standards Board (JSB)

Since the advent of the World Wide Web earlier this decade, there has been a literal explosion in the availability of Web-related products for the end-user. In just browser technology alone, the path from the original *Mosaic* to the commercial *Netscape* browser and the subsequent entry of Microsoft's *Internet Explorer* browser has been disruptive for many users. According to the Intelligence Community's recently convened *Joint Intelligence Lessons Learned Working Group*, this plethora of Web browser options for many of the existing intelligence systems has been partially responsible for "single source reporting, speculation, lack of quality control and lack of properly identifying sources, causing precious resources to be expended on disproving the negative." Since the Intelligence Community does not measure its success in terms of profit, the end result of these problems is a pronounced decrease in customer satisfaction. On the other hand, effective standards are intended, in the words of IMO Director Jim Peak, "to increase your market penetration and get your products to more customers faster, and in better order." Peak continues, "What the Intelligence Community produces is extremely perishable. Information that is beyond price one day is suited only as evidence for inquiry in an 'intelligence failure' the next day. Get it to the customer in time or forget it."

There have been many short-term, creative *ad hoc* fixes to the problem of defining and using standards. In February 1997, many Intelink users convened at the United States Space Command (USSPACECOM) Headquarters at Peterson Air Force Base near Colorado Springs, Colorado. They were able to participate in an IMO sponsored Intelink conference to discuss and agree upon a number of plans, conventions, procedures, and standards designed to improve Intelink services. Standards have been developed for Web homepages and common security procedures have been defined to more easily move material from one instantiation of Intelink to another, e.g., from *Intelink-SCI* to *Intelink-S*. Perhaps the single most important decision made at the conference was to follow the lead of the global Internet's World Wide Web Consortium (W3C). As we discussed in Chapter 2, IMO chose to follow the lead of the W3C, implementing their adopted standards and certain other activities, after waiting a six-month period of time to ensure stability. For example, Intelink mandated the use of HTML 3.2 effective October 1997, six months after the W3C adoption in April 1997.

In spite of these efforts to develop and use standards, according to Bill Fleming, these fixes are still not enough. He cites *Joint Vision 2010*, which states:

> *Throughout history, gathering, exploiting, and protecting information have been critical in command, control, and intelligence. The unqualified importance of information will not change in 2010. What will differ is the increased access to information and improvements in the speed and accuracy of prioritizing and transferring data brought about by advances in technology. While the friction and the fog of war can never be eliminated, new technology promises to mitigate their impact.*

Fleming believes that in order for the Intelligence Community and the Department of Defense to fully address the emerging importance of information superiority as articulated in *Joint Vision 2010*, the Intelligence Community should establish an integrated and coordinated approach to *all* Intelink standards. This need is reiterated for the Intelligence Community in its own *Information Systems Strategic Plan*, mentioned above and detailed in Chapter 10. Furthermore, Fleming points out, the mission of interoperability for Intelink (referred to as "jointness" in *Joint Vision 2010*) must extend *beyond* the U.S. Intelligence Community to the allies and global partners of the United States. In the section entitled, "Imperative of Jointness," *Joint Vision 2010* states:

> *It is not enough just to be joint, when conducting future operations. We must find the most effective methods for integrating and improving interoperability with allied and coalition partners.*

Responding to the mandates of *Joint Vision 2010*, specifically the call for improving interoperability with allied and coalition partners of the United States, Fleming is implementing a "Joint Standards Board" to function in a fashion similar to how the W3C operates to support the global Internet. The W3C has hundreds of members representing most computing and telecommunications companies that have a significant stake in the global Internet, as well as many government agencies (US and otherwise—the Intelink Management Office itself became a member), and several non-profit groups. Membership fees range from a few thousand dollars to $50,000 or more. The stated goal of the W3C is "to realize the full potential of the Web."

Just as the W3C is oriented towards the global Internet, the Intelink *Joint Standards Board* will be geared toward the Intelligence Community. It will consist of 16 primary members representing the United States Department of Defense and the U.S. Intelligence Community, as well as several partnering foreign intelligence and NATO related organizations. Hosted and chaired by the IMD, they plan to meet annually in conjunction with the Worldwide Intelink Conference. In addition, the IMD will provide all necessary staff support for the new Board. Bill Fleming, whose ideas have been warmly received by the Intelink Community as he travels around the world explaining this new concept, proposes the following initial board membership:

1) Intelink Management Directorate (Chair)
2) Department of Defense
   - Office of the Assistant Secretary of Defense for Command, Control, Communications, and Intelligence, or "C3I"

- Defense Information Systems Agency (DISA)
- Joint Staff (J3)
- Joint Staff (J6)
3) US Intelligence Community
   - Defense Intelligence Agency
   - Central Intelligence Agency
   - National Security Agency
4) North Atlantic Treaty Organization (NATO) Related Members
   - NATO (NC3A)
   - SACLANT (Supreme Allied Commander, Atlantic)
   - JDISS/LOCE (Joint Deployable Intelligence Support System/Linked Operations [Intelligence] Capability-Europe)
   - BICES (Battlefield Information Collection and Exploitation System)
   - CRONOS (Crisis Response Operational Network Open System)
5) Intelink-Commonwealth Organizations
   - United States (Defense Intelligence Agency)
   - United Kingdom (DIS)
   - Canada (J2)
   - Australia (DIO)

The stated overall goal will be to facilitate Intelink, helping it to realize its full potential within the Intelligence Community. Specifically, the JSB will provide the growing Intelink Community and its partners with a *neutral forum* on Web standardization. Essentially, members get a "seat at the table" of a Board designed to:

1) Improve information management by coordinating the implementation of new Web technologies across the Intelink Community;

2) Respond to the threat of divergent information technologies and the resulting impact on interoperability of intelligence systems;

3) Achieve a consensus on standards decisions through a simple majority vote.

In addition, the *Joint Standards Board* will provide members with the opportunity to present working papers, briefings, and recommendations on selected areas of interest. Through workshops, working groups, and even informal meetings, the JSB would facilitate the sharing of ideas and potential technical solutions on all aspects of Web publishing and other related areas such as security standards and training support. Initially, the JSB plans to focus its standards activities on the formatting, production, and archiving of intelligence, as well as standards for homepages, metadata (which we define and explain in the next section), and security. However, Bill Fleming's long-term plans include an extensive array of information management challenges responding to *Joint Vision 2010* including:

- *Defining* US/NATO interoperability in a Web environment such as Intelink

- Using Web technology to balance information systems interoperability with security concerns

- Ensuring an uninterrupted flow and exchange of information during the operations with U.S. allies and coalition partners

- Sharing technology and intelligence information with U.S. partners

The concept of a *Joint Standards Board* for the Intelink Community, including our foreign partners, holds much promise for success. As such, it represents a key element in the plans of the U.S. Government to forge new ways of doing business in the new Web environment. Affording an easy method to gain understanding of integration issues, share information management ideas, and contribute to interoperability solutions, the *Joint Standards Board* is also a critical step in the evolution of the U.S. Intelligence Community to the future world of *managing its information as an enterprise.* We will discuss this important information management theme in detail in the remaining chapters of this book.

7.1.2 Use of Metadata

Finding specific information or data, or a special report, or other items of interest can be very difficult on the global Internet. Queries to the most popular search engines will often return tens of thousands of webpages to the frustrated searcher, as we discussed in Chapter 6. Unfortunately on Intelink, and in many large corporate intranets as well, the situation is no different. Indeed, one of the major complaints from the Intelink user community is the inability to find, quickly and easily, information located on its servers. There are a number of efforts underway to alleviate these concerns, including the improvement of current search engines, the addition of new engines with enhanced capabilities, and the definition and use of *metadata*.

The term metadata is often defined in various information systems glossaries as "data about data," or "data which relate to other data." Metadata refers to machine-readable document "tags" or other data that provide descriptions for collections of distributed information. The concept originated in information management systems designed for large collections of objects, such as a library. Today, the use of metadata is increasing rapidly in all forms of digital data collections. There have been a number of recent, high-profile proposals using the concept of metadata, including the World Wide Web Consortium proposal known as the *Platform for Internet Content Selection* (PICS), which allows parents and teachers to control what children access on the global Internet. The PICS specification uses metadata associated with Internet content for use in filtering software. Today statisticians use metadata to describe sample spaces and biases in experiments, database designers use it for relational schemas and data dictionaries, and mass storage designers use this concept to describe how their data is catalogued and stored. In all of these applications, "metadata," "document tags," "labels," and "collections" provide insight into the structure and content of data, and therefore, can facilitate their subsequent discovery using various search and retrieval tools. Metadata becomes even more useful when it is employed in conjunction with these query tools and other advanced capabilities such as "user interest profiles."

7.1.2.1 Metadata Implementation on Intelink

In July 1997, at the annual Intelink Users Conference, a set of guidelines for the use of metadata in the dissemination of finished intelligence on Intelink was approved. The guidelines had been developed earlier, by a task force chaired by Intelink's *Dr. Surf*—Randy Marks—with representation from throughout the Intelink user community. Among the task force representatives was Mark Kelly, an internet/Web technology expert from the Defense Intelligence

Agency, assigned to the Intelink Management Office. Kelly, who has become
the driving force behind Intelink's metadata implementation activities, and the
other members of the task force kept the initial set of required metadata tags for
finished intelligence small, and easy to understand and implement.

According to Kelly, simplicity is especially important for metadata
generated by the authors of finished intelligence. "However," he says, "the use
of good metadata will be so beneficial to the Intelink Community that
additional sets of metadata are envisioned for other communities of interest
such as imagery and mapping."

The *Guidelines for Use of Metadata on Intelink* carefully explain the
purpose and use of metadata for authors of finished intelligence. This document
stresses that "the key to success is a balanced approach of well-structured
metadata with the requirement that it be manageable by the individual authors
and producers." There are three primary categories of metadata tags for
Intelink:

• **Required Tags**

These tags are required to meet the minimum standards for metadata.
Examples include security classification, the name of the intelligence
agency that has produced the information, title, and date of creation.

• **Required if Applicable**

Various other tags may be required, depending on whether or not they
refer to special organizations, relate to certain types of finished
intelligence, or merely because it is deemed as "good publishing
practice." Examples include topic country, additional security tags, and
specific "URLs." (Uniform Resource Locator; like the global Internet,
this refers to a specific address for a particular file on Intelink).

• **Optional Tags**

These metadata tags will be used to provide additional information that
the author feels will facilitate the search engine registration process, or
aid in some other way during the retrieval process. Examples include
tags for non-Intelligence Community security classifications, finish

intelligence summaries, and a tag to cite an expiration date for the product.

The use of Intelink metadata tags was required on three Intelink instantiations—*Intelink-SCI*, *Intelink-S*, and *Intelink-U*—in October 1997. Any new "finished intelligence" being posted on these networks after that date must include the *Required* and *Required if Applicable* metadata tags. In addition, authors are now encouraged to include all reasonable *Optional* tags that pertain to their products. To facilitate this process, Mark Kelly established a *Metadata Home Page* on Intelink to assist in the coordination of metadata implementation (Figure 7-1).

By May 1998, almost all intelligence producers that use Intelink as their publication and dissemination medium were providing metadata for their finished intelligence. Monitoring this process very closely, Mark Kelly observed, "Most producers jumped on the bandwagon quickly, while others took some coaxing to begin participating in this Intelligence Community-wide venture." He added that many producers have even gone beyond the Intelink metadata and produced their own local metadata extensions. The National Air Intelligence Center (NAIC), for example, is now producing the *NAIC InfoSource Directory*, which uses various metadata in addition to the basic set of Intelink standards. Another example is the Office of Naval Intelligence (ONI), which we shall discuss in detail as a case study in Chapter 8. ONI has created many new metadata tags to facilitate implementation of their *Netscape Catalog Server*. Indexing of the metadata provides the needed details to allow easy navigation through ONI's Intelink site.

7.1.2.2 The Future of Metadata on Intelink

While the Information Management Directorate is pleased with the initial response of the Intelligence Community to implement metadata, much remains to be done. For example, documents do not always follow the format specifications in the metadata standards. An approach to quality control issues needs to be resolved and developed. In addition to fixing these obvious problems, however, Mark Kelly is approaching the future of Intelink metadata on three fronts. Tools for creating and searching metadata, expansion of metadata, and metadata for U.S. allies are described on page 211.

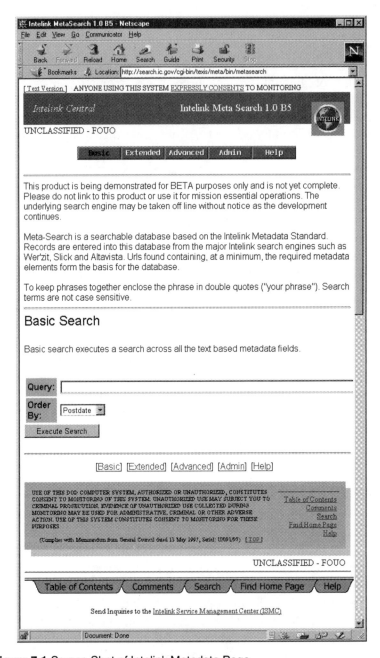

Figure 7-1 Screen Shot of Intelink Metadata Page.

• Tools for Creating and Searching Metadata

One of the main tools for using metadata on Intelink has been the use of search engines or other tools specifically modified for this purpose. In Chapter 6, we discussed the *Strategic Locator of Intelligence Community Knowledge*, (i.e., SLICK), a search engine developed in-house by the Intelink Service Management Center, and *Wer'zit!?*, the ISMC developed equivalent of the popular *Yahoo* on the global Internet. To enhance the search process, *Wer'zit!?* has been modified to read the HTML tags used for metadata. Since intelligence producers using Intelink are required to "register" their search topics and sub-topics on *Wer'zit!?* as we explained in Chapter 6, the ISMC has developed a new *Meta Search Tool* that is able to take advantage of the now available HTML metadata. While many problems remain, the idea is to eventually be able to read metadata from the Web "crawlers" for the other Intelink search engines. In addition to metadata search tools, various metadata creation tools have been developed to aid in the intelligence production process. Indeed, according to Kelly, "The increased automation of metadata creation is one of the chief goals of the IMD."

• Expansion of Metadata

The second major future thrust for metadata is to expand the set of tags used. This will include providing tags for both "subject access" and "content markup," as well as the addition of new tags. The new tags being considered include indicators for geographical coordinates, additional security tags, and intelligence disciplines—such as "signals intelligence" or "human intelligence." The effort for "subject access" refers to the security classification of the particular intelligence subject and other keywords. We mentioned in Chapter 5 that Intelink has caused the Intelligence Community to reexamine how security classifications are standardized across the entire enterprise. As part of the metadata effort, several organizations have expressed a requirement for a standardized keyword list addressing subject access.

The IMD recognizes the importance of SGML, and the new XML, in future World Wide Web and Intelink operations. They laud the

efforts of Major Lee Hopson and his Digital Production Office at the
Joint Intelligence Center, Pacific (JICPAC), which are detailed as
another case study in Chapter 8. As we will learn, JICPAC has created
an SGML-compliant "information space" using SGML tags. One of the
features of this new system facilitates the dissemination of intelligence
on Intelink-S by automatically flagging material at the correct security
classification. The idea is to author an intelligence report only once,
and then distribute it automatically. In addition to JICPAC, the
National Air Intelligence Center (NAIC) and the National Ground
Intelligence Center (NGIC), have been active in metadata for "content
marking." The IMD will coordinate all of these efforts.

• Metadata for U.S. Allies

Cooperation with *Intelink-Commonwealth*, the latest instantiation of
Intelink, continues to grow. In Chapter 2, we mentioned that Intelink-C
is the network that serves the association of the United States and three
of its allies, the United Kingdom, Canada, and Australia, and is not
under the formal purview of the Intelink Management Office. However,
the strong working relationship between the IMD and the Intelink-C
community has led to their adoption of all of Intelink's initial metadata
standards. In addition, talks are ongoing with North Atlantic Treaty
Organization (NATO) personnel to explore the possibility of
standardizing metadata in order to facilitate exchange of information
between the U.S. and NATO. Obviously, this is an extremely important
thrust for the IMD.

7.1.3 Web Publishing Standards: SGML/HTML/XML

In Chapter 1, we discussed the role of Web publishing standards in processing
the information carried over the World Wide Web on the global Internet, and
similarly, on intranets such as Intelink. We explained the necessity of the
primary standards in use, including HTML, XML (the newest W3C standard),
and SGML, which allows computers to recognize the *structure* and *content* of

information, not just its presentation *format*. SGML has been critical to the success of electronic publishing in general, and publishing on the Web in the form of HTML. In addition, XML—a true subset of SGML—holds great promise for optimizing the use of SGML in a Web publishing environment.

Since the advent of the Web earlier this decade, the decision on what standard to use for a given application has been an important information management concern of the Intelligence Community. It should be no surprise, as a result of the many differing objectives, and subsequent resulting conflicting priorities of the U.S. Government, including the Intelligence Community, that there were advocates of a number of specialized, proprietary, i.e., *non-SGML* methodologies for document management and information dissemination systems. Indeed, during the period in which SGML was being developed in the late 1970's, and until it became an International Standard in 1986, the "electronic publishing" industry consisted of various automated "typesetters" linked to a number of proprietary computer operating systems. The entire process was oriented towards the production of a paper document, itself a product of the legacy of printing presses originally developed some 500 years ago. Few people had any vision of an International Standard that would allow information reuse, based on the structure and content of the information, in a number of output formats. Fewer still were able to foresee the greatest application of all—the World Wide Web. Fortunately, SGML bridged the gap between paper and these new electronic output forms by providing a highly customizable, standardized methodology. As a result, the advocates for proprietary, non-SGML solutions were largely unsuccessful.

The U.S. Intelligence Community has a significant investment in SGML, and plans to continue its use. Indeed, we chronicle a sampling of five major case studies on the use of SGML and intranet technology within the Intelligence Community in Chapter 8, providing details on their development and the implementation issues that each encountered.

Most intranets such as Intelink use the simplicity of the SGML application called "HTML," developed by Tim Berners-Lee, for publishing documents on the World Wide Web of the global Internet. HTML defined the necessary element types to display a rendition of a complete document, including text, pictures or other images, and any other supporting media. The real key to HTML, however, was its ability to create special hypertext links between the document and other documents on the Internet. Intelink, like many corporate intranets, follows the lead of the World Wide Web Consortium in the use of

HTML. Since its inception, HTML has been improved many times and has served the Web well.

Nevertheless, many people believe that there is a need for—in the words of Jim Peak—a "stripped-down version of SGML," that is optimized for publishing on the Web. As a result, XML was developed as a subset of SGML. XML does not contain the complexity of SGML, but of course, it also cannot do many of the things that SGML can do. As a comparison, SGML took an international committee many years to develop and its specification contains 300-some pages, while XML was developed by a review board that met *electronically* most of the time, and the specification is about 30 pages.

The W3C Recommendation Document for the XML Specification states its overall goal:

> *The Extensible Markup Language (XML) is a simple dialect of SGML...The goal is to enable generic SGML to be served, received, and processed on the Web in the way that is now possible with HTML. XML has been designed for ease of implementation and for interoperability with both SGML and HTML.*

The Intelligence Community plans to invest in XML in the future, just as it has done with its superset, SGML. With XML's formal and concise design that is optimized for Web delivery of information, and with the initial support shown by industry, it is expected to be a winner. In the words of Jim Peak, "XML won't just supplement the Web. It will be the Web." Noting the W3C design goals for XML also published in its Specification, Peak says, "These [design goals] will happen. Visions often die when they try to be all things to all people. XML won't. Its job is making visions be all things to all people." That is a strong endorsement of XML and reflects the attitude of the Intelligence Community towards this new standard.

7.1.4 Push and Pull Technology

The final area of Intelink standardization activities being addressed by the Intelink Management Directorate involves the concept of *selective* automated delivery of intelligence. The automated delivery of intelligence itself is not so difficult; Intelink is a very capable mechanism by which intelligence may be transmitted electronically. Rather, it is the *selective* transferal of desired intelligence that has become the elusive dream of intelligence users and producers alike.

The most recent incarnation of this dream was in full bloom early in 1997, around the same time that several companies announced new or improved products to automatically deliver content to audiences on the global Internet. Collectively known as "push technology," these products provided users with the capability to select, and then automatically receive, various types of information directly at their desktop. For example, early "push" products delivered news, weather, and stock quotes to interested recipients. The information can also be filtered to match a specific user interest "profile."

This new approach to data delivery can be contrasted with what is termed as "pull" technology, in which the user must actively go out and retrieve the information that he desires. This latter approach could be automated to some extent, say through a subscription service in which a user configures their browser to pull information from the network. However, push technology was intended to fully automate data delivery, and when first introduced, it quickly became the latest rage on the global Internet.

Perhaps the most prominent company offering push technology during that period was *PointCast*, Inc. This company pioneered the concept of content push supported only by advertising, i.e., there were no fees to the user of the service. *PointCast*'s own website says:

> *[Push technology is] like having your very own personal assistant... someone to take care of gathering all the information you want to know and then presenting it to you on a silver platter. With* PointCast, *you get the news you need to stay on top—effortlessly.*

Although a number of small companies entered this seemingly lucrative market, many were overtaken when both *Microsoft* and *Netscape* began to offer push capabilities as part of their browser products. However, *PointCast* remained one of the primary industry leaders. Indeed, according to the June 1997 issue of PC World, *Microsoft* signed on *PointCast* as a content provider.

Anxious to enter into "niche markets," *PointCast* executives approached Jim Peak in 1997 to explore the use of *PointCast* to deliver intelligence content over Intelink. With the previous *PointCast* business model revolving around the concept of advertising, a number of discussions were held before agreement was reached on a feasible approach. The result was *Project Spitfire*, the working prototype of an Intelink *PointCast* model. The idea was to implement the *PointCast*-based content distribution infrastructure, including development of the specialized tools that would be needed to deliver intelligence information. In the pilot, the intelligence customer would receive the capability to select examples with very high granularity from all of the various possible offerings, even including some of the *PointCast* commercial content.

Unfortunately, *Project Spitfire* had to be cancelled. Intelink had an absolute requirement for a version based on the UNIX operating system, which is currently unavailable from *PointCast*. Perhaps even more significant, many users are having second thoughts about push technology as a way to receive intelligence information. Specifically, several have expressed similarities between push technology and "spam," the colloquial term for unsolicited e-mail. So while selective automated delivery of intelligence may be a dream of the Intelligence Community, push technology in its present form may not be the answer.

With the demise of *Spitfire*, the quest continues within the Information Management Directorate to find the right balance between selective, automated delivery of intelligence and the old, traditional method of delivering intelligence "messages" to a distribution list of recipients—"*push* with a vengeance," according to Jim Peak. Fortunately, a better balance may be in sight. Rob Sims, an information technology expert in the IMD, has proposed a new "push" study that would use existing Intelink system capabilities, utilities, and delivery methods. Sims proposes a methodology that would modify the user profile capabilities of Intelink's homegrown search capability called *Wer'zit!?* to allow a selection of specific topics of interest, and then create a personal page of the results for an interested user. In addition, Sims proposes taking advantage of certain metadata tags that could enhance the user's ability to find desired information. Indeed, according to Sims, "Intelink Smart Push/Brilliant Pull can be a reality using existing desktop tools and current Intelink search capabilities."

7.2 IMPROVING OPEN INFORMATION MANAGEMENT SUPPORT

The second area of information management challenges facing Intelink involves improving services and support to users. Since Intelink, like most corporate intranets in use today, was originally implemented on top of an existing information technology infrastructure, it had to be capable of being integrated into the existing information systems within the Intelligence Community. This, in turn, resulted in the need for an overall management framework to address all of the information systems related to the intranet, as well as the intranet (Intelink) itself. In addition, Intelink provided a new opportunity for the Intelligence Community to manage its resources as an enterprise. The result of this new management approach allowed the Intelligence Community to attain significantly higher levels of knowledge sharing and data integration, the ability to foster and maintain specific "Communities of Interest",[17] and an overall improvement in customer relationships.

Addressing all related information systems and taking advantage of these new capabilities required an effective distributed systems management framework. The Intelink Information Management Directorate developed this new framework in order to:

- Improve Intelink's service and user satisfaction

- Provide better budgetary control and reduce systems costs

- Improve overall system planning and reduce duplication

- Implement necessary security controls

The following section will provide additional detail about this framework, specifically highlighting training and a new concept referred to as the *Site Intelink Information Managers* (SIIM) infrastructure.

7.2.1 Site Intelink Information Managers (SIIM) Infrastructure

Jeanie Layton, head of the IMD's Consumer Requirements area, developed a unique approach to the development of the necessary distributed systems management framework for Intelink. She was convinced that a properly trained

---

[17] For additional detail, see Chapter 6.

and indoctrinated team of full-time professionals was needed to collectively respond to the unique set of management issues facing the new global Intelink. The result was the *Site Intelink Information Managers* infrastructure.

The core concept of SIIM was to have *every* Intelink-related organization (i.e., both intelligence user organizations as well as intelligence producers), to designate a specific person to serve as the primary focal point within that organization for all matters pertaining to Intelink. The new infrastructure was tasked with a set of roles and responsibilities designed to facilitate information management within the Intelink Community. To facilitate the establishment of this new team, Layton issued a general call in June 1997 encouraging the Intelink Community to participate. In her request, she stated:

> *In spite of the way several organizations are traditionally structured, Intelink brings many intelligence functions and considerations into an integrated information service environment—requirements management, security, production, publishing, librarian and dissemination services. To provide improved Intelink information services, it is beneficial for the Site Intelink Information Manager to have a high level of understanding of internal procedures and national policies across the various intelligence functions...*

According to Layton, each individual site manager must keep current with all new requirements, policies, and efforts originating from Intelink, while maintaining the perspective of the user or consumer. She feels that it will require a full-time effort to respond to the coordination, electronic publishing and dissemination, security and other policies that are necessary to improve Intelink service and prevent duplication. The SIIM must assess the impact of potential changes, and report the results to the Intelink Management Directorate. "Regardless of the particular instantiation of Intelink," Layton says, "this SIIM position is the critical link to the rest of the Intelink Community, and will result in improved support directly to the sites from the IMD."

The ideal site manager, according to Layton, would be an individual "capable of resolving issues related to the organization, availability, and usability of intelligence information, who possess an in-depth understanding of who the consumers are and what they think about Intelink." An effective site manager would be in constant communication with their own customer base and be able to accurately and effectively communicate their views to the IMD.

Although the concept of SIIM is still evolving, the IMD defines five essential components to the set of roles and responsibilities for *Site Intelink Information Managers*:

1) Intelink *Infosphere Road Map*

The IMD uses this term to describe the information structure of an organization. The *Infosphere Road Map* is a tool for developing and maintaining the necessary knowledge of a particular organization's overall information structure and flow as they relate to their own requirements as well as those of their customers.

The *Site Intelink Information Manager* should have an understanding of the current information flow into and out of the organization, including an understanding of what that flow *should* be, and a comprehensive knowledge of what is and what should be connected to Intelink (such as databases to enhance intelligence reporting). To do this, the SIIM must have an understanding of the various classes of information at his or her site, including an extensive knowledge of the database interfaces for information that is created at the site for Intelink. Most importantly, the SIIM must be able to assess the impact of changes in the flow of information to Intelink users at all levels. All proposed changes must be approved by the site as well as by the IMD.

2) Intelink Policies, Procedures, Guidelines, and Standards

The SIIM is the primary point-of-contact for any questions or issues that may arise from both internal and external users of the Intelink site. To prepare for this role, a SIIM must establish and rely on a number of mechanisms to acquire the necessary customer feedback, such as customer surveys and specific requests for information. To respond to the customer set, the SIIM must issue monthly reports, special on-line postings, and other innovations to report on issues relevant to their sites or intelligence products. In essence, this individual represents the organization in all matters of policy, planning, and budgetary matters related to Intelink. He or she also acts as the Intelink advocate to the organization, serving as the site proponent for Intelink policies and guidelines. For example, the SIIM is responsible for ensuring that Intelink standards decisions, such as the recent transition to HTML, are smoothly implemented at the site. Finally, this individual is responsible for bringing resource issues, technology implementation concerns, and other potential problem areas to the attention of the IMD.

3) Intelink Training and Education

Assisting the IMD with the promotion of various Intelink capabilities is another key responsibility of the SIIM. This requires both formal education and classroom training and informal on-the-job training of Intelink users at the individual sites. It also includes determining, documenting, and forwarding future training requirements to the IMD for incorporation into an Intelligence Community-wide training program.

4) Intelink Consumer/Producer Forums

There are a number of regularly scheduled conferences and other forums to promote and enhance Intelink. These forums include a wide variety of topics at every level of expertise, from the novice to the very technically oriented person. They include discussions on every aspect of Intelink operations from security to technology. The annual Intelink Conference has grown significantly over the years and now typically includes a vendor exhibition of Intelink-related products and services. This conference attracts intelligence users and producers from throughout the Intelink Community, as well as speakers and participants from industry, academia, and government. Each SIIM is required to attend and participate in these conferences, working groups, task forces, and other forums. It is also the SIIM's responsibility to ensure coordination within his or her own organization on all matters that evolve from the various forums.

5) Intelink Security

The *Site Intelink Information Manager* security role is highlighted as a separate responsibility because of its importance. The SIIM serves as the focal point for the implementation of all Intelink security plans, addresses security-related architectural concerns, standards, and policies, and assists other site security personnel.

Recognizing the value of enthusiastic, involved and empowered Intelink users, achieving "buy-in" from the Intelink Community on the SIIM concept was extremely important to the IMD. The *Site Intelink Information Manager* concept is fostering a new environment of Intelligence Community-wide participation in providing a powerful tool for improved service and user satisfaction, budgetary control, systems planning, and effective security. It is contributing to the dialogue among users that is absolutely necessary to the success of an intranet.

7.2.2 Training and Education

In addition to the concept of full-time Intelink site managers, the IMD has invested heavily in training and educating the Intelink Community as part of its effort to improve open information management support. According to Debra L. Hinrichs, who heads up all Intelink training activities, "Training increases awareness and facilitates progressive thought and understanding among intelligence users and producers. Therefore, it is as important as the new Web-based tools and techniques being implemented on Intelink." Accordingly, she has implemented an overall framework for the development of the necessary training strategies and methodologies, as well as acquiring the necessary resources to support the Intelink environment.

According to Hinrichs, the IMD will use new and emerging training technologies to ensure that the Intelink Community has a well-trained cadre of intelligence professionals with the necessary expertise to operate well into the next millennium. These training technologies include self-paced computer-based training (CBT) techniques, computer assisted instruction (CAI), informal on-the-job training, and, of course, conventional instructor based training. IMD will also examine the concept of a "virtual university," or "distance learning."

All electronically distributed training will focus on desktop delivery mechanisms over Intelink, using a variety of training methods. Hinrichs estimates that 70 to 80% of the Intelink user Community can be trained using electronic methods as opposed to formal classroom training.

Initial training has been standardized on three basic user categories in order to reduce training costs as well as reduce the overall organizational impact on individual intelligence agencies, elements, and supporting military commands. These three basic user categories are:

1) Management Users

This category encompasses individuals who need a general overview of the tools, capabilities, and issues associated with the use of Intelink. Typical students are those who require a broad high-level overview of Intelink, including all levels of management and strategic planners.

2) Production Users

Production users include the specific intelligence analysts, officers, and others who use Intelink on a daily basis to produce finished intelligence. Typical students would include intelligence producing authors, webmasters, and editors. Unlike the management users, these individuals require a training program that is comprehensive, detailed, and for many, technically-oriented.

3) Consumers

The consumers refer to the set of individuals—the customers—who receive and use intelligence information from Intelink that the producers create. Like production users, consumers also require extensive training in order to optimize their use of Intelink's product offerings, such as how to use search engines effectively.

An effective and comprehensive training program for Intelink requires the cooperation and full support of the various training efforts that currently exist within the Intelink Community. In the Washington, D.C. area, this has been accomplished through cooperative arrangements with on-going efforts within the major agencies of the Intelligence Community. By posting course offerings on Intelink, these users are made aware of the Intelink offerings within their own agencies.

In addition, Hinrichs has received support from a number of training schools and centers outside of the immediate Washington, D.C. "headquarters" area. The following listing demonstrates the breadth of involvement.

- Navy and Marine Intelligence Training Center (NMITC)

- [Pacific Command] Joint Intelligence Training Activity, Pacific (JITAP)

- Fleet Intelligence Training Center Pacific (FITCPAC)

- Air Force Intelligence Welfare Center (AFIWC)

- [Strategic Command] Regional Joint Intelligence Training Facility

- [European Command] Regional Joint Intelligence Training Facility

- Joint Military Intelligence Training Center (JMITC)

A recent user survey conducted by the IMD quantified the estimated current user population, by training category, for *Intelink-SCI*. Similar surveys were conducted by the *Intelink Service Management Center* for *Intelink-S*, and by CIA's *Community Open Source Program Office* (COSPO) for *Intelink-U*. Future training requirements for both Intelink-S and Intelink-U are expected to grow into the hundreds of thousands as support to the warfighter through Intelink continues to gain momentum.

7.3 IMPROVING *INTELINK-S* TO THE WARFIGHTER

The final example of Intelink's response to open information management challenges involves the response to early criticism of *Intelink-S*, the instantiation of Intelink used predominantly for providing intelligence information to the warfighter. As such, Intelink-S users include supporting military commands, and even communities outside of the Department of Defense, with most users being customers or consumers of intelligence information rather than intelligence producers. Intelink-S carries information with a security classification up through Secret level only, and became operational in January 1997, some three years after the inception of the first instantiation of Intelink. The Defense Information Systems Agency estimates that the number of individual computers with access to Intelink-S is approximately 265,000, clearly showing the important role of Intelink.

Essentially the early criticism of Intelink-S involved the quality of its services, as well as its intelligence production and dissemination capabilities, especially the information content that was available. These problems varied among the various user organizations, and included problems ranging from the inability to conveniently access an Intelink-S workstation, to issues such as insufficient bandwidth or communications capability, and concerns over the availability of necessary training.

These problems were addressed immediately by the Intelink Management Directorate. A special "Intelink-S Task Force," chaired by IMD Director Bill Fleming, was formed to identify shortfalls and recommend solutions to the Intelligence Community. Interestingly, much of the dialogue was conducted in cyberspace using various Intelink collaboration tools and facilities. Membership in the task force came from across the entire Intelink Community, including the various military services and unified commands, as well as all of the major national-level intelligence organizations and agencies. The recommendations of the task force were reviewed at a special session held in March 1997 at Colorado Springs, Colorado, as part of the annual Intelink User Conference series.

The recommendations put forth by the *Intelink-S Task Force* included a corrective plan of action that responded to five specific action items. The action items were:

1) Moving Intelligence Information from Intelink-SCI to Intelink-S

Perhaps the most often heard criticism of Intelink-S was the lack of clear procedures and security guidelines for moving intelligence information from Intelink-SCI, the highest classified instantiation of Intelink, to Intelink-S. Much of the material classified Top Secret or higher could be modified or summarized at the lower Secret level to make it available to the warfighter on Intelink-S, yet comprehensive security and procedural guidelines for "posting" this information were desperately needed to facilitate the transition. The Task Force Recommendations included sharing local ad hoc solutions to this problem with the Intelink Community as a whole as well as the development of a comprehensive set of security guidelines and policies within six months. As part of this dialogue, a recommendation was made to adopt the standards and guidelines of the World Wide Web Consortium with a six month delay for stabilization.[18]

2) Standards for "Homepages" and Disseminating Finished Intelligence

While standards for the development of homepages tend not to be an issue in much of the private sector, the *Intelink-S Task Force* felt that the Intelink Community was exposed to so many different methodologies and approaches in creating organizational homepages that it was adversely affecting the users' ability to locate information. In addition, the varying styles of homepages made the access and use of intelligence products significantly more difficult. In response to this issue, the task force agreed to IMD development and implementation of a set of standards for homepage development within several months. In particular, these standards promote the use of various hyperlinks between the table of contents of their homepages and the homepages of higher echelon organizations. By mandating this structure of hyperlinks, Intelink-S users can be assured of some level of consistency in the pages that they access.

3) Technology Integration Procedures

The *Intelink-S Task Force* felt that the lack of a comprehensive set of guidelines and standards for Web-based tools, services, and other related procedures on Intelink-S inhibited the ability to take advantage of such new technology. They reiterated the need to follow the standards and guidelines of the W3C in order to facilitate technology insertion. They also agreed to a number of specific recommendations relating to registering finished intelligence topics on the *Wer'zit!?* search tool.[19] Finally, they agreed to seek additional funding for more modern browsers than were currently deployed in many organizations using Intelink-S.

---

[18] As we discussed in Chapter 2 as well as Section 7.1.1, above.

[19] As we discussed in more detail in Chapter 6.

4) Implementation of Metadata Standards

Clearly an issue that is not limited to Intelink-S, it was determined that metadata standards are needed to increase user confidence in the results of search queries. According to this criticism, users have unnecessary difficulty in locating both new and archived information on Intelink-S. The task force not only recommended the use of standardized metadata,[20] but agreed to require intelligence producers to enforce their use in their respective organizations. As a result, quarterly progress reports on the use of metadata are now forwarded to the IMD, where compliance is monitored.

5) Training and Education

Although not limited to Intelink-S, the task force recognized the importance of training in the implementation of the other action items. They felt that a comprehensive Intelligence Community-wide program was needed to ensure consistent and effective Intelink training. The Task Force recommended the development and coordination of an *Intelink Training Management Plan* that would take advantage of existing government-sponsored programs for Intelligence Community-wide application. They also agreed to seek additional funding for training, further underscoring the commitment to this need. Finally, they recommended the establishment of a special topical page, to be posted on all instantiations of Intelink, on training information.

In addition to the five specific recommendations, the *Intelink-S Task Force* formulated two additional general findings. These two overriding concerns were:

• Funding Requirements

All Intelink-S sites must allocate an appropriate level of funding, in terms of both resources and manpower, in order to effectively implement the five task force recommendations.

---

[20] As we discussed in Section 7.1.2, above, this has been accomplished.

• Bandwidth Capacity/Management

The *Intelligence Systems Secretariat* of the *Intelligence Community Management Staff* must lead a series of discussions with telecommunications personnel at the National Security Agency, the Defense Information Systems Agency, and the program office of the new Joint Intelligence Virtual Architecture (JIVA) program in an effort to begin to resolve bandwidth deficiencies.[21] Proper bandwidth is absolutely critical, as warfighters in the field of battle must be assured of getting the information they need immediately.

Through these recommendations and findings, the task force identified Intelink-S shortfalls and developed a set of corrective actions that are in the process of being implemented. The results of this effort were particularly significant to the Intelink Community for two primary reasons: First, most of the Intelink-S problems and concerns were also applicable to the other instantiations of Intelink. Metadata, standards, and technology insertion, and training are all issues facing Intelink in general. Secondly, Intelink-S serves the American warfighter, and constitutes the most promising intelligence delivery method developed to date. Intelink-S should go far to prevent in the future what happened to Air Force pilot Captain Scott O'Grady in Bosnia because intelligence information failed to reach him in time.[22] Similar concerns were expressed by General H. Norman Schwarzkopf after the 1991 Persian Gulf War. The failure of intelligence information to reach the warfighter at the time it is needed is one of the most significant intelligence dissemination issues. It has become clear that Intelink-S will play a major role in solving this problem. As a result, improving Intelink-S has become a primary information management challenge for the Intelink Community.

7.4 HOW DOES THIS RELATE TO BUSINESS?

It can be useful to step back a moment once again and assess what these experiences might mean to other government entities and to the private sector.

---

[21] The new JIVA program is discussed in more detail in Chapter 10.

[22] See Chapter 1 for additional detail.

Examining the approach of Intelink to its own information management challenges can be very useful to the business leaders of today. To accomplish this, we summarize a number of the basic lessons or conclusions relating to information management that a business enterprise could apply to its own intranet application. For example:

• **Work with Your Users**

Never underestimate the value of your user community. If your users do not support your project, it will be doomed from the outset. The *Intelink Management Directorate* learned that the best way to improve the usability and effectiveness of the intranet is to interact closely with the customer as they did as part of the *Intelink-S Task Force* and are doing through the *Site Intelink Information Manager* infrastructure. Furthermore, your need for user support and the value of their contributions is ongoing—it continues throughout all phases of the life of an intranet.

• **Training to Increase Awareness of Users**

In addition to working with your user community, you must ensure that they are capable of taking advantage of all the intranet has to offer. The best way to do this is through a strong training and education program, backed up by a management plan that is supported throughout the community. Be aware, however, that it is a "seller's market" for highly skilled intranet professionals. Retaining these experts can be a challenge as your competitors are very willing to offer substantial salaries and other benefits to lure them away.

• **Standards Are Important**

The importance of the level of consistency and stabilization that can be achieved in an intranet environment through the use of specific guidelines and standards cannot be overemphasized. This has been reiterated throughout this book, and the lessons learned from the experiences of Intelink in standardizing their operations are particularly useful. The Joint Standards Board, adherence to a guiding body such as the W3C, and metadata standards are all excellent examples.

Chapter 8

Implementation Case Studies

Many commercial and governmental enterprises today are information based. The true assets of the enterprise are the data and the intellectual resources that transform that data into information. Clearly for the Intelligence Community, information is its most critical resource, and successfully managing that resource is its *number one* priority.

Chapter 8 contains five case studies—two detailed descriptions and three summaries—that describe the experiences of the Intelligence Community in managing its information through the use of document management standards and Web-based technology. The detailed experiences of one of the U.S. Military's Intelligence Production Centers located in Hawaii and known as the "Joint Intelligence Center, Pacific" (JICPAC) is presented first, followed by the Office of Naval Intelligence headquarters in Suitland, Maryland. These are the "real" stories, i.e., the people, events, and specific products that made these two efforts so successful. The remaining three stories are summaries of several efforts at the National Security Agency, the Foreign Broadcast Information Service of the CIA, and the Intelligence Community's newest member: the National Imagery and Mapping Agency. These case studies examine the unique experiences of these organizations, including how they were able to realize tangible cost savings as well as significantly improve their capabilities.

In each case, Intelink provides the catalyst for their success. In addition, all of them are taking advantage of the International Standard known as SGML, or derivatives of SGML such as HTML or the new XML. Their experiences provide insights into the issues, problems, and solutions for any business or other organization desiring to take advantage of these technologies.

8.1 JOINT INTELLIGENCE CENTER, PACIFIC (JICPAC)

Now that we have a good understanding of Intelink, we can move to a harbinger of the future. We learned that Intelink fosters interaction and collaboration among the analysts and intelligence analysts of the U.S. Intelligence Community. We also learned that electronic publishing was the *"killer app"* that makes Intelink the new strategic direction for intelligence dissemination. Since Intelink has become the foundation of the electronic publishing services of the future for the Intelligence Community, the opportunity exists to create an entirely new electronic publishing paradigm for the next millennium. In this new paradigm, aptly referred to by many as the concept of an *"information space,"* the Intelligence Community has access to an integrated information infrastructure and a common set of tools and information repositories that they can use to produce, update, collaborate, and exchange intelligence information. In this first case study, we gain perspective on how the Joint Intelligence Center, Pacific (JICPAC) has evolved towards this new concept. As this case study will show, JICPAC is moving from an almost exclusively hardcopy environment to a Web-centric environment based on Intelink. As such, they represent the true prototype of the future intelligence production world, a very "agile" environment where information is shared and managed as an enterprise.

The story is quite detailed, but deserves close attention. After providing some necessary background, it explains how Intelink came on the scene and changed the way JICPAC had been producing intelligence for decades. It details the grass roots work done by a special quality improvement effort called the *"Living Document Working Group."* It then explains how the use of SGML and JICPAC's own concept of an *"information space"* were perceived as the best approaches after they had examined a number of alternative solutions. Their decision process is detailed in the story, including the formation of a special office, and how they convinced senior management that this was the best way to go. Implementation details are also provided, including their budgeting and funding process, team approach (including some valuable team lessons learned), use of commercially available products, and even the DTD development process. The story concludes with their current status and overall project lessons learned.

8.1.1 Who Is JICPAC?

Support to all worldwide military operations, whether they are humanitarian in nature or part of an armed conflict, is a primary goal of the U.S. Intelligence Community. Several of the thirteen primary Intelligence Agencies are designated as "Combat Support Agencies" within the Department of Defense. This means that their mission also includes providing intelligence to various military commanders and their forces not only to keep them out of harm's way, but also to exploit the operational environment of their adversaries.

The *Joint Intelligence Center, Pacific* is a key element in this process. Located in Pearl Harbor, near Honolulu, Hawaii, JICPAC is the U.S. military intelligence production center for the Pacific Rim and Indian Ocean areas. They are responsible for producing general military intelligence, targeting, and operational intelligence information for over forty countries in this geographical area. According to his official "mission and function" statement, the JICPAC commander is responsible for the production and publication of intelligence information to the U.S. military's Commander-in-Chief in the Pacific Ocean. In accomplishing this mission, he must ensure that the intelligence he delivers is a compilation of all of the information available from all intelligence sources, and that it is delivered fast enough to be of use. In addition to his local responsibilities, the JICPAC commander must also accommodate the broader needs of the Intelligence Community at the national level, both military and governmental, for intelligence regarding the Pacific Theater.

8.1.2 What Was the Issue at JICPAC?

The production and publication of regional intelligence information for the Pacific Theater is the primary business of JICPAC, and by all accounts, they have been doing an outstanding job. But in order to continue doing that job well, they found that they needed to respond to a much wider variety of intelligence requirements than ever before. Furthermore, the amount of information that they needed to process in order to meet these expanded objectives continued to grow rapidly. Perhaps most constraining of all, doing that job right was becoming more expensive at a time when resources, both funding and personnel, were being cut.

Like their sister production centers elsewhere, and not unlike much of the corporate and business world today, JICPAC lived in a "hardcopy," paper-based world. Their intelligence reporting consisted primarily of text-based messages that could be sent electrically over communications lines and the production of paper documents that were printed and eventually distributed to their recipients. "Re-using" information, i.e., taking information from one format to another (and then another), was not possible.

Even when Intelink appeared on the scene, with all of its obvious potential, they continued to struggle with paper. In fact, with the introduction of Intelink, JICPAC's production process actually became more cumbersome at first. From their perspective, the additional burden of converting the data from its hardcopy format into something suitable for the Intelink Web environment quickly became overwhelming. Intelink was a new medium, the technology was somewhat immature, everything had to be developed in-house, and the other media requirements still existed. It quickly became apparent that information "re-use" continued to be a very inefficient operation. JICPAC's Military Capability Studies, Country Fact Sheets, and Special Reports were considered to be the premier "General Military Intelligence" (GMI) products of the entire command. The processes being used to produce them were too manual and time consuming and could no longer keep up with the dissemination and update requirements. They knew something had to be done—something far reaching.

8.1.2.1 Background

JICPAC has always been a forward-looking organization. For example, before implementation of their "*information space*" prototype, even somewhat before the implementation of Intelink, the intelligence production methodology at JICPAC was beginning to take advantage of newer technology. Their strategy proved very useful later on.

They began to examine ways to leverage the advantages of Intelink. Part of this new approach involved intelligence analysts using commercially available word processing and desktop publishing tools to create various textual products. Once the product was in a final draft format, it was converted to the Microsoft Rich Text Format (RTF) standard and passed electronically to both the publishing and graphics departments of the organization. The RTF file was imported into the desktop publishing package *FrameMaker* where it was composed and laid out with all appropriate figures, illustrations, and graphics. A galley proof of the product was then set on paper and given back to the author for final review and approval. Once the product obtained final approval and was ready for dissemination, publications personnel used a customized version of *Harlequin Webmaker* to convert the *FrameMaker* file into HTML for display in a Web environment.

Unfortunately, this first galley was rarely the last as authors frequently made substantive content changes to the galley that resulted in another composition and print phase. This was a semi-automated process that required human review to ensure the conversion was completely successful. And especially on lengthy documents with many graphic elements, manual clean up was normally required.

8.1.2.2 The "Living Document Working Group"

To its credit, JICPAC is an active participant in the quality management program of the Department of Defense. As part of this program, JICPAC encourages its people to think about problems and potential solutions to these problems. This encouragement frequently comes from their "quality council" which is called the "Executive Steering Committee" (ESC). This august group, which consists of the Commander, the Deputy Commander, and all senior managers in the command, addresses all pertinent JICPAC issues, particularly when they address cross-functional matters. This is accomplished by forming "process action teams" or other working groups that are empowered to examine a particular process or issue of concern, and make recommendations to the quality council: the JICPAC Executive Steering Group.

It was within this quality management framework that a group of frustrated analysts in the South Asia Department first raised their concerns about their inability to produce and update quality intelligence products in a timely manner. What they wanted was the ability to produce a dynamic, "living document" of intelligence. Without any formal structure (not even a designated chairperson), but blessed by the ESC, they called themselves the *"Living Document Working Group"* and became the driving force behind efforts to change the entire intelligence production process at JICPAC. These people knew that this future intelligence environment had to be Intelink-based, contain shared data, and be managed as an enterprise, i.e., embody the notion of what later would be called an *"information space."*

The grass roots *Living Document Working Group* (LDWG) was composed of several of the South Asia Department's intelligence analysts who originally raised the issue, representatives from the webmaster shop, visual information specialists, and several other multidisciplinary technical experts from across the Command. The tasks of this group were then formalized and approved by the ESC—they were to evaluate the emerging automation technologies of the time (early-mid 1996), and recommend possible alternatives to the slow, unwieldy, and somewhat unresponsive intelligence production process then in use. The working group recognized two strong influencing factors for changing JICPAC's system:

1) Inefficiency of the Current Process

The first factor was partially a result of the tremendous increase in requirements for intelligence dissemination in multiple media. In turn, this caused significant increases in the workloads of both the traditional publishing departments and their respective information systems departments. At that time, all products were still derived from a paper-based production environment, and that environment simply was not optimized for CD-ROM and Web media. As a result, the processes were largely manual, people intensive, and fraught with errors.

2) Concerns of Analysts/Authors

The second push came from the authoring side as intelligence analysts became more familiar with Web-based technologies and wanted to take immediate advantage of that dynamic environment. Their initial focus, however, was not on meeting all production requirements. Instead, analysts tended to look only at Web dissemination. One of the most difficult challenges was to convince them of the benefits of a complete reengineering approach.

8.1.2.3 SGML Was the Solution

The *Living Document Working Group* went out and looked for the best solution. What they found was SGML. While there was no single event that put the JICPAC problem into focus, there were several related concerns that seemed to point to SGML as the best solution:

1) The Overall Requirement for Web Publishing

This was clearly a significant factor, and it highlighted their need to raise awareness of the various intelligence production problems of the existing system.

2) Creation of Metadata

At that time within the Intelligence Community, there was much attention being devoted to the problem of finding, in a timely fashion, relevant intelligence on Intelink. One possible solution was the concept of tagging potential data to be searched, essentially creating "data about the data," or "metadata." The creation of metadata, it was believed, would significantly improve the ability of intelligence analysts to use Intelink search and retrieval engines. An Intelligence Community-wide effort to develop standards for metadata[23] was initiated. From the perspective of JICPAC, this created yet another requirement for Web publishing, further underscoring that need.

3) Automating the Process of Creating Metadata

The manual recording of metadata for HTML postings on Intelink proved to be extremely labor intensive. Therefore, either it was simply

---

[23] See Chapter 7 for additional detail on this effort.

not done, or if it was attempted, it could not keep up with intelligence postings. As a result, when an intelligence user was attempting to find a particular topic or intelligence report using the various Intelink search engines, the "hits," or matches, were spotty at best. In turn, this diminished the "return on investment" of producing the information in the first place. An automated means of populating metadata fields for the search engine database was needed. To do that, a standard production environment was imperative, and some "capture" function was desirable to see what an analyst was writing about as he or she went about the business of producing an article.

Given the overall Web publishing requirement, since SGML seemed to provide both the standard production environment that was needed as well as the capture feature for automated mapping of information to metadata fields, it became the major contender for the JICPAC prototype.

8.1.2.4 Possible Alternative Solutions

The *Living Document Working Group* looked everywhere for the best solution. Through participation in various intelligence forums, and in both government and industry conferences, it was obvious that similar problems were being experienced everywhere. The subject of SGML was always raised during those forums as a possible solution; however, it was acknowledged that the start-up costs would be high and the payoffs might be difficult to quantify. Therefore, before the working group went forward to senior management with its recommendation of an SGML-based solution, they knew that they needed to consider a number of simpler alternatives.

As they examined various alternatives, one in particular stood out as a possible solution: the use of structured authoring templates in conjunction with their existing desktop publishing software. The plan was to push the templates out to the authors where they could tag appropriate sections, paragraphs, tables, and other elements. However, after extensive experimentation, it was decided that this approach would create more problems than it would solve, and was discarded. The primary problem was that desktop publishing tools could not enforce or validate use of the templates or appropriate tags in specific locations.

Acknowledging the inadequacies of authoring templates and choosing SGML, the *Living Document Working Group* had now completed the task given to it by the Executive Steering Group. They were convinced that a complete intelligence production process reengineering based on the use of Intelink and SGML, was necessary for JICPAC to continue to meet its intelligence production objectives.

8.1.3 The Decision: Process Reengineering

At JICPAC, a process change of this magnitude must be approved by the Executive Steering Committee (ESC). Closely monitoring the work of the *Living Document Working Group*, the ESC considered the group's recommendation to look at the potential for an SGML solution, spoke with additional technical experts, and ultimately decided to follow the working group's suggestion. Buy-in was slow, and took place over approximately six months. Several briefings were presented to the ESC, outlining the concepts of SGML, the benefits for the command and the consumers, and high-level proposals for implementation. Because of the complexity of the subject matter, it was necessary to present the information from a process and production viewpoint rather than in terms of the technical benefits. The final decision was based, in large part, on extensive research by and recommendations of experienced staff members. Then the real fun began!

8.1.3.1 The Digital Production Development Office

The Executive Steering Committee knew that it had to put some real teeth in its decision to explore SGML as a solution to its production problems. This meant providing both the personnel and the resources needed to establish a development team of government and contractor personnel. The end result was the establishment of the "Digital Production Development Office." U.S. Air Force Major Leland (Lee) R. Hopson, a career Intelligence Officer assigned to the Command, was selected to lead a group to develop an SGML solution. Major Lee Hopson then began to assemble what turned out to be an outstanding team of on-site experts. The implementation team, which included Ms. Joan Smith, Ms. Gail Picard, and Ms. Peggy Fraga, was assisted by a team of experts assembled from key areas throughout the command. This group of 12 people was further augmented by contractor support, located external to and distant from JICPAC. Together, they would assemble a prototype of the future intelligence environment, a new paradigm for managing information and disseminating intelligence. However, as they learned more about the concepts and strategies of information management, and as they began to see the benefits of reengineering the entire production process, it became clear to Major Hopson and his team of experts that the problem set was much larger than first envisioned.

8.1.3.2 The Mission: Develop an Information Space

The group's first mission was to look into the SGML recommendation of the *Living Document Working Group* and develop a workable proposal to solve the problem. Their first approach was limited to their requirement to publish hard copy intelligence reports. So they took their existing products and created a set of rules known as a "document type definition" (DTD) to describe the structure of those documents. These rules defined which SGML tags could be used, what they meant, and their context, for a specific application. However, while this approach was ideal for that one requirement, the team soon realized that this would not get them where they needed to go in the long run. Rather than only publishing hardcopy documents electronically, what they really wanted was to provide users with quick, easy access to all available on-line intelligence. They wanted to move from a line of separate and distinct publications to a system where information was available in small, modular packets, which could be updated individually as new information became available. The user or reader could then query and view only those packets of information that were of interest to them at that moment. What they really wanted was a true "information space," accessible by all appropriate users, which contained many components in addition to the reports themselves. The additional information (which would include other databases and imagery data, for example) could be maintained in one place, combined with other packets of information and repackaged as needed for various requirements. They believed that their SGML solution would provide the foundation for this new approach.

8.1.3.3 Information Space Modules

What did this new SGML-based information management, electronic publishing, and distribution system look like? Using SGML to create, manage,

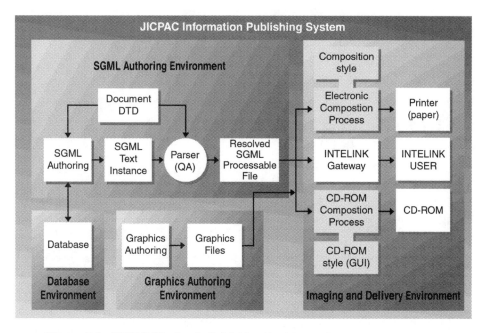

Figure 8-1 JICPAC Electronic Publishing Environments.

and maintain the necessary databases for their own local information space, as well as to produce and deliver intelligence documents over Intelink, the new system consists of four primary system environments (Figure 8-1):

- **SGML Authoring Environment**

The authoring environment is used to create, edit, import, and mark up character-based documents.

- **Graphics Authoring Environment**

Graphics are created at workstations using special development software. They are stored in formats defined by the development team and are referenced in the SGML documents.

- **Imaging and Delivery Environment**

Graphics are integrated into the document, and documents are output to Intelink, or produced as print or in CD-ROM format.

• **Database/Data Management Environment**

This environment includes database software and structures for storing, manipulating, and managing SGML documents and associated data.

8.1.3.4 Realizing the Advantages of an SGML Approach

At JICPAC, reuse of information was the primary decision driver rather than cost or personnel savings. Major Hopson recognized several key strengths of an SGML approach that needed to be considered in order to make this type of decision: information reuse, cost-savings, requirements for on-line or networked publishing, platform or product independence, and sound information management. All of these are important to JICPAC, but by far the most critical was that SGML would provide them with a way to reuse information once it was written. To JICPAC, information reuse meant that intelligence information in a database could be published on a CD-ROM, and then the same information could be printed in another report and even later published electronically over Intelink, and this could be accomplished, if necessary, on different information systems.

This concept of information reuse, with product and format independence, was critical to JICPAC. As a quick fix, some people advocated direct authoring in HTML. Upon further study, however, JICPAC became convinced that the frequent changes to the HTML standard as well as proprietary extensions implemented by several vendors made this approach an unwise proposal. Although JICPAC has not quantified their cost savings in a formal fashion, they are beginning to measure their savings. To them, the importance of providing information that could be reused and tailored by their customer or consumer to satisfy their own individual needs was a key savings factor.

In summary, it is important to reiterate that cost and personnel savings were never a major factor in selling the concept of production process reengineering using SGML. Instead, JICPAC focused on the inability of the current process to support the number one priority requirement of disseminating intelligence using Intelink. From several experiences it was apparent that the command was ill equipped to respond to the dynamic environment of the Web and consumers' requests for more information in less time. They believed that

SGML would allow them to better manage change in order to meet the current and rapidly evolving requirements of the user community. JICPAC strongly believes that providing authors with a tool that allows them to write once and reuse the data in multiple ways will ultimately increase production and allow analysts to focus on more in depth intelligence reporting.

8.1.4 Implementing the Decision

Major Hopson knew what had to be done. He and his team understood that their SGML solution would be the keystone of an overall information management strategy that would allow intelligence dissemination across multiple media, information databases with retrieval of "intelligent" information, and interoperability with intelligence repositories throughout the intelligence community—again the concept of an "information space." They realized that since SGML was an International Standard that was being mandated as *the* standard for data interchange within the Intelligence Community, it was a very reasonable approach. They also recognized that it would be a long and difficult process to implement—and their experiences to date have definitely confirmed that fact.

8.1.4.1 Marketing their Decision

Their decision to build an "information space"—to change the way business was done at JICPAC—and to employ SGML—was not an easy one to sell. Once the office reached its conclusions and was ready to go forward with necessary procurements and project development, it took several months to obtain the approvals they needed from the JICPAC Executive Steering Committee. Securing ESC approval was largely an educational process. As is frequently the case in any military organization, there had been personnel changes on the ESC and there were vocal opponents to the proposal among the committee members. Once again, familiarization briefings were required and Major Hopson and his group countered each objection. It is important to mention that the ESC's objections were *not* unfounded—the SGML standard can be costly and difficult to implement, and JICPAC was lacking in the necessary expertise. However, when the negatives were compared to the positives of implementing an SGML solution, the choice became obvious. The steering committee realized that the command had to move forward and could not achieve its information strategies using current processes and tools.

And this buy-in had to occur at all levels: internally within JICPAC, within the broad JICPAC customer base, and within the Intelligence Community at large. To facilitate the development process, the command's South Asia Subcontinent Division, within the Directorate of Operations, was designated to provide several intelligence analysts/report authors to assist in solution development. The active involvement of these and other analysts in the Functional Team's data analysis project was critical to a complete and accurate portrayal of JICPAC's intelligence production tasks. For example, the authors' efforts in developing a common "help" function provided specific examples of the data type required for each section of JICPAC's General Military Intelligence product. In turn, this gave them a valuable tool that should shorten their learning curve. The Implementation Team, again with input from the analysts, developed some JICPAC-specific enhancements to the software. The close interaction of Major Hopson's Digital Production Development Office and the working analysts accelerated and smoothed the development process and lessened the fears and natural resistance of the authors who were faced with yet another system/process to learn. This same kind of close interaction is continuing as awareness spreads to the other geocentric analytical work centers within JICPAC.

Selling the process to potential customers was also hard. Customers at all echelons and locations were persuaded to the SGML solution through orientation and familiarization briefings, observed and hands-on demonstrations, and an active Intelink presence. Major Hopson and his team approached the larger Department of Defense and Intelligence Community through their active participation in conferences, seminars, and other large group sessions. Locally, they took every opportunity to conduct desktop briefings and demonstrations and conducted countless briefings at Pacific Theater and JICPAC sponsored meetings and conferences for theater-wide intelligence and operational groups. Through it all, JICPAC always placed the customers first.

8.1.4.2 Funding: How Much Did It Cost?

Similar to many situations in the business world, budgeting for resources was a problem. Not only did JICPAC find itself with no firm estimate of the costs of the program, they knew that in field prototype projects like this, they would have a tough time finding some start up money. Meanwhile, back in Washington, the Intelligence Community's "Electronic Publishing Board" had sent out a data call to all intelligence organizations on funding needs. This helped to focus the JICPAC initiative, and provided Major Hopson with other potential future funding sources. In 1997, competing at home directly against other command requirements, approximately $300,000 was secured for contractor development of the first (product specific) DTD, and an additional $250,000 was granted for technical training and DTD tool procurements. With these funds, the project was able to begin in earnest.

Basic technical training for team members provided them with enough expertise to begin development, but their limitations quickly became obvious. In order to keep pace with their stringent development schedule, Major Hopson's group began to look for ways to use outside contractors for several tasks. While "in-house" JICPAC personnel have done much of the work, the early plan was to have most discrete tasks accomplished with contractor support. This included such functions as DTD completion, Web publishing, database research, CD-ROM publishing, and configuration management.

They are continuing to refine their fiscal needs as they learn more about the process. They are also continuing to seek out and explore other funding avenues that open up to them as the scope of their efforts expand to meet, not just JICPAC, but Community needs. Support for project funding is growing as the Community becomes better educated about what SGML implementation means to the Community as a whole, not to just this one command. These efforts have paid off, and the entire Intelligence Community has benefited. For example, JICPAC convinced the Intelink Director, James P. Peak, to invest in this effort. An apparent strong believer in the old adage, "put your money where your mouth is," Peaks' Intelink Management Office has committed an additional $500,000 for tools evaluation, procurement and other funding, as needed. Major Hopson and his group are using those funds, in part, for small, one-time purchases of software, which will facilitate their development process. This infusion of Intelink funds has—in effect—resulted in JICPAC being designated the de facto beta site for SGML utility within the Intelligence Community.

In the overall scheme of things, the total of these funds is obviously very small relative to the millions of dollars spent in the Intelligence Community on intelligence production and dissemination. When compared to similar initiatives within the private sector, the JICPAC investment even falls below what many organizations have spent. Yet it is not the dollar amount that is most important here, but rather the *process,* including the contribution by interested parties like the Intelink office. After all, this is the prototype of the future of the U.S. Intelligence Community.

8.1.4.3 Team Approach

Implementation began cautiously. We learned earlier that the implementation team Major Hopson assembled immediately following approval by the JICPAC Executive Steering Committee was designated as the "Digital Production Development Office." Even the *naming* of this office assumed significance and was done very carefully as the group sought to avoid specific terminology (such as "SGML" or "Intelink") which could potentially polarize people at the early stages of the project.

Since the new office was specifically tasked with taking JICPAC through the transition to their new digital environment, Major Hopson knew that he needed top-notch help. In addition to himself and Ms. Joan Smith of the MITRE Corporation as his Technical Advisor, he formed two teams:

1) The Functional Team

This was a user-oriented team led by Ms. Gail Picard, the technical editor. It initially consisted of a military targeting officer, a military current intelligence non-commissioned officer (NCO), and a contracted intelligence expert. More recently, an additional civilian technical editor has been hired. The Functional Team's primary tasks were to evaluate the content of the General Military Intelligence product, determine the needs of the intelligence analysts, articulate analyst's requirements to the Technical Team, and test and evaluate Technical Team solutions.

2) The Technical Team

This team was led by Ms. Peggy Fraga and consisted of a DoD civilian computer programmer/analyst, two DoD civilian graphic artists/visual information specialists, a military computer programmer and a military NCO computer operator. The Technical Team has developed the tools used by the analyst, ensured the ability to incorporate all graphics required for the products, and developed the overall "look and feel" and conversion scripts. This was done for both the authoring environment and for product delivery, in multiple formats and to multiple media. This team also addressed all automation questions relevant to the project.

Development priorities were immediately established without any regard to who would actually be doing the work. The intelligence "product lines" were analyzed and information types (i.e., traditional subject headings) were categorized across the two separate and distinct JICPAC product lines:

1) General Military Intelligence (GMI); and

2) Target Intelligence.

Of the two, GMI is the more textually-based product, and since that made it a better candidate for the initial DTD development, work began immediately with contractor support. Work on the second type, Target Intelligence, will begin at a later date, using in-house resources. The more time sensitive, less durable, operational intelligence products will also be examined as an area for future SGML development.

The in-house teams then completed numerous SGML training programs and completed all necessary tools testing for the initial SGML authoring software selection. When the DTD was delivered from the contractor, the Technical Team began extensive modifications to the DTD to correct identified problems and to incorporate additional capabilities and requirements that they had identified during their learning process. Simultaneously, they began developing a template for the authoring environment and brainstorming for the envisioned new publication process. It was only at this point that Major Hopson's group realized several things:

1) JICPAC's own proficiencies had increased much more quickly and substantially than had been anticipated.

Task assignments were reviewed and major changes were made. The Technical Team took an earlier and more active role in developing the

DTD, tailoring the user interface and formatting data for output. The fact that one of the primary contractors was not physically on-site during development was deemed to be detrimental to the project. As a result, contractor tasks were redefined to include tasks such as product testing, long-range planning, and consulting.

2) Creating the authoring environment (i.e., what the individual intelligence analyst actually sees when beginning to compose intelligence reports) should also be accomplished entirely with in-house personnel.

Functional Team members with intelligence analysis experience conducted a series of extensive data analyses and researched numerous administrative details such as security requirements, use of foreign names and terms, and peripheral data (e.g., points of contact, source material, etc.) which should be captured. The results of their analyses fed the DTD and style development phases. The development of both the authoring and the output *Formatting Output Specification Instances* (FOSIs) has been an iterative process open to refinement and change as necessary.

3) The tasks of maturing the DTD and developing the authoring interface should be combined.

As a result, the Technical Team's learning curve from the time of their initial training to the time when they could be considered SGML experts was shortened significantly.

4) The Functional Team should do all beta testing of the authoring environment.

This involved cutting and pasting legacy data into the SGML structure and updating that information with some original writing in the SGML environment. The Technical Team's greater understanding of the DTD and the FOSI made incorporation of Functional Team recommended changes a relatively painless procedure. The same can be said for changes recommended by authors who have assisted in the beta testing process. Major modifications have been essentially nonexistent.

At the end of this process, JICPAC had learned an extremely important lesson: In order to optimize the overall development results, you must *deeply immerse* your in-house project people into the development process. That is, you must have them working and solving their own problems, as this ensures not only the development of expertise, but also guarantees organizational buy-in.

8.1.4.4 System Components—COTS Software

As is the practice throughout the Intelligence Community, commercial off-the-shelf (COTS) products are being employed extensively in this prototype. Fortunately for JICPAC, the SGML industry has matured sufficiently to allow them wide latitude in the selection of specific products and tools for the myriad of tasks.

What were some of the COTS products selected by JICPAC for this prototype? They include the *ADEPT* series of software from *Arbortext* for development and authoring. The *Arbortext* product *Document Architect* is the tool used for creating and maintaining the DTDs and the style sheets or FOSIs. *ADEPT Editor and Publisher* is being used for authoring and convenience printing.

The system will generate *Omnimark* scripts to transform the SGML data into HTML for Intelink delivery and for querying relational databases for automatic population of SGML tabular data. The team is working closely with the JICPAC Web development office to take advantage of UNIX operating system scripts like *Perl* to automate the appearance and behavior of the Web delivery applications.

As JICPAC completes this prototype of the future intelligence production world, where information is managed as an enterprise in a true "agile" environment, all within a Web-centric environment based on Intelink, their next step is an automated Content Management System. This is needed to manage all of the information components and involves developing a single database of all information, processing the workflows, and providing a means for controlling access. JICPAC is completing the requirements definition phase and will be evaluating additional SGML commercial products, such as *Texcel Information Manager, Chrystal Astoria*, and *Xyvision Parlance Document*

Manager. Content management and Web delivery solutions continue to evolve and merge, making it very difficult to decide on a commercial product for implementation. However, JICPAC expects to make a decision very shortly and implement their pilot Content Management System with an integrated Web delivery capability.

8.1.4.5 DTD Development Details

The DTD was designed by the in-house team working closely with an external contractor support team. Primarily because the two teams were geographically separated, the process was iterative. It required on-site visits by the contractor on several occasions to demonstrate the DTD to determine whether it met the stated requirements. As a result of these visits, additional changes were made to the DTD and tested by JICPAC personnel. The DTD has now been completed and delivered by the contractor and JICPAC is enhancing and maintaining it. Currently, the DTD is in constant revision and will be throughout the test period. Indeed, changes will be necessary over the entire life of the DTD, due to periodic changes to the regulatory guidelines under which JICPAC must operate. The regulatory guidelines ensure that the modifications to the DTD cannot be avoided nor, to any substantive degree, anticipated. For the future, the expectation is that the current Technical Team will become tasked with maintaining and updating the DTD, while the Functional Team will become the technical editors who ensure analysts/authors comply with the DTD requirements and provide more traditional editing support.

Steps in the Development Process

Extensive data analysis was the first step. Those members of the Functional Team with intelligence analysis experience performed the necessary analysis, working closely with the Technical Team members and the external contractor. An in-depth review of the command's GMI products and associated intelligence production guidelines revealed that over 1400 headers and titles were being used to label information. Through scrupulous review of content, that number was nearly halved to a lengthy but more manageable 750. The results of this analysis became the basis for developing the initial DTD. Combined meetings of the Functional and Technical Teams were conducted to ensure the requirements for the application were understood as the DTD was being developed. After several iterations, a baseline GMI DTD was completed and development of the Authoring Environment module began.

The overall style or "look and feel" of the Authoring Environment module is defined through the use of FOSIs. As in the DTD development, FOSI development was also an iterative process as team members attempted to enter information while using the application. The Technical Team is responsive to authoring requirements based on input from the testers. The goal was to make the environment look fairly close to what would be seen in an on-line dissemination environment without spending an inordinate amount of time on a page layout. An additional feature of the design of the Authoring Environment module was to provide an on-line help capability that explains each data element and attribute. This customized help function is in addition to the system help function. It deals with content (e.g., sample input) rather than traditional software help. Members of the Functional Team created the help data as they tested the Authoring Environment component.

How Many DTDs are Needed?

In an implementation of this magnitude, the question of how many DTDs are needed to fulfill the intelligence production requirement is a common one. In the case of JICPAC, it is not a simple question to answer. In their current environment, there is an overall master DTD for General Military Intelligence data that has been subdivided into modular pieces based upon subject matter. The totality of these pieces creates the information base about a particular country or specific target, and it will be possible to pull these various pieces together, when required, into a single report or other example of finished intelligence. Additional DTDs, which may or may not blend with the overall country DTD concept, will be developed in the future. These additional DTDs will support targeting, operational intelligence, and other, more specialized, intelligence production needs.

However, this approach does not support JICPAC's overall goal of focusing on *information* instead of the specific product or type of finished intelligence. Through close coordination with its customers, JICPAC has come to believe that they are interested in *topical* considerations such as naval capabilities, target sets, or weapon systems rather than the type of finished intelligence.

8.1.4.6 Success Variables

Only time will tell just how successful this new digital production system, an "information space" based on SGML, will be as a component of the interactive intelligence development process required by JICPAC. According to Major Hopson, its success will depend on a number of variables:

1) Data management systems

2) Powerful search engines

3) Systems compatibility

4) Willingness of customers to accommodate new technologies and techniques

5) Willingness of the Intelligence Community to develop a process with flexibility (through JICPAC as the initial beta test site)

One thing is clear, however: The Intelligence Community will reap the rewards of their success. They are beginning, now, to be more agile in sharing their information and knowledge resources for the common good of the intelligence process. As we approach the 21st Century, we know the era of *"virtual intelligence"* is coming!

8.1.5 Current Status—Impact on Other Projects

Where does JICPAC stand now? They are currently migrating the development software of the Authoring Environment module of this prototype to the operational environment. They have been in a limited operational mode since February 1998. As a result, this has had a major impact on a number of organizations, and even caused fundamental changes in the way they had been doing business for some. For example:

1) Training

JICPAC has begun to provide in-house training for the intelligence analyst "beta groups" and for support personnel, to include the document review chain, systems personnel, and graphics support staff. A three-pronged SGML training program is near completion. Two components, an initial awareness briefing presented to all newcomers, and an in-class, one and one-half day training session, are in place. The third component, a Web-based training course, is still in development.

In addition, the "information packet" format used in the DTD necessitates a new way of writing. Because the packet is modularized to facilitate export to the Intelink servers operating at various security levels (Top Secret, Secret, and others), the analysts must ensure that each module can stand alone as a complete and meaningful piece of intelligence data. While this means that the analysts no longer need to rewrite products for the various security levels, it also means they must rethink how they write. A training program, similar to the three-pronged SGML training is envisioned. Each of the two training efforts includes an active Web site, available on both JICPAC's internal intranet and on the Intelligence Community's Intelink. Beta test personnel are now authoring in the SGML environment and training of the entire analytic staff is underway. This training, testing, and operational production cycle will continue until all divisions have been incorporated into the SGML environment. When fully operational later this year, the prototype will be fielded throughout the remaining three operational departments of the command.

2) Transition Planning

As the group neared the end of the DTD and FOSI development phases, they began to do some transition planning. They looked at all the things that needed to happen before their new product could become operational on Intelink, before the next CD-ROM could be produced, and before any customer could have any SGML-based product. In actuality, they began to look at whether the old production process was still valid. For instance, the old document review process was closely scrutinized. Intensive discussions were held with senior analysts, division and department management, and foreign disclosure and security personnel to determine the optimal procedure. Members of the review chains were provided with specialized training that enhanced their understanding of what on-line review entailed so that they might better evaluate their options. The Technical Team, using some *ADEPT* capabilities and some creative programming, has developed assists to the review process. Systems personnel in the Information Systems Department of the Directorate of Support are assisting through the development of on-line tracking capabilities as information passes through the approval process.

3) Revamped Graphics Department

One of the major changes in the way JICPAC has traditionally approached production is the revamped function of the Graphics Department in the Directorate of Support. This group had, in addition to creating graphics, done all composition and layout, HTML conversion for export to Intelink, and preparation of CD-ROMs. A sizeable portion of the production cycle involved the Graphics Department. In the new process, Graphics is tasked with graphics creation and CD-ROM creation. Layout is now a function of the FOSI and graphics are stored in the file system by Graphics and referenced by the SGML instance through the analyst's designation of a file name. This last change has highlighted the need for creation of a Graphics Digital Library for the storing of all graphics used in JICPAC's products. The Graphics Department, with close support and coordination from the command's Webmasters and the Digital Production Development Office, is working to define the requirements for the Graphics Digital Library.

4) Changes to Handle Legacy Data

The existing Intelink home pages do not always support the kind of production JICPAC is doing. In addition, since legacy documents are not being converted to SGML, existing products will remain on JICPAC's country home pages for several years. Thus, new home pages are being developed to reflect the new production. Again, coordination between all parties has been the key to a fruitful effort.

5) Impact on Other Intelligence Community Elements

It is apparent that the efforts of JICPAC have had a profound impact on the Intelligence Community, and that the commitment to this process continues to grow rapidly. Support from the Intelink Management Office, from the various Service and Joint Intelligence Centers, and from the potential customers becomes stronger every day. Other agencies are looking, not only at JICPAC's approach, but at the SGML implementation efforts of other commands to determine which of the solutions available are right for their needs. The other commands include the Office of Naval Intelligence (ONI) that is detailed below in Section 8.2, as well as the National Air Intelligence Center (NAIC) and the National Ground Intelligence Center (NGIC).

8.1.6 Lessons Learned—Future

What did they learn? Well, for one thing, that there is always an easier, better, faster way of doing things. Unfortunately, the reverse is also alarmingly true. For example:

• Technical Skills Are Critical

New and specialized skills and training are required when undertaking a project of this magnitude. This would be true no matter what technical solution was chosen since the digital production and dissemination environment is so different from a hardcopy paradigm. Technical personnel selected for such a project should have strong programming language experience and exposure to markup languages like HTML.

• Multidisciplinary Approach

Creating an integrated team of subject matter experts, SGML experts, information systems, and publishing personnel is paramount to success of a project like this. All aspects must be considered with no one functional area taking precedence over another. On-site SGML expertise would have shortened the development cycle by as much as one-third and given the technical team members opportunities to learn from experienced developers. Even so, a careful selection process and wise, early use of training resources can greatly shorten learning curves (as was true in the case of JICPAC). Better trained people can do more, better, and faster. Scarce contractor resources then become available to deal with the thornier issues of tool evaluations and future development.

• Grass Roots Support

With the original "spark" of this fire coming from the analysts raising their own concerns about their ability to get the job done, success was inevitable. Indeed, the original *Living Document Working Group* was responsible for initiating actions that resulted in a number of other improvements to JICPAC's on-line delivery process. For example:

1) The LDWG suggested that JICPAC's geo-centric products could best be displayed on country-specific home pages. That idea, which has since gained wide acceptance in the Intelink community, groups all products or links to products for a given country on a single home page. The production center itself becomes less important as a way for the customer to locate information.

2) The LDWG also pushed for an end to the mandated 2-3 year production cycle in favor of a means to continually update intelligence whenever information becomes available.

3) Finally, they sought ESC empowerment for the individual analysts to post directly to the Intelink server, cutting out excessive review and approval processes then in place. This last effort resulted in the development of the Intelink Staging Area. From the staging area, the analysts, key people in the review chain, production personnel, and "special access" individuals can all review the products on line. The analyst and the "special access" individual actually post the material.

• Incremental Approach

Major Hopson believes that in the best of efforts, new or enhanced capabilities must be delivered in steps. This measured, incremental approach validates the approach that is being taken and serves several purposes:

1) It provides a demonstration of what may have been an unwanted or poorly understood concept.

2) A capability, even a limited one, which whets the appetite of the user, goes a long way toward sustaining enthusiasm for the migration.

3) Feedback from each step provides critical information and is a principal contributor to determining actions needed in subsequent steps.

4) Iteration is inevitable. As users' understanding of new processes increases, their desires shift or grow.

It is more than a mere truism, as Major Hopson put it, that "the customer always wants more than you gave him, after you gave him more than he had."

JICPAC's future is firmly wedded to an SGML-based production environment. As it begins its "initial operational capability" (or IOC in government parlance), JICPAC looks to the national community for the unifying guidance required to ensure that they always maintain interoperability of their various SGML efforts—indeed, that the Intelligence Community maintains its goal of managing information as an enterprise.

But, in the meantime, JICPAC continues to look to the future: the Center continues to search for answers to data management and warehousing questions. It continues to wrestle with security issues and to tailor its efforts to the eventual support of a multi-level security dissemination system. And it continues to look outward, to examine emerging technologies. JICPAC proudly states that their technology goal, within the limitations of decreased budgets, is to follow the mantra of Intelink's Jim Peak and stay within an increasingly short distance of industry's cutting edge.

8.1.7 Summary

JICPAC is a leader in the development and application of information technology. Their prototype implementation of the "information space" concept, an interoperable information infrastructure that supports collaboration and knowledge sharing among intelligence users and producers, exemplifies the evolution toward an "agile" intelligence enterprise. As implemented on Intelink, this concept provides the critical tools and capabilities needed by the intelligence analyst of the 21st century, including:

- Publishing and Dissemination Tools,

- Searching and Accessing Tools,

- Various Presentation and Analysis Tools, and

- Information Directory Services;

all within a secure environment protected from unauthorized access or tampering.

With the initial implementation of their new system in March 1998, JICPAC has become the herald of the future world of "virtual intelligence" within the U.S. Intelligence Community. We can learn from them and reap the rewards of their pioneer efforts, as we shall examine in more detail in Part Three of this book.

8.2 OFFICE OF NAVAL INTELLIGENCE

On 23 March 1882, the Honorable William H. Hunt, Secretary of the Navy, signed General Order 292 establishing the Office of Naval Intelligence (ONI). ONI is the oldest continuously operating intelligence agency in the nation. For 115 years, it has provided vital, timely and accurate worldwide maritime intelligence assessments to the Navy and the nation. The many men and women who have served in ONI over the years can take pride in a distinguished legacy of having contributed to the security of the country...

– Extracted from the Intelink ONI homepage

This second case study examines the process used by the Office of Naval Intelligence in the production and publishing, including softcopy delivery on

CD-ROM, of classified handbooks of the various characteristics of the world's Naval ships. This effort employed an SGML process that proved to be most successful, with significant, documented manpower savings coupled with real dollar cost savings. But most important of all, the end product was vastly improved.

8.2.1 Who Is ONI?

The Office of Naval Intelligence (ONI), now resident in its new headquarters in Suitland, Maryland, is the national production center for global maritime intelligence for the United States (Figure 8-2). As such, it has become the nucleus of their expertise for all important maritime issues, including sea related weapons systems, foreign naval sensor systems, submarine platforms, and ocean surveillance systems. ONI supplies a large variety of maritime products to Naval and Joint Forces, ranging from large scientific and technical (S&T) handbooks distributed to a wide customer base to short threat summaries for limited distribution to decision-maker audiences. For ONI and other intelligence centers, the products are extremely perishable. Intelligence that is delivered either late or in the wrong format has lost both its impact and usefulness to the customer. Collectively, *Naval Intelligence* products and services constitute one of the thirteen primary components of the U.S. Intelligence Community.

8.2.2 What Was the Issue at ONI?

In the past, ONI's production unit was staffed and oriented toward printed media production exclusively. However, in 1991 the Persian Gulf War changed their thinking. Lessons learned from intelligence production in support of Operation Desert Shield/Desert Storm had exposed a serious weakness in traditional intelligence delivery methods using printed media. The rapid build-up and entry into combat outstripped the long production times for traditional publishing, which simply could not keep up with the demand for printed intelligence in large volumes. Worse yet, the delivery of some products as huge pallets of paper documents was completely inconsistent with the rapid deploy-

Figure 8-2 Logo for ONI Headquarters.

ment and movement of those military forces. The sheer weight and volume alone made it extremely difficult to deliver paper documents to mobile theater units and it was difficult for the units to transport the products with them.

ONI knew that they needed an intelligence production method capable of putting intelligence in the hands of naval and joint forces quickly, and in a form that was compatible with their mobility requirements. They also recognized the potential of electronic dissemination of intelligence over other media. It became obvious to ONI that the advantages offered by CD-ROM technology were compelling, and that automating this capability would go a long way towards meeting their needs.

At about the same time, Intelink arrived on the scene. Since Intelink was designated as the primary medium for rapid intelligence dissemination, the stage was now set: ONI, (like JICPAC), and indeed *all* intelligence production centers, now faced the challenge of simultaneously bringing both of these new technologies into their worlds.

There were other problems. The demand for "peace dividends" within DoD resulted in a steadily declining workforce and severe budgetary cutbacks. However, there was no reduction of production requirements; in fact, the opposite was true. Units were directed to move into electronic media, but because all units were not connecting to Intelink or had not installed CD-ROM drives, paper production was still required. The aggregate publishing requirements for all media were rising as fast as ONI publishing personnel resources were declining.

8.2.3 The Decision: Automated CD-ROM Capability

Two years after the Persian Gulf War, ONI's Services Directorate publishing unit established a CD-ROM production capability in order to satisfy their immediate requirement for more viable, timely electronic production and delivery method. (Of course, this effort could also facilitate their longer term requirement of publishing on Intelink.) They also got some help from headquarters: reinforcement of their action by a directive known as a *"Chief of Naval Operations (CNO) Instruction."* This directive, OPNAVINST 5230.24, sought "to facilitate the smooth and effective transition of the Navy and Marine Corps to Compact Disc (CD) technology as the preferred media for storage and dissemination of data and information." It gave them all the ammunition that they needed.

In 1993, a small core of ONI personnel began their task. Led by Mr. Joseph F. Fisher, Jr., the head of the Electronic Publishing Division within their Services Directorate (ONI-3), this group began extensive work with a new Department of Defense officer, Navy CDR Bill Lyda. As the DoD "Executive

Agent" for CD-ROM development for the military services, Lyda was in charge of a special program that eventually purchased production suites, software, and licenses for 15 national and theater intelligence production centers before the program's scheduled termination in September 1996.

By the end of 1995, thanks to this special program, ONI was equipped with Sun computers running the UNIX operating system, and commercial off-the-shelf document management software, including the *INSO Corporation* (formerly *Electronic Book Technologies*) product known as *Dynatext*. This gave ONI the potential ability to move quickly into an automated, SGML compliant production environment for a number of its intelligence products.

8.2.3.1 SGML Was the Answer

In order to become more efficient, extensive production automation was viewed as critical to success. And, like JICPAC, the ability to reuse the same information in a number of different applications, delivered, perhaps, over different media, was also a driving factor. They also knew that automation using proprietary standards would provide a quick, short-term solution, but with potentially expensive retooling requirements for the future. On the other hand, the Standard Generalized Markup Language—as an International Standard—almost guaranteed future independence from both proprietary hardware and software. Even with the potentially greater start-up costs, SGML was the favored solution.

Collaboration was another reason to consider SGML. ONI's maritime mission responsibilities as part of the National Maritime Intelligence Center (NMIC) were expanding. Partnerships with other federal agencies such as the FBI, ATF, Immigration, the Coast Guard, DEA, and others argued for conversion to the commonly accepted and government sanctioned SGML standard. Indeed, collaboration with a growing number of foreign governments *required* the exchange of intelligence in standard international formats.

8.2.3.2 Automation of Handbook Process

Given their decision to use SGML, they needed to focus on a specific intelligence product. ONI's intelligence products can be broadly classified into two categories.

1) Text-based products developed on word processors

2) Handbooks derived from databases

The handbooks were the foundation of ONI's knowledge base regarding foreign naval platforms, weapon systems and associated electronics. They accounted for approximately sixty percent of ONI's intelligence production volume in terms of page count. Unlike the text-based publications, the information source was well defined, and highly structured. In particular, since SGML tags could be used within *Dynatext* to identify document objects within a specified product structure, they were convinced that they could quickly and successfully automate the handbook production process.

8.2.4 Implementing the Decision

ONI's main scientific and technical database is the Naval Intelligence Database (NID). It is an Oracle relational database that contains information on all foreign military equipment that could be a threat to U.S. naval forces. With the budgetary cutbacks at ONI, there were no resources available to do any serious internal modifications to this proprietary database. All efforts to develop a CD-ROM capability would have to be done using the standard report outputs of the NID. But there was good news, also. ONI knew that by applying SGML tags during the extract, the NID database could remain intact.

8.2.4.1 CD-ROM for Naval Ship Characteristics

To get started, they needed to select a specific handbook to convert to CD-ROM. They decided to focus on converting the naval ship characteristics handbook series published by the ONI Services Directorate (ONI-3). The head of the Electronic Publishing Division, Joseph Fisher, called an informal meeting with the head of the Ship Systems Branch, Claire Jeffries, and the lead technical analyst of the Naval Intelligence Database Branch, Tim Johnson, in February 1996 to outline the project. The concept was to develop scripts to automatically substitute SGML markup for the normal data and field delimiters during an extract. The resulting SGML/ASCII data stream would then be loaded into the *Dynatext* software with a *document type definition* (DTD), then indexed and combined with browsers/readers for multiple operating systems. This would be supplemented with thousands of photos and drawings of the naval platforms, hyperlinked at multiple locations within the data.

Two individuals with unique backgrounds did the critical aspects of this very important work: Jack Webb and Tim Johnson. Webb had been in charge of production at the JICPAC, and Johnson was intimately familiar with the NID data content and how customers used it at sea. Together, they bridged the traditional gaps between analysis, programming, and production. Within one month, the initial programming script had been written to extract data, the DTD had been prepared, browsers within the EBT software had been selected and combined, and hyperlink tests of images had been conducted. This effort proved to be so successful that the method by which the actual operation itself was done could be streamlined.

Traditional publishing had been a labor-intensive process for both analyst and production staffs. Weeks before a document was scheduled for publishing, the analytical units would ensure that all data fields in the database were accurate and up-to-date for a specific geographic ship characteristics volume. While the production staff labored to prepare it for printing, the analyst staff moved on to the next volume. Because the analytical staff was much larger than the production staff, the production staff was always under heavy pressure to keep up.

The first prototypes of the new process quickly revealed that the tables had turned. With a methodology that could extract the entire world's data in a few hours and prepare it for publication on a CD-ROM, the heavy pressure now shifted to the analytical staff. Now the entire world's data had to be up to date before production began. The resulting adjustments streamlined the entire process, allowing ONI to significantly reduce the overall production cycle for the handbooks (Figure 8-3).

The finished version of the new CD-ROM for the Naval Ship Characteristics Handbook was cut in June. It began to reach customers in late July 1996.

8.2.4.2 DTD Development

The Inso Corporation *Dynatext* software was chosen because it has a strong SGML capability and would work with ONI DTDs that were already designed. A year earlier, ONI had led a Joint-Service Working Group to create DTDs for

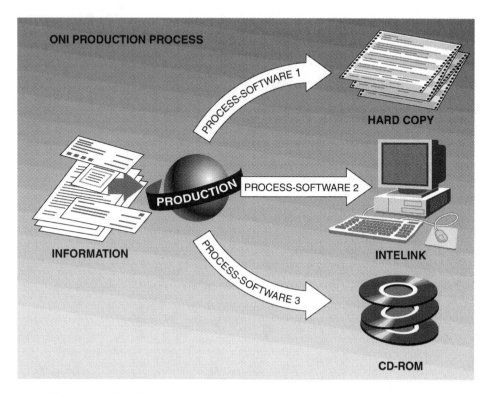

Figure 8-3 ONI Production Process.

the three most heavily used publication formats of the Defense Intelligence Agency. This work was accomplished with a lot of help from a brand new organization known as the Intelligence Community SGML Resource Center. Hosted at the CIA, the SGML Resource Center was instrumental in providing general expertise, training, and consulting resources to intelligence organizations that were implementing SGML related projects.

The DTD for the *Defense Intelligence Reference Documents* (DIRD) was selected as the starting model. This DTD was written originally to define the structure for a printed textual intelligence report. It contained much more structural detail than was required for the highly formatted Naval Ship Characteristics Handbooks; thus, many components were deleted for this project. The subsequent DTD was designed for a document that would be rendered much like the original paper version, but instead of viewing pages, the customer was seeing streamed data in a pleasing format.

The initial design of the screen view closely matched the paper format to keep the product familiarity for the customer. But in the new design, the locally printed versions had to differ greatly from the original document. This was necessary to ensure that customer-selected extracts could be printed on virtually any type of local printer, from dot matrix to high-end laser. The DTD ensures that security and informational elements are available to be printed as headers on each page.

Extensive liaison with the analysts/authors was done throughout the design period to work through the rationale for DTD modifications, print/view requirements, and the like. The driving objective was to try and put the ONI developers in the place of the customer. How would they access and use the product? What kind of display would be best? How can ONI make their access task easier? Working from the user backwards helped ONI define how the product should look and operate.

The entire development was done in small component builds that were individually tested and then combined with others and tested as a complete entity. In this way, problems were quickly identified and corrected. Sometimes several tests a day would be conducted to evaluate the results. In the end, the script was virtually error free when it was run in a final form.

8.2.5 Results

Using SGML, ONI developed an automated document production system for CD-ROM with options for printing and electronic dissemination over Intelink. ONI was then able to use this system to put intelligence in the hands of naval and joint forces quickly and in a form that was compatible with their mobility. The CD-ROM format was especially important as it allowed ONI to reach customers where Intelink was not available. This effort provided a significant, documented manpower and real cost savings.

Even more important than the manpower and cost savings, the quality of the intelligence was vastly improved. For example, it is now easy to tailor a unique product for a specific audience. The customer gains the ability to process more information in a medium that has virtually no space or weight restrictions. It was clear to ONI and the Intelligence Community that the results of this project exceeded virtually every original expectation and objective.

8.2.5.1 Impact on the Organization

This new production method has dramatically changed the commitment of analysts to their databases and the way they update material. They can see a clear benefit to loading the NID for more efficient support to customers in the form of formal publications and in providing customized CDs on demand for special situations. Likewise, they are freed from their former cycle of updates to meet a production schedule. Currently, each geographic ship and submarine analyst ensures that his/her area of the world is continually up to date.

For the production services staff, they can now keep ahead of the handbook authors and focus their attention on other products and other media, especially publication of intelligence information on Intelink.

Training for the authors turned out to be easy, since there were no major changes to their way of producing reports. Authors continue to input information directly to the Oracle database system as they did in the past. Training for the production staff involves ensuring that they are familiar with several new areas, including image scanning, sizing, manipulation, storage, and transfer. No extensive knowledge of SGML is required because the extract scripts do the tagging, but a working knowledge of the tags and how they are used is necessary.

8.2.5.2 Cost and Time Savings

This new process allows ONI to produce its former intelligence product volume with only about five percent of the previously required resources and in less that 1 percent of the time. The process also makes it easy to tailor a unique product for a specific audience. The customer gains more information that is easily accessed and searched in a medium with virtually no space or weight restrictions—easily meeting their mobility requirements.

The traditional paper version of the Naval Ship and Submarine Characteristics Handbook series consisted of 11 regional volumes of about 1,000 pages each. These volumes were distributed to over 900 customers around the world at a total cost of approximately $250,000. The cost to produce the new CD version is about $10,000, or less than five percent of the paper version.

That's not all. In addition to the production cost savings, the production labor that it takes to produce the handbook series has been cut from approximately 204 person/weeks to only 1 week. And similar levels of reduction have been experienced for the authoring and labor and mailing savings. Moreover, the CD contains additional information, is fully searchable, and offers more ways to view the information.

The technology and process is entirely exportable to any other Intelligence Community entity, or commercial organization that has a requirement to produce reference material from a database. With the automated scripts and use of SGML, similar savings can almost certainly be achieved.

The ONI efforts, as well as the JICPAC digital production effort detailed in the previous section, clearly demonstrate that SGML can be an extremely efficient and rapid means of delivering information to intelligence customers. Much credit goes to the early work performed by the development team at ONI, which received a Meritorious Unit Award from the Director of Central Intelligence in 1996. In addition, it was recently learned that ONI will play a pivotal role in the development of a true digital production environment for the Intelligence Community. ONI will further the work performed at JICPAC as the Intelligence Community evolves towards the concept of virtual intelligence.

8.3 NATIONAL SECURITY AGENCY

Information Superiority for America—One Team, One Mission

Intelligence and information systems security have always complemented each other. Intelligence gives us an information advantage over our adversaries and competitors. Information systems security prevents others from gaining a comparable advantage over us. The two functions serve as the offensive and defensive squads of a team dedicated to a single goal—information superiority for America and its Allies.

– NSA Vision Statement

The third case study summarizes some of the activities at the National Security Agency (Figures 8-4 and 8-5) in the production, publishing and dissemination of what the NSA calls "end-product." The later efforts rely on both Intelink and the Standard Generalized Markup Language (SGML), and have significantly improved the way in which NSA produces intelligence information.

8.3.1 Who Is NSA?

The National Security Agency is the official cryptologic organization of the United States, employing world class mathematicians, computer scientists and engineers, linguists, and other experts as both "codemakers" and "codebreakers." Founded in 1952, NSA has a proud tradition of serving this nation with critical intelligence that has consistently shaped our strategy and helped to win the Cold War. Indeed, in November 1997, NSA received the *National Intelligence Meritorious Unit Citation* from the Office of the Director of Central Intelligence. The prestigious award cited the accomplishments of NSA throughout the Cold War era over five decades.

NATIONAL FOREIGN INTELLIGENCE COMMUNITY
CITATION
NATIONAL SECURITY AGENCY
is hereby awarded the

NATIONAL INTELLIGENCE
MERITORIOUS UNIT CITATION

in recognition of the exceptional performance of its members between 1 November 1952 and 1 June 1997. The members of the NSA displayed high levels of technical skill, dedication, and understanding of the Community's need for intelligence information. The expertise in producing Signals Intelligence displayed by the Agency during this period allowed U.S. policymakers, military commanders, and Community intelligence officers to understand and counter the threat posed to U.S. national interests by world-wide Communism. The standard of excellence and the uncommon dedication to duty displayed by the men and women of NSA reflect great credit upon themselves, the Agency, and the Intelligence Community.

Figure 8-4 National Security Agency Fort Meade, Maryland Headquarters
Building.

Although NSA is like the Defense Intelligence Agency and the new
National Imagery and Mapping Agency in that it has been designated as a DoD
Combat Support Agency reporting to the Secretary of Defense, it is also a
separately organized intelligence agency, under the Director of Central
Intelligence. In essence, the "codemakers" protect the security of U.S. signals
and our own information systems and the "codebreakers" derive intelligence
information from the signals and information systems of our foreign
adversaries. This process of providing and protecting information supports a
wide customer base: literally, from the battlefield warfighter, through his
commander, to policy makers and ultimately to the Commander-in-Chief in the
White House.

In the Intelligence world, *information superiority* is usually defined as the
unimpeded capability to collect, process, and distribute information while
preventing an adversary from doing the same. As the NSA vision statement
above explains, *information superiority* constitutes the true business of NSA.
But their requirements and goals are no different than many companies and
commercial enterprises today. Many businesses today have the same set of
problems, concerns, and opportunities.

Figure 8-5 National Security Agency Fort Meade, Maryland Complex.

8.3.2 What Was the Issue at NSA?

So, how has the National Security Agency fared in its quest for *information superiority*? NSA has always been at the forefront of technology, particularly information technology. Early on, they established partnerships with industry that evolved into critical roles in the development of automation systems. Indeed, for decades prior to the advent of the personal computer in the 1980's, NSA was actually shaping and *driving* the computer industry in a number of directions that played key roles in today's modern computer and information systems. For example, the extensive computing needs of early cryptanalytical research being carried out at NSA was a driving factor in the development of the first "large-scale" computer, as well as the first solid state computer, leading to mainframe computers and today's modern systems, including super-computers.

Yet despite this significant role in the development of modern automated information systems, the reporting and publication of NSA's "end-product" or "finished intelligence" remained a difficult, paper intensive dissemination process until relatively recently. For example, well into the 1990's, a prominent staple of NSA that was produced daily and known as the "SIGINT Summary" or SIGSUM was still published on paper and manually distributed. It was available to NSA's customers electronically, but only as a simple text file with no graphics. It contained a *feast* of the world's most significant events of the day that were derived from the codebreaking side of NSA's mission. That *feast* was the product of the various intelligence resources of NSA—resources on which our government has spent hundreds of millions of dollars over the years—and was an NSA example of our *information superiority*. Yet it was published and distributed by techniques that would be used if the SIGSUM were not much more than a club newsletter. It became painfully clear to NSA's leaders that the time was overdue to capitalize on commercial electronic publishing techniques and the concepts behind the World Wide Web.

There were many senior leaders at NSA that were involved in improving the production and delivery of NSA's finished intelligence to its customers. Early-on was Vice Admiral William O. Studeman, NSA's Director from 1988–1992.[24] More recently, Air Force Lt. General Kenneth Minihan (NSA's current Director), Vice Admiral J. M. (Mike) McConnell (his predecessor), and Barbara A. McNamara (formerly NSA's Deputy Director for Operations and recently confirmed as the current NSA Deputy Director), have set the course for future collaboration—cutting across organizational and geographical boundaries to unify intelligence support. But the person that many people believe played the most significant role in guiding NSA's role in electronic publishing—particularly automated electronic publishing—was William P. (Bill) Crowell. Many organizations have a technical expert in the senior management ranks, and for NSA, Bill Crowell always filled that role. Crowell was a senior executive at NSA for seventeen years, serving in many positions—including the Deputy Director for Operations with responsibility for

---

[24] Later, as the *Deputy Director of Central Intelligence*, Admiral Studeman signed the directive that waived the "Need-to-Know" security principle that allowed Intelink to begin operations, as we explained in Chapter 2.

publishing finished intelligence—and recently retired as the NSA Deputy Director.[25]

Several attributes separated Crowell from other leaders. He was a "geek" in the most positive sense. He programmed in several computer languages. He understood technology. He knew the intelligence business—coming up through the ranks—and served in a number of diverse areas. He also knew the private sector, having recently served for a year as Vice President at *Atlantic Aerospace Electronics Corporation*. But most important of all, Bill Crowell is a true *visionary* who knows how to effect change in a large organization. Predicting the significance of the personal computer, its societal impact and the resulting changes at NSA as early as 1977 and 1978, he went on to a series of assignments that allowed him to implement many of his thoughts on the application of automation to NSA's challenges.[26]

8.3.3 NSA Improvements

Bill Crowell was involved early on in the challenge of improving the way in which NSA produces its finished intelligence. Responsible for the area of NSA that was tasked with producing intelligence on the former Soviet Union (at the time clearly the largest NSA intelligence production organization), Crowell became convinced that utilizing commercial off-the-shelf technology was the correct path to improving intelligence production and dissemination. Later as the Deputy Director for Operations, and a champion of the concept of Intelink, he oversaw the development of a number of intelligence distribution improvement projects based on Web technology and document standards such as the Standard Generalized Markup Language.

8.3.3.1 The Center for Applied Technology

Several years before the efforts of Tim Berners-Lee and others at CERN in Geneva, Switzerland, resulted in the development of the World Wide Web, Bill

---

[25] Bill Crowell was a mentor to the author, and was the driving force behind the approvals necessary for publishing this book.

[26] Shortly after retiring from the National Security Agency, Crowell joined the *Cylink Corporation*, a leading supplier of encryption-based network security solutions, as their Vice President for Product Management and Strategy.

Crowell established the *Center for Applied Technology* (Figure 8-6), or the "CAT" as it was known. The purpose of the CAT was to provide NSA with an opportunity to examine and evaluate various high technology computer hardware and software products, determine their applicability to NSA requirements, and to develop new approaches and techniques for intelligence analyst automated systems. His plan was to ensure that NSA stayed current with the latest computer technology, exploit the "open systems" concept that was gaining momentum at the time, and to use commercially available hardware and software products whenever they were cheaper, easier, and appropriate for the application.

The author was fortunate to have been chosen by Bill Crowell to serve as the first Director of the CAT. Teaming with Thomas E. Hassing, a senior level NSA computer systems and telecommunications expert, our task was to ensure that the Crowell vision for keeping abreast of technology flourished.[27] Tom Hassing and I were able to recruit not only the best and brightest from NSA, but also to enlist the support of many organizations external to NSA. For example, we were able to forge special relationships with a number of high technology companies in the private sector, ranging from very small companies (most have grown to much larger companies) to large ones such as IBM, Sun Microsystems, and Sybase. We also formed partnering relationships with several high technology universities including the Massachusetts Institute of Technology (MIT), Carnegie Mellon University, and the University of Michigan.

8.3.3.2 BEAMRIDER: An Early Electronic Reporting Prototype

The Center for Applied Technology used its array of in-house talent and partnering relationships to build proof-of-concept prototypes demonstrating the feasibility and applicability of interesting new technology. An early NSA solution to the electronic dissemination of finished intelligence was the brainchild of Michael V. Limcangco, one of the early members of the Center's

---

[27] Hassing is now retired from NSA and serves as the Chief Technology Officer at the Sun Microsystems Federal Division near Washington, D.C.

Figure 8-6 NSA's *Center for Applied Technology.* F. T. Martin, M. Lazar, and M. V. Limcango.

staff.[28] Limcangco demonstrated the *essence* of the Center's founding principles: a working prototype—using commercially available tools—that met a critical NSA need.

Project BEAMRIDER was an electronic reporting proof-of-concept prototype based on commercially available desktop publishing (*FrameMaker*) and database technology (*Sybase*). BEAMRIDER used *FrameMaker* and *Sybase* to electronically disseminate highly classified intelligence reports, over secure NSA communications lines, to customers in the Washington, D.C. area. With its own graphical user interface, this project was a precursor to the Web-based dissemination systems of today. It embodied many of the concepts that are now part of Intelink, and represented a fundamental change in the way NSA

---

[28] A good friend, Michael Limcangco is now a senior executive at *Analytical Graphics Inc.* (AGI), one of the early partnering companies of the CAT. AGI markets a number of products, including the *Satellite Tool Kit.*

disseminated its intelligence information. As such, BEAMRIDER played an important role in the evolution of automated intelligence reporting systems.

8.3.3.3 Recent Improvements

After the advent of the World Wide Web, Bill Crowell and others at NSA actively explored ways to take advantage of this new technology. To set policy and coordinate the development of the various resulting intelligence distribution projects, Bill Crowell's Operations Directorate used a very effective mechanism known as the "*Reporting and Dissemination Steering Group*" (RDSG). Essentially, the RDSG had overall responsibility for all NSA finished intelligence dissemination, including efforts to build the necessary information systems to automate the process. According to Ed O'Conner, one of the NSA intelligence reporting experts and a driving force behind the establishment of the Steering Group, it was effective because it bridged the entire NSA organization. Initially chaired by the director of the senior NSA reporting element, Bernard Elliker, it included representatives from each of the analytical reporting groups, and even included people from the various NSA support organizations.

NSA is moving forward one step at a time. The RDSG commissioned a special study, appropriately called *Neogenesis*, which blessed several initiatives that have become part of their strategy for wisely moving forward towards managing their information as an enterprise. These new initiatives were categorized into three primary areas:

1) Long-Term Storage

2) Authoring

3) Dissemination

These efforts exploit new technology and new opportunities for information sharing across the Intelligence Community, but are carefully transitioned to ensure backward compatibility with other existing systems. In each of the new projects, Intelink provides the catalyst. In addition, all of them are taking advantage of the Standard Generalized Markup Language, or derivatives of SGML such as HTML or the new XML. According to Katheryn Travers, the senior manager driving the development of these new systems, examples within each category include the following.

1) Long-Term Storage: Project Oceanarium

Oceanarium was the first Agency-wide implementation of an automated system to improve and modernize the storage, processing, retrieval, and publishing of NSA "end-product" or finished intelligence from Signals Intelligence (SIGINT) sources. It stores multimedia intelligence reports and makes them retrievable not only at NSA, but across the Intelligence Community through media such as Intelink. Project leader Calvin R. Wylie explained that Oceanarium mandates full SGML compliance, uses commercial off-the-shelf software products, and institutes common production processes across the reporting elements of NSA. Oceanarium capabilities include multimedia databasing, video streaming, and integration into NSA's internal intranet, known as Webworld.

When fully operational later in 1998, Oceanarium will allow all participating NSA intelligence analysts and reporters to leave the world of printed reports maintained as text files with few or no database technologies that they have known in the past. Instead, they will be equipped to enter into the new multimedia world of an information space of sharable databases allowing intelligence data reuse for electronic publishing and other applications. The bottom line will be significant production cost savings, increased efficiency of the intelligence analysts, and, most important of all, a significantly improved set of end-products across the entire Agency.

2) Authoring: Project Skywriter/Infowriter/Hightide

Project Skywriter/Infowriter/Hightide is an individual application of the Oceanarium automated storage concept for a specific target set within NSA. Built from a broad set of commercially available SGML products tailored to NSA requirements, this project focuses on the concept of metadata to enhance search engine capabilities and otherwise facilitate intelligence reporting.[29]

---

[29] In this application, metadata is "tagged" information, and becomes literally data about intelligence data. Metadata is considered to be an *enabler of change* with high potential, and has become a major Intelink thrust. Refer to Chapter 7 for additional detail.

The Skywriter/Infowriter/Hightide multimedia authoring and reporting system uses, according to Project Leader Marian P. (Patti) Chandler, several excellent SGML commercial products, including *Information Manager* by *Texcel*, *Adept Editor* by *Arbortext*, and *Translator* by *Omnimark*.

3) Dissemination: Project Tugboat

Tugboat was designed to automate the process of disseminating multimedia intelligence reports to consumers, including the delivery to Oceanarium for long-term storage. The long-term goal of this project is to achieve what Project Leader Michael Kiser refers to as "sanitation," or the ability of intelligence reporters to write an intelligence report once and have it automatically disseminated to consumers at multiple security classification levels. Only limited "sanitization" has been achieved to date, but work continues.

Collectively, these new long-term intelligence storage, authoring, and dissemination systems will enable NSA to meet the future challenges of a worldwide virtual intelligence environment, including the support of collaboration and knowledge sharing, thereby increasing its overall value to intelligence customers.

8.3.3.4 National SIGINT File

So what happened to the publication and dissemination of the prominent but paper-based "SIGSUM" or daily summary of NSA's most important intelligence information? As a result of the efforts of a number of organizations across NSA, brought together in particular by the *Reporting and Dissemination Steering Group*, the SIGSUM slowly evolved into a sophisticated and much enhanced, electronically published report known as the NSA *SIGINT Digest*. The *SIGINT Digest* was produced using commercial desktop publishing software and disseminated electronically to its authorized consumers. But the most important milestone was reached recently in October 1997 with the inauguration of what is referred to as the *National SIGINT File*.

The National SIGINT File (NSF) completely replaces the electronic version of the *SIGINT Digest*. Essentially, it is a virtual window into NSA SIGINT finished intelligence, tailored to provide various options for the customer to electronically retrieve, or "pull," items of interest. The following NSF services have been implemented to date:

• National SIGINT Update

This replaces both the executive and regular versions of the former *SIGINT Digest*. National SIGINT Updates can be pulled as a single file, or can be specifically tailored by region, topic, and specific articles of interest. It is updated periodically throughout normal business hours.

• Broadcast Program Listing

This feature provides the consumer with a complete program listing of available SIGINT finished intelligence—in an easy to read "TV Guide" format. It is updated daily, Monday through Friday.

• Digital Video on Demand (DVOD)

This feature, still operating in test mode, disseminates finished intelligence in a video format, including the option of displaying information in a window on the user's screen. The latest version, updated daily Monday through Friday, has improved audio synchronization, and interoperability with additional types of computer workstations.

• Recent *CRITIC* Reports

A "CRITIC" is an intelligence report that is considered to contain information on an event that is so important, or critical, that it must reach the White House and be available to the President within ten minutes or less from the time that it occurs. For example, the initial report that Saddam Hussein had attacked Kuwait in 1991 was a "CRITIC." This feature provides access to CRITIC information after completion of the specific CRITIC event. For on-going CRITICS, a flashing message appears on the top left corner of the screen. This is updated, obviously, as necessary—around the clock.

• Hot Spots and High Interest Topics

This feature automatically provides all relevant SIGINT finished intelligence relating to key issues or statements of interest that have been defined by the user—an example of "smart" push to the customer.

Figure 8-7 NSA's National Security Operations Center.

The list itself is updated on a daily basis; however, the finished intelligence reports themselves are updated bi-hourly.

• SIGINT Search Capability

This capability provides a quick search option against SIGINT that has been previously issued. It is updated hourly, and can be retrieved by the "serial number" of the product, title, or by certain predefined keywords.

• Latest SIGINT

This service offers the subscriber a topical breakout of the most recently published SIGINT finished intelligence. It is updated daily.

• SIRO Press Review

This feature provides the user with daily press reviews compiled by the Senior Information Resources Officer (SIRO), i.e., the duty officer-in-charge at the NSA command center known as the National Security

Operations Center (NSOC) (Figure 8-7). Updated daily, these press reviews are developed for use as background information by intelligence analysts and serve as indicators of significant world-wide events that may be reflected in SIGINT.

The NSF completes the transformation of the archaic paper-based SIGSUM into a state-of-the-art electronic dissemination tool that exemplifies the ability of the U.S. Intelligence Community to leverage and apply technology. It also represents the ability to manage information across the enterprise, enhancing their capability to deliver timely intelligence information.

8.4 FOREIGN BROADCAST INFORMATION SERVICE

A proper analysis of the intelligence obtainable by these overt, normal and aboveboard means would supply us with over 80 percent, I should estimate, of the information required for the guidance of our national policy.

—Secretary of State Allan Dulles to Congress, April 1947

8.4.1 Who They Are

The Foreign Broadcast Information Service (FBIS) (Figure 8-9) was created just prior to our entry into World War II in 1941 with a mission of listening to and analyzing foreign radio broadcasts. In a sense, it was a forerunner of the Signals Intelligence (SIGINT) mission of the National Security Agency, except that it was directed at "open" or publicly available information. Today the FBIS, with its bureaus located around the world, collects a huge volume of publicly available information that is related to various foreign national security policies. Known as "open source" information due to its unclassified and publicly available nature, it is normally technical information obtained from various foreign sources. These sources include radio and television; print media

Figure 8-8 NSA's Broadcast Network.

such as books, newspapers, and periodicals; and even so-called "gray literature"—information that is unclassified, but not generally available by subscription, such as company reports, financial reports, information databases, and technical conference proceedings.

From the earliest times (as cited by Secretary of State Allan Dulles 50 years ago), FBIS has enjoyed a reputation for providing accurate and timely foreign open source political, military, economic, and technical information as well as comprehensive reports about this information. These reports have included translations and transliterations, summaries, and even original analytical products written for U.S. policy and decision-makers and members of the Intelligence Community.

Figure 8-9 Foreign Broadcast Information Service Icon.

From its humble beginnings in the 1940's with a few senior-level linguists, analysts, and editors, the FBIS has grown to be a major supporting component of the U.S. Intelligence Community. Its products, customer services, media delivery options, and of course, issues and challenges, are very similar to commercial publishing concerns within the private sector. Revealing the magnitude of their operations, FBIS products and services are now available from a number of worldwide electronic information handling systems, including both the Intelligence Community's Intelink, and the Internet.

These products and services include:

• **Publications Procurement**

With officers and analysts stationed both abroad and in the US, the FBIS is able to procure many hardcopy and electronic forms of unclassified, open source information, such as newspapers, telephone books, journals, commercially printed books, and even CD-ROMs of databases. Clearly the highest volume product, FBIS presently purchases and distributes over five million publications and other products each year.

• **Regional and Topical Reporting**

Reporting includes translations, transliterations, and other summaries of open source materials, including detailed media analysis reports, centered on both regions (East Asia Daily Report, Latin America Daily Report) and specific topics (Arms Control and Proliferation Report, Narcotics Report, Terrorism Report)

• **Foreign Language Glossaries**

These are comprehensive guides to foreign language terminology with a format similar to a dictionary.

• World Media Guides

These are catalogs of information about both the print and electronic media of various countries. The Guides include various political affiliations, policy positions, and broadcast and circulation data for a specific country or region.

• Maps

Maps are always needed to perform the decision making and analysis functions of our government. FBIS is the distributor of unclassified reference maps produced by the Central Intelligence Agency to other government organizations.

• Foreign Video

In one of its most popular products, FBIS produces videos (for official U.S. Government use on a strictly controlled basis to comply with copyright restrictions) that include selected footage from foreign television programs and other sources, in the original language of the broadcast. These videos include unique—and frequently otherwise unavailable—coverage of internal events such as riots or uprisings, foreign satellite launchings, and political public appearances.

• Gray Literature Procurement

For official government use, particularly within the U.S. Intelligence Community, FBIS obtains large quantities of valuable information that is not generally available to the public, and cannot be obtained by commercial subscription, known as "gray literature." Much of this information—procured in response to specific customer requests, and tracked in a special summary database known as the Gray Literature Tracking Database—has been collected by FBIS analysts at facilities overseas.

• Linguistic Support

Usually on some sort of fee-for-service or payback mechanism, FBIS continues to provide a multitude of linguistic services to official government customers. These services range from instruction in a particular foreign language to various translation services such as treaty monitoring assistance and specific source translations (classified and unclassified) such as audio and video.

Clearly this is a perfect environment for Web-based technology with distribution over Intelink, and the use of SGML.

8.4.2 How They Are Using Intelink and SGML

How did they get started? According to Ralph Steiniger, an electronic publishing expert retired from the CIA, it was an evolutionary process that started in early 1990. At that time, FBIS management began reviewing their existing computer and communications systems to determine what changes to their production workflow might need reengineering to support future customer requirements. This was especially driven by requests for electronic delivery of daily publication, while still maintaining hardcopy delivery. And, with receiving locations all over the globe, another driving factor was the ever-increasing distribution costs.

Perhaps influenced by the early successes in the CALS initiative, SGML was considered immediately as a possible answer. In fact, by late 1990 there were a number of studies that indicated that a migration to an SGML-tagged product database, with commercially available tools, could provide FBIS with the capability to deliver their multiple formatted documents.

In came Carlton Neville, a long time FBIS employee and a recognized SGML expert who had recently formed his own consulting company, *Neville and Associates*. As a consultant to FBIS, Carlton performed a complete analysis of their existing product line and proposed the adoption of SGML. By 1993, FBIS had implemented a rudimentary magnetic tape distribution process, based on SGML-tagged data, for limited dissemination to several government agencies. Distributed on a weekly basis, these tapes were produced by adding the SGML tags after the paper copies were produced. It was a start, but unfortunately this process was found to be unsuccessful since most organizations were not able to deal with SGML-tagged data on their existing mainframes.

By 1994, electronic publishing on CD-ROM was a clear Intelligence Community requirement. This new requirement necessitated a complete redesign of the FBIS publishing/composition process, the staff and their equipment. Another contractor was hired by FBIS and they developed a system that was more "SGML oriented," taking advantage of a number of improved SGML tools that had arrived in the market place. Although it took many extra months to complete the initial operation of this system, primarily due to the training of FBIS production staff and analysts, by the end of 1994 the new system was operational.

By October 1996, it had become clear to FBIS that it would be possible to eliminate the production of most hardcopy products entirely. They knew that achievement of this goal would result in significant distribution cost savings with no compromise in the quality of their product. Their plan was to use Intelink to deliver all Web-based products to members of the Intelligence Community and use the Internet for Web-based delivery to other government agencies and to the public.

The National Technical Information Service (NTIS) is the host for FBIS items on the Internet. As part of its "FedWorld" service, there is currently no charge for accessing the extensive list of available items. Check out URL http://www.fedworld.gov/fbis.

Personnel cuts were not possible, despite eliminating most hard copy distribution. This was due to the increased demand for CD-ROMs, which significantly increased the workload of the production staff.

They continue to look at the future and improve their product. This year, the FBIS organization has begun the integration of this technology to their overseas facilities so that translated information is tagged in SGML prior to arrival at FBIS headquarters. And as they become more "agile," they plan to include the integration of more robust products (for example, the use of audio and video clips) into their product set.

8.5 NATIONAL IMAGERY AND MAPPING AGENCY

In the final case study, we briefly summarize work going on at the National Imagery and Mapping Agency (NIMA) (Figure 8.10). NIMA, the newest member of the Intelligence Community, is a designated DoD *combat support agency* that was chartered in October 1996 to provide timely, relevant, and

Figure 8-10 NIMA Icon.

accurate imagery, imagery intelligence, imagery-derived products, and geospatial information. It was formed by consolidating a number of very diverse organizations: the former Defense Mapping Agency, the Central Imagery Agency, the National Photographic Interpretation Center, and other smaller DoD organizations and resources. In remarks presented in March 1998 at AIPA'98, the annual symposium presented by the Intelligence Community's *Advanced Information Processing and Analysis Steering Group*, the first

Deputy Director of NIMA, Mr. Leo Hazelwood, spoke of a number of NIMA's unique attributes. For example, NIMA is the only component of the U.S. Intelligence Community with mission personnel who are "uncleared," i.e., they do not hold a security clearance authorizing them access to the classified reports produced at NIMA. Similarly, NIMA is the only member of the U.S. Intelligence Community that employs unionized labor for part of the workforce. The uniqueness of NIMA within the Intelligence Community clearly presents special security needs.

One response to these special security needs involves the use of Intelink. In order to enhance their publication of various products, including softcopy delivery on CD-ROM, NIMA recently turned to the SGML standard with implementation on Intelink. As in the previous case study examples, manpower and other cost savings were achieved, but most important were the enhanced capabilities and a vastly improved product.

It all started in July of 1995. Managers at the former National Photographic Interpretation Center were driven by challenging electronic publishing objectives developed by the Intelligence Community's newly formed *Electronic Publishing Board*, chaired by Barbara Sanderson (later Avis Boutell) of the CIA. As a result, these same NIMA managers developed a plan for implementing SGML, using Intelink, through an ongoing organizational effort known as the "Softcopy Program." The driving force behind NIMA's plan was their COTS Integration Support Branch. Through their leadership, this important project has progressed to the implementation phase and has been successful in achieving its initial goals.

The Integration Support Branch knew that whatever implementation decision was made, no matter what system was developed, there were two long-standing and cherished NIMA goals that had to be met:

1) Produce and distribute information in the most timely manner possible; and

2) Enable the archiving of information in a format that would remain stable over time.

NIMA based its decision to implement SGML, using Intelink, after recognizing three primary benefits of SGML that the Integration Support Branch knew would foster accomplishment of these goals.

1) Authoring in an SGML environment protects the investment placed in information because it is a widely supported standard that is vendor and platform neutral.

2) By enforcing document structure, an SGML environment ensures the validity and consistency of the documents produced.

3) SGML enables multiple distribution formats from one document source. A document can be produced one time and distributed to print, CD-ROM, the World Wide Web, and to a document database.

The SGML migration plan by NIMA management directed initial concentration on one of their more common documents, the NIMA Imagery Intelligence Brief (NIIB). Following that direction, a team of NIMA editors and SGML specialists created a document type definition (DTD) for the NIIB, defining its elements and structure. Once the DTD was developed, a thorough analysis of all SGML authoring tools was conducted to determine the best application for NIMA to use in producing SGML documents. As did JICPAC, NIMA selected *FrameMaker+SGML* by *Adobe* as the tool offering the simplest, most efficient, accurate, and flexible means for authoring documents in SGML. *FrameMaker+SGML* is cross-platform and has a WYSIWYG user interface, allowing users to generate SGML documents without having to understand SGML or the DTD. It also ensures validity of the document prior to distribution.

Using *FrameMaker+SGML*, system developers created a template for the NIIB and set up a beta site for testing its use. While testing of the template took place, a means for converting the SGML data directly to HTML for publishing on Intelink was developed using a commercial conversion tool called *Omnimark*. This conversion tool was then provided to the Intelink team for testing. Both the testing of the template and the conversion to HTML proved successful and the new SGML process was implemented within all of the NIMA Synergistic Support Teams.

In this new environment, once a user produces the NIIB in *FrameMaker+SGML*, it is sent directly to the Intelink server where it is automatically converted to HTML and published. There is no longer a need to manually convert the documents to HTML. In addition, the document is sent to the Consolidated Products Database (CPD), where the SGML data is used to automatically populate metadata fields within the database, also a process that was previously done manually. The automation that has resulted from the implementation of SGML has increased the speed at which the NIIB is distributed on Intelink. But most importantly, the information is stored in a document database in a format that will be retrievable on any computer with any software capable of reading ASCII text. Clearly, the NIMA critical goals have been met.

Given the success of SGML for production of the NIIB, NIMA now plans to begin development of a DTD, template, and conversion program for another NIMA product, the Intelligence Memorandum (IM). They are even considering expanding the use of SGML to include all production support personnel as well as all originating authors of documents. This will further optimize the use of SGML and increase the speed at which documents are delivered. And, of course, development continues with full consideration given to applications of XML, with the design being maintained to comply with both specifications.

The more NIMA embraces the use of Intelink and standards like SGML/XML, the closer the agency will move in the direction of a more "agile enterprise" within the Intelligence Community.

8.6 HOW DOES THIS RELATE TO BUSINESS?

It is worthwhile to step back, once again, and examine the "lessons learned" from these success stories and how they apply to the business enterprise of today. What can you gain by reading these case studies? The answer is *Illumination*. These case studies provide detailed examinations of the unique experiences of specific Intelink applications within the U.S. Intelligence Community. They document the cost savings and improved performance achieved through the use of Web technology and information management improvements. More specifically, these five case examples demonstrated:

   • **It is imperative to clarify all funding and manpower issues.**

Time and time again, across all agencies and organizations, the selection of a particular path was derailed because the resources were insufficient, or later evaporated. Occasionally, the simple lack of planning for resources that would otherwise have been available has doomed important projects.

- **The value of the "team approach" cannot be underestimated.**

Every success story involved an organization that took full advantage of the synergistic effect of teaming. The teams should consist of the *grass roots* leaders, experts, and consultants from similar organizations, outside contractors, or teams from the "problem" or mission side of the house interacting with the information systems professionals. Never underestimate the value of your user community's support. An intranet project is doomed from the start if the users do not support it.

- **Carefully sort out the role of contractors and consultants versus in-house resources.**

Establishing good contractor relationships is very important. *Deep immersion* of your own in-house project people into the development process, however, is highly recommended. Having them working and solving their own problems guarantees organizational buy-in and simultaneously ensures development of needed expertise.

- **Intranet development is a process of *continuous* problem solving.**

This is the bottom line. Following the experiences of the Intelligence Community organizations depicted in these success stories can help to avoid many problems, but no two organizations are alike. Understanding their experiences will at least alert you to potential pitfalls that can easily be avoided. Hopefully, building on their experiences will assist you in developing creative solutions to your own individual problems.

Part Three
The Future: "Virtual Intelligence"

Chapter 9

Challenges for the U.S. Intelligence Community

Since the fall of the Berlin Wall in November 1989, the traditional view and many of the basic assumptions of intelligence have changed drastically. As a result, the U.S. Intelligence Community is facing significant challenges as it adapts to the post-Cold War era. As one begins to understand the background of the U.S. Intelligence Community (as outlined earlier in this book), the role of Intelink as the Community's primary intranet/extranet for intelligence analysts and users (as discussed in Part Two), and specific case studies of improved intelligence analyst collaboration and electronic publishing activities (Chapter 8), a clear picture of *improved* government begins to emerge. The concepts of *Open Information Management* have played a significant role in meeting these

Figure 9-1 Logo of Intelligence Systems Secretariat.

challenges. The Intelligence Community *really* has improved the way in which it handles and manages its information assets using networking, Web-based technology, and International Standards such as SGML.

What does the future hold? In what direction does the Intelligence Community plan to go as we reach the millennium and beyond? For an answer, we will turn to several visionary leaders of the Community, including Mr. William P. Crowell, former Deputy Director of the National Security Agency, Dr. Ruth A. David, currently the Deputy Director for Science and Technology at the CIA, Mr. Richard J. Wilhelm, Executive Director for Intelligence Community Affairs, and Mr. Ronald D. Elliott, the second Director of the Intelligence Systems Secretariat (Figure 9-1) of the U.S. Intelligence Community Management Staff. These senior policy and decision-makers were instrumental in a cooperative effort to implement what could be termed *Virtual Intelligence* across the U.S. Government. This *Virtual Intelligence* concept is generally considered to encompass all electronically networked intelligence environments and architecture initiatives. And as you would expect, the direction that they have been taking the Intelligence Community is no different from how smart leaders in private industry are steering major corporations.

To gain insight into the future, Chapter 9 will first cite the need for change, as articulated in a number of commissions and studies of the U.S. Intelligence Community. Intelink, of course, represents a big part of that change, but much more needs to be done. We will then look at what Mr. Elliott terms the "Information Revolution of the Third Millennium," including the impact of recent legislation passed by Congress. After that, we will examine the impact of information technology and the global Internet including economic considerations, relating that to the business community. Finally, we will take a reassuring look at the direction headed by the Walt Disney Corporation as well as some future predictions by Mr. Bran Ferren, Executive Vice-President of Walt Disney Imagineering, and a frequent advisor to the U.S. Intelligence Community. All of these factors have influenced and motivated the U.S.

Intelligence Community by reiterating the necessity to achieve a more "agile" intelligence enterprise, as envisioned by Dr. David, and supported by Mr. Wilhelm and other senior leaders throughout the Community.

9.1 ENABLING OPEN INFORMATION MANAGEMENT IMPROVEMENTS

The need for improved open information management across the U.S. Intelligence Community has been apparent for some time. But a number of recent Presidential and Congressional studies has provided a renewed catalyst for change. This has led many leaders in the U.S. Intelligence Community to recognize the need and potential value of a worldwide "virtual intelligence" environment that provides a flexible and rapid collaboration capability. Perhaps the two most influential studies have been:

- **"Commission on the Roles and Capabilities of the U.S. Intelligence Community"**

This Presidential Commission, later known as the *Brown Commission*, was established by the Intelligence Authorization Act of Fiscal Year 1995. It was initially chaired by former Defense Secretary and Wisconsin Congressional Representative Les Aspin until his death in May 1995, and subsequently by former Defense Secretary Harold Brown. The Brown Commission investigated many aspects of the U.S. Intelligence Community and issued its final report in March 1996. Many expected the Commission to call for a major restructuring of the Intelligence Community, although in the end, it did not recommend that. Instead, the Brown Commission strongly recommended that the size of all of the intelligence agencies be reduced and that the authority of the Director of Central Intelligence, who doubles as the Director of CIA, be significantly strengthened. To accomplish this, it recommended adding a second full-time CIA Deputy Director to allow the Director to spend more time managing the entire Intelligence Community. The need to manage the entire Intelligence Community as an enterprise was clear.

- **The Intelligence Community in the 21ˢᵗ Century**

This study, known as "IC21," was undertaken by the Permanent Select Committee on Intelligence in the House of Representatives of the 104ᵗʰ U.S. Congress. Rather than concentrating on recommendations to "reform" the Intelligence Community, it focused on the exploration of new opportunities. The study was comprehensive, with 12 formal staff panels with expert witnesses. The study kept close touch with the Brown Commission and other efforts that were examining the Intelligence Community. For example, two members of the House Permanent Select Committee were also members of the Brown Commission. In March 1996, it released a large number of findings and recommendations. They were all-encompassing, ranging from the role of the Director of Central Intelligence to reiterating the need for the Intelligence Community to be fully compliant with emerging standards. But the primary theme of "corporateness" was so prevalent that the IC21 Study cited the success of the Goldwater-Nichols reforms for the Department of Defense in 1986. The central, unifying theme of the Goldwater-Nichols reforms was the concept of "jointness," the notion that the individual branches of military service had to improve cooperation, and that the central authority—the Joint Chiefs of Staff—had to be strengthened. The IC21 Study's major findings included the following two related recommendations:

The Intelligence Community should put greater emphasis on functioning as a true corporate enterprise, in which all components understand that they are part of a larger coherent process aiming at a single goal: the delivery of timely intelligence to policy makers at various levels.

The Intelligence Community would benefit greatly from a more corporate approach to its basic functions. Central management should be strengthened, core competencies (collection, analysis, operations) should be reinforced, and infrastructure should be consolidated wherever possible.

In addition, IC21 stated that the results of this corporate approach would be stronger and better intelligence products from all sources "through synergistic collection management and collaborative analytic efforts via a *virtual analytic environment.*" The stage was set, the mandate was clear: Intelink was the cornerstone of a new networked Intelligence Community.

9.2 INFORMATION REVOLUTION OF THE THIRD MILLENNIUM

The rapidly approaching new millennium is bringing what some call an information revolution of the scope experienced in past millennia in agricultural and industrial revolutions.

— Ronald D. Elliott, August 1997

The offices of the Intelligence Community Staff under the direction of Mr. Richard J. Wilhelm, and the Intelligence Systems Secretariat, the office that launched Intelink under Steven Schanzer and later Ronald Elliott, agreed with the thrusts of the Brown Commission and IC21. Indeed, according to Mr. Elliott, in order to ensure the support of national security in the 21st Century, it is absolutely essential to "take advantage of the information revolution, adapting the national intelligence enterprise to this new paradigm." He goes on to say, "We must work towards providing the necessary common processes, procedures and organizational relationships within the Intelligence Community to enable the application and improved exploitation of these Web-centric information services. Although we have Intelink, our national security information services must go further in effectively applying, on a worldwide basis, the information hypermedia that is needed by our operating forces." Mr. Elliott also believes that we need to move much faster towards Web-centric services in order to improve the manner of "pushing" the information needed to those needing it (at all echelons)—and in the appropriate context and format. This means delivery of specific, tailored information in a dynamic manner across our networks. It would involve access of multimedia information repositories directly by the warfighters in the field who need the best possible "knowledge" of their situation without having to wade through reams of paper or hundreds of messages or computer files. It certainly would have made a big difference to Capt. Scott O'Grady, the Air Force F-16 pilot downed over Bosnia in 1995.

9.2.1 Basic Assumptions

The Intelligence Systems Secretariat, like many leaders of corporate America, is taking the lead and beginning to move towards this new paradigm. For the Intelligence Community, according to Mr. Elliott, this means subscribing to a number of basic precepts that will reshape how intelligence is exploited, processed, and shared:

1) All authorized users must be able to access all relevant available information no matter where it resides.

This will be a fundamental, revolutionary change in the Intelligence Community. For a number of reasons, ranging from how the intelligence agencies were chartered by Congress to valid security issues, this has never been the case. But today, it is recognized that information and information-based services must be managed as the most critical resources of the intelligence enterprise, the "raw material" and "engine" of intelligence. Intelink, as the intranet/extranet of the Intelligence Community, is serving as the catalyst for this critical requirement.

2) Information is a "capital resource" and must be used to realize its value.

In the past, the Intelligence Community thought of its information related capital resources as the physical plant associated with the production of what was primarily documents—the actual computers, information systems, and other tangible items that had been successfully budgeted for previously. Now they must view and evaluate the information dollar value to the mission. No longer can their valuable resources be stored and lose their value over time in data repositories. It is now understood that the value of information is directly related to time. Information must be continually accessible across the intelligence enterprise in real time or near real time in order for it to contribute towards key decisions that are critical to our national security. Thus, intelligence information is becoming an economic commodity, and our support must be cost effective. Again, Intelink represents the beginning of this new approach.

3) We must have a strong, focused, and proactive Intelligence Community corporate leadership in order to fully realize the opportunities of the "information revolution."

Unlike much of the corporate world, within the government and certainly within the specialized secret world of the U.S. Intelligence Community, "stovepipes"—strong individual bastions of expertise and specialized functional areas—are prevalent. As a result, while high-level senior oversight does exist, we are not always able to fully exploit and leverage opportunities and that would enable us to be a more cohesive corporation. Much is being done within the Intelligence Community to address this issue, including strengthening the role of Mr. Wilhelm's Community Management Staff. Even Congress has become involved, as we see in the next section.

9.2.2 Information Technology Management Reform Act (ITMRA)

The U.S. Congress has always had a strong interest in the information management needs of the federal government. In fact, Congress recently passed important legislation to improve the way federal agencies manage information technology investments and streamline the acquisition process. Known as the *Information Technology Management Reform Act* (ITMRA) and signed into law in August 1996, it requires each federal agency (including the intelligence agencies, of course) to implement a process to optimize the value of information technology acquisitions. It also established the position of Corporate or Chief Information Officer (CIO) in every federal agency to serve as the senior information technology manager or official. While the role, which is defined as a strong advisory and advocacy component, may not be as strong as we have seen in the corporate world, the groundwork has been laid for the future. Each of the thirteen agencies comprising the Intelligence Community has now selected their individual "Corporate Information Officers." Indeed, Mr.

Elliott chaired a special group known as the "SIM Panel" or Senior Information Management Panel, to provide the very focus needed. The group continues to meet on a regular basis, and provides not just a dialog for interaction, but makes operational decisions and policy recommendations to the Intelligence Community Management Staff.

The ITMRA legislation, also known as the *Clinger-Cohen* Act, has special significance to many members of the Intelligence Community—namely those in the Department of Defense—since the current Secretary of Defense (former Representative and Senator from Maine from 1979-1997) William S. Cohen was the primary author. The new legislation has led to the formation of a number of forums, such as the SIM Panel, that have facilitated exchange and cooperation of mutual information technology concerns. This, in turn, has helped to focus on the information technology needs of the Intelligence Community as an enterprise and the examination of the value of a collaborative environment using intranet technology.

9.3 IMPACT OF TECHNOLOGY AND THE INTERNET

Few people question the impact on open information management and the benefits of the global Internet, World Wide Web, and other technology advances that we have seen in the last decade. And most experts agree that the right tools are critically needed to navigate us through the sea of information that is now available to us. In March 1998, Paul Saffo, a director for the *Institute for the Future* in California, and a prominent information technology forecaster, spoke to the Intelligence Community at their annual symposium sponsored by the *Advanced Information Processing and Analysis Steering Group* (AIPASG). In his address on the future of information processing, he discussed the inadequacy of current technology tools to handle "information overload," i.e., the inability to take advantage of the amount of information that is really available. A classic example of this would be using a single phrase in a search request and then getting back thousands of hits. As part of an article in the September—October 1997 *Harvard Business Review* on the same subject, Saffo stated that information overload is "not a consequence of the amount of information confronting us but rather of the gap between the volume of information and the effectiveness of the sense-making tools that technology has made for us."

Improved collaboration tools can narrow that gap for the U.S. Intelligence Community. A case in point would be the linguists at the National Security Agency. According to former Deputy Director William P. Crowell, NSA linguists were 700% more effective in 1997, in spite of downsizing that has seen the NSA workplace shrink 33% since 1993. As recently as 1992, according to Crowell, NSA linguists "still walked downstairs, picked up their tapes for the day, then typed and put little pieces of paper in the tapes to mark content." There was no other way for the linguists to recognize where the voice cuts existed, certainly no database of voice material. Today, networked computers have made the difference, with new improved collaborative working tools and methods for the linguist. The bottom line, according to Crowell, is that the Intelligence Community needs to create a "virtual" collaboration environment, addressing several open information management improvement areas. He describes three necessary "direction vectors" for this new environment:

• Improved Collaboration and Collaborative Tools

The Intelligence Community needs a combination of Web-based tools that will allow an intelligence analyst driven environment. A culture change is occurring, but more needs to be done to alleviate the negative ramifications of existing "stovepipes" throughout the Intelligence Community. Intelink, of course, is the beginning, the *prototype*.

• Improved Search Tools

Better search engines are needed by the Intelligence Community. While metadata and other tagging approaches are innovative, a *cognitive* or "smart" search engine is needed, rather than the ones that are based on words as we have today. As we discussed in Chapter 6, the Intelink Management Office is exploring several novel approaches.

• Improved Security

The primary problem facing the implementation of a "virtual intelligence environment" is security. Despite recent hacker attacks, Crowell is confident that it is possible to design government and commercial security products that can protect networks and keep them highly secure. These are urgently needed and must be fully exploited wherever possible.

All three of Bill Crowell's "direction vectors" relate to what he considers to be the most difficult problem: overcoming the cultural barriers that separate the various members of the Intelligence Community. This is a *major* issue, as we will discuss further in Chapter 10, in spite of the theme of unification that Intelink represents.

9.3.1 New World Order of Connectivity: the Economics

Ron Elliott, and other Intelligence Community leaders, believe that intelligence information is becoming a measurable, economic commodity, as cited in Section 9.2.1 (see above). This concept was articulated in an article published as part of the Intelligence Community's own scholarly series known as "Studies in Intelligence," which is available on the global Internet from the *Center for the Study of Intelligence* as part of the CIA's Web page at URL http://www.odci.gov. In a 1996 article entitled, "Adam Smith Examines the Intelligence Economy," author Todd Brethauer equates finished intelligence to the classical economic theory that says customers will tend to buy those products that give them what they need for the least cost. According to the author, his novel new economic arrangement where intelligence producers and consumers *pay* for services rendered is simple: On an annual basis, the Director of Central Intelligence, with the concurrence of the President and the Congressional intelligence committees, would allocate a budget from a fixed pool of "Dulles Dollars" to each branch, department, and agency. This idea of bringing a business model to intelligence, of course, is the norm for the private sector. He explains:

Intelligence consumers could buy products off-the-shelf or have them tailor-made. Inefficient producers would eventually be forced to improve or leave the market. For example, an intelligence user today concerned about the threat to regional stability in Asia from AIDS could request, justify, and eventually receive a multi-source study about the incidence of AIDS in Asia and its consequences...When subject to budgetary discipline, the user could still request the same study. Now, however, when confronted with the prospects of having to "pay," the World Health Organization study that addresses 90% of the issues and that is available free over the Internet would begin to look attractive.

The scheme also could bring the efficiency of the marketplace to the intelligence collection process. Under such a system, intelligence collectors would bid for the work of satisfying consumers' requirements for information. The collection discipline able to meet the requirement on time and within bid would win the contract. The number of Dulles Dollars the user would be willing to pay would reflect the value of the collection effort to his mission...Consortiums between collection disciplines might form and should be encouraged. This would reduce duplicative, competing, and inefficient tasking. It also would encourage effective use of low-cost open sources.

The Intelligence Community may not yet consider the economics of intelligence information in terms of "Dulles Dollars." But every organization should recognize that a fundamental shift in the economics of information has occurred. Earlier in this book we discussed the global Internet phenomenon, where millions of people are now connected electronically using universal, open standards. According to Philip B. Evans and Thomas S. Wurster of the Boston Consulting Group, in an article entitled "Strategy and the New Economics of Information," published in the September—October 1997 issue of the Harvard Business Review, "This explosion in connectivity is the latest—and, for business strategists, the most important—wave in the information revolution." They feel that all executives—not just those in high-tech or information companies—must completely rethink the fundamental strategies of their businesses based on this new "connected" world.

This article is an in-depth discussion of the economic aspects of information. However, there are three primary points in this article that particularly apply to both government and private enterprises concerning the impact of our new, electronically connected, world order.

1) Your business is an *information* business.

It is clear that the U.S. Intelligence Community is in the information business—information is its most critical asset, and managing that information is its most important challenge. But, according to Evans and Wurster, "*Every* business is an information business." Even in businesses not normally associated with information, the cost of processing information critical to that business is enormous. For example, about 1/3 of the total cost of U.S. health care—over $300 billion dollars annually—are the costs associated with handling information such as patient data, physician data, test data, insurance data, and the like. Furthermore, information can define competitive relationships among competitors. Whether a company is using its presence on the World Wide Web, exploiting some electronic commerce advantage, or merely using advertising to its best advantage, that company is relying as much on information to compete as they are on their physical product.

2) Existing companies can be victims of their own obsolete infrastructure.

Take, for example, the near demise of the *Encyclopedia Britannica*, perhaps one of the best known names in the world. Publishing encyclopedias on CD-ROMs seemed to come from nowhere and destroyed the printed book encyclopedia business that existed for decades. Grolier, Incorporated, publishers of the popular *Encyclopedia Americana*, published their first general reference publication on CD-ROM as early as 1985.[30] And, of course, the *Microsoft Encarta* CD-ROM encyclopedia is available for about $50, assuming that you did not already get it free as installed software on your new personal computer. The cost of printing and distributing a set of encyclopedias—the *Britannica* sold for approximately $1500 to $2000—is less than about $300. The cost of producing a CD-ROM is

---

[30] Grolier now maintains all source data for their publications, and electronic versions, in SGML, as chronicled by Chet Ensign in another book in this series entitled, *$GML: the Billion Dollar Secret*.

less than $1.00. Furthermore, in the case of *Microsoft Encarta*, the content was licensed from Funk and Wagnalls encyclopedia, which was sold in grocery stores. Microsoft initially spiced up the content by inserting publicly available movie clips and pictures. Evans and Wurster point out that parents had been purchasing encyclopedias for their children out of a desire to foster a proper learning environment. Today when parents make a purchase to foster a proper learning environment for their children, they buy them a computer. Thus, the *computer* became the real competitor of *Britannica*. Eventually, the company did issue a CD-ROM version, but instead of pricing it competitively, they charged nearly the same price for a stand-alone CD-ROM as they did for the print version. As a result, sales declined, and many people left the company. Finally sold and now under new management, they are trying to rebuild the company around the global Internet.

3) New businesses will emerge from this newly connected world.

Businesses like retail banks and newspapers will continue to exist, but their basic strategic directions will change. Components of the newspaper, like the classified ads, can be unbundled from the paper. Home electronic banking will change the retail banking landscape. In addition to these fundamental changes, there will be completely new businesses built around the new world of connectivity. Take for example, Amazon.com. As perhaps the largest and most prominent of the global Internet on-line booksellers, they have had a revolutionary impact on the industry, partially due to the seemingly infinite supply of potential customers. Furthermore, with the near infinite choices given to people in our connected world, there is now a navigation problem, i.e., a problem finding exactly what they want, at a price they are willing to pay. According to Evans and Wurster, the solution to the navigation problem "could be a database, intelligent-agent software, or somebody giving advice. The navigator could be a brand providing recommendations or endorsements." And in each one of these scenarios is a potential new business.

The phenomenal explosion in electronic connectivity must be recognized by all business executives. And all leaders, within the governmental and private sectors, must either exploit or capitalize on the capabilities of the technologies associated with this connectivity.

9.3.2 Example of How the Private Sector Is Coping: Walt Disney Imagineering

In the context of information, there are many parallels between the U.S. Intelligence Community and the private sector. Much insight can be gained by an examination of the direction being taken by leading organizations with similar information related challenges. One such enterprise is the Walt Disney Corporation.

The Walt Disney Corporation continues to be one of the fastest growing enterprises today, with revenues of over $21 billion last year. The Disney empire includes the ABC television network, Miramax and Touchstone movie production companies, Hollywood Records, the ESPN sports cable network, a professional hockey franchise, a major league baseball team, and numerous magazines, newspapers, trade journals, and other businesses. Furthermore, some of the world's smartest computer and information science experts are now employed by a subsidiary of Walt Disney known as *Walt Disney Imagineering*. Indeed, the fact that Disney has brought on-board an entire cadre of computer science luminaries was described in an August 11, 1997 *Newsweek* magazine article by technology correspondent Katie Hafner. Known as *Disney Fellows*, they include MIT artificial intelligence pioneer Marvin Minsky, computer interface pioneer Alan Kay, and computer/education expert Seymour Papert. Hafner concluded in her *Newsweek* article that "Disney is becoming a player along with Microsoft in the research and development arena at a time when corporate research is more important than ever." The person responsible for the *Disney Fellows* concept is Mr. Bran Ferren, a nationally recognized technologist working in theater, film, special effects, product design, architecture, and the sciences.

Bran Ferren is Executive Vice President for Creative Technology and Research & Development at Walt Disney Imagineering. With about 2400 people, Imagineering is responsible for theme park master planning, research and development, and implementation at The Walt Disney Company. Mr. Ferren's responsibilities, which include managing all research and development, extend beyond Imagineering to include technology development with potential value throughout the Walt Disney Company. And he works closely with the U.S. Intelligence Community. He holds a top-level security clearance and is a frequent speaker at Intelligence Community conferences and symposia. A key advisor from the private sector, he was appointed to the *Army Science Board* in 1995, the *National Security Agency Scientific Advisory Board* in 1997, and the *National Reconnaissance Office Science Board* as well as the *Senate Select Committee on Intelligence Technical Advisory Group* in 1998. His views, consistent with Intelligence Community leaders, have helped to shape the future direction of open information management.

9.3.2.1 Walt Disney Imagineering Predictions

The number one and *driving* conclusion from Bran Ferren at Walt Disney Imagineering is that the global Internet is clearly, and absolutely, the *enabler of the future*. While the application of computers and automation were not always used effectively against many intelligence related problems as recently as five years ago—such as the linguist example at NSA—the global Internet and the advent of the World Wide Web has the potential to change everything. This belief was stressed in a March 1997 interview with Bran Ferren by the author at Walt Disney Studios in Burbank, California, and followed up with a presentation at the Operations Research Symposium held at the National Security Agency in October 1997. It was again reiterated in a colloquium in February 1998, entitled "Managing Intelligence in a Networked World," held in the "Bubble" Auditorium at CIA Headquarters in Langley, Virginia. In his remarks, entitled, *"The Global Impact of the Internet Phenomenon and Why We Should Care,"* Bran Ferren compared the Internet to the discovery of fire. To put this in the proper context, he explained that some inventions—such as the CB-radio[31]—have a very brief impact on society. Other inventions or discoveries—such as fire—have had a profound impact on society. Yet the "fires" of today consist of the same basic "technology" as those of 10,000 years ago. Ferren strongly believes that the impact of the global Internet falls on the

---

[31] While very popular in the 1970's and early 1980's among consumers, CB-radios joined eight-track tape players as obsolescent technology and are used today on the highway almost exclusively by long haul truck drivers rather than the public in general.

"continuum of societal impact" right beside fire—it will be with U.S. for a very long time. The following paragraph provides additional insight into Ferren's beliefs/philosophy concerning the Internet and networking technology:

9.3.2.1.1 Ferren View of the Future

Due to rapidly changing technology, computers will be barely recognizable just ten years from now. Indeed, in 20 years Ferren suggests, we will have more computing power on our desktops than an NSA supercomputer of today. The UNIX, NT, and Windows battles will be over, because operating systems as we know them will go away. Everyone will use very small or portable PCs and everything will go over the networks, both public and private. Networked applications will be the driver behind everything we see and do on the global Internet. Security will be an "endpoint-to-endpoint proposition" and firewalls, as we now know them, will cease to exist. We will be using "Object Oriented" code exclusively, like Sun Microsystems's JAVA, which will take over all of these network applications. Finally, Bran Ferren believes that alternative computing paradigms—leading-edge concepts such as optical, DNA, or even quantum computing—will become commonplace, and even have the potential to "put much of the intelligence community out of business, unless we take these concepts seriously." He further states, "The supercomputer of today will be replaced with distributed network based computing concepts necessary to support the processing tasks of the future. This is necessary to support next generation data warehousing concepts like the MOADB (Mother Of All Data Bases). The concept is simple: Remember everything and find it instantly."

What does he mean by all of this? We take a closer look at some of these emerging technologies in the next section.

9.3.2.2 Optical, DNA, and Quantum Computing

The end of Moore's Law—which states that computer chips double in power every two years as discussed earlier in Chapter 4—is relatively near, and we must begin to think about the technology or technologies that will replace the silicon computer chip. This is necessary because the simple combination of economic and physical limitations will put an end to the phenomenal growth in chip power that we have seen over the past several decades. After several more generations of the silicon chip over the next five to ten years or so, what is next? One possibility, of course, is to further optimize existing technology. To that end, the recent advances in massively parallel computing are encouraging. However, these three radically new technologies could play a significant role in diverting chip designers from their silicon plateau, with a corresponding impact on the future of computing:

1) Optical Computing

This very promising innovation is based on the fact that certain materials have very unusual and fascinating optical properties. For example, certain materials have the ability to change their opacity depending upon the intensity of light that is passed through them, e.g., clear eyeglasses that become sunglasses in bright sunlight. An article entitled, "The End of the Line," appearing in the 15 July 1995 issue of Economist magazine, explains: "By shooting light through such materials from tiny lasers, millions of which can be packed on to a single chip, engineers can create optical switches. Linked together, these could make computers in which signals would run at the speed of light—much faster than the electrical impulses in conventional computers. Nor do light signals interfere with each other to produce the 'crosstalk' that bedevils electric circuits when the connections are close enough together for electrons in one wire to interact with those in neighboring wires." A drawback to the concept of optical computing, however, is that the necessary laser chips require significant amounts of power, which in turn present serious overheating problems. Solving this problem will be expensive, slowing down the promise of optical circuit technology.

2) DNA Computing

The pioneer behind this technology was a University of Southern California (USC) professor, Dr. Leonard M. Adleman. A mathematician by training, Adleman met colleagues Ronald Rivest and Adi Shamir while serving as an assistant professor in MIT's mathematics department. Together they developed and patented the "RSA"—an acronym of their last names—public key encryption system, and later founded RSA Data Security Inc.[32] According to an article by Wyman E. Miles published in the September/October 1996 issue of *NetWorker*, Adleman was struck by a resemblance between the way biological enzymes are able to "read" DNA and the principle behind the "Turing Machine." DNA is an abbreviation of "deoxyribonucleic acid," from which scientists can extract a sequence of molecules that uniquely determines the shape, form, and other functions of every living organism. A "Turing Machine," a computational model invented in 1936 by theorist Alan Turing, is a straightforward methodology that can be used to formalize the notion of computable mathematical functions. Intrigued by this, Adleman developed the concept of DNA Computing by solving a well known mathematical problem often referred to as the "traveling salesman problem" —a classic conundrum whose solution is the set of optimal routing paths among a number of departure and destination points. Attempting to find the most efficient routing among seven cities, Adleman encoded strands of DNA to represent each of the cities and paths between cities, and quickly reached a solution. According to Miles, "Because of DNA's extremely small size and amazing computational speed, Adleman's molecular computer holds the potential to solve problems far beyond the scope of any existing electronic computer." In 1995, Adleman founded the Laboratory for Molecular Science at USC, where research on DNA computing continues today. Their next challenge, according to Miles, is to solve the Digital Encryption Standard approved by the National Security Agency. While this issue is beyond the scope of most computers, the theoretically huge parallel processing capabilities of DNA Computing are ideally suited to complete the task.

3) Quantum Computing

A "quantum computer" is a hypothetical machine that uses the concepts of the field of quantum mechanics to perform its computations. Since we are very near the limits of conventional chip design which are constrained by the laws of physics—Moore's Law—quantum computing offers an intriguing possibility of constructing new types of logic gates and secure

---

[32] As discussed further in Chapter 4.

cryptosystems. A quantum processor can theoretically perform a single command or operation operating on many different numbers simultaneously through the use of a special algorithm. Questions remain as to whether a computer can be built that can process a quantum algorithm. However, according to quantum computing pioneers Peter W. Shor from Bell Laboratories and Seth Lloyd of MIT, an algorithm for quantum computing that factors large numbers and is capable of breaking the RSA public key cryptosystem, was recently discovered. "If developed," they said, "quantum computing has implications for the future of computing that are astounding and revolutionary." Indeed, Ferren calls quantum computing "potentially the *Manhattan Project* of cryptanalysis."

These three concepts represent potential new directions, with correspondingly new opportunities, for both the U.S. Intelligence Community and the private sector. And, in particular, any new technique with a potential to affect network security could impact Intelink and intranets in general. Therefore, they are examples of important developments that must be tracked as we enter the next millennium.

9.3.2.3 Steganography: Additional Security

It is clear that Bran Ferren believes the government and the Intelligence Community—as well as the private sector—must understand and take advantage of the Internet and Web phenomenon to succeed. A less known concept related to Intelink (and related to the private sector interested in more secure exchanges of data) that has serious potential for the Intelligence Community is the field of steganography. Although steganography, or "data hiding," has been around for centuries (hiding information in the teeth or scalps of messengers in medieval times, or more contemporary examples such as "disappearing" or "invisible" ink), the advent of digital data and the global Internet presents an astounding array of new data hiding opportunities.

Today, the field of steganography encompasses all aspects of stealth-like communications, data compression, and media exploitation. A simple example would be to take one piece of information and hide it within another piece of information. Since all computer files on the Internet (a digital GIF image, for example) contain unused or insignificant areas of data, information to be hidden could be placed into those areas. The files can then be transmitted over the unclassified Internet without anyone suspecting that an encrypted or hidden message was present.

According to Thomas Kraay, Chief Scientist of the Washington DC-based *Secure Solutions* Directorate of the *BSG Corporation*, a subsidiary of the *Medaphis Information Technology Company*, steganography provides "unique, stealth-like communication, data compression and media exploitation." From his office in their *Computer Forensics Laboratory*, Kraay explained how steganography could work:

> *For a personal computer, a typical image has a resolution of 640 x 480 "pixels," or picture elements. It is possible to represent color images using 24 bits, with 8 bits allocated to each of the three primary colors (red, green and blue). Since the human eye is not capable of seeing fine variations in colors, it would therefore be possible for someone to hide a message by using the least significant bit of the color information. A person could even hide a message in some subset of the available pixels for a specific image. On top of this, the hidden message could itself be* encrypted *by some additional mechanism, rendering an additional level of security.*

This could easily be done on a Usenet news group or website accessible to the public. Ferren quickly points out that a person could use these steganography techniques and covertly disseminate information by *breaking* into a commercial Internet website and then surreptitiously adding data. "For example," he says, "entertainment industry sites receive anywhere from 7 to 20 million hits per day. Conceivably it might take weeks (if ever) before anyone knew a site had been violated."

9.3.2.4 Changes at Walt Disney Imagineering

According to Mr. Ferren, the final and most difficult challenge to consider is how an enterprise is going to survive the "reinvention" necessary to keep pace with changing technology. Walt Disney Imagineering R&D recently completed a task that can be very difficult for any enterprise to do, particularly one within the government: They have completely modernized their information systems infrastructure, not just by simply upgrading the equipment, but actually by replacing everything. The new infrastructure is geared toward the use of the Internet and Web-based technologies. The challenge is to operate as an "agile" enterprise, with the ability to be adaptive with each new management issue or challenge. Indeed, according to Ferren, Disney's strategy and policy on many issues literally changes every month.

As an example, Disney is grappling with how to effectively monitor its employee's use of the Internet, but still maintain their individual rights to privacy. They know that if they lock out or restrict employees from the Internet, they would be keeping them from what Ferren considers to be the most important movement of the century. Indeed, according to a December 1997 study by the Alexandria, Virginia based *Society for Human Resource Management*, 70% of organizations polled had no written Internet access policy, and 50% had no policies that addressed e-mail usage. Uncertainty about how to draft such policy is one reason that many companies avoid this issue. Disney believes that the global Internet is the biggest enabler of our time, but also that it provides the biggest challenges to security. The harnessing of the Internet is, therefore, a number one priority at Walt Disney Imagineering.

9.4 WHAT THIS MEANS TO THE INTELLIGENCE COMMUNITY—AND YOU

The Intelligence Community has always been a leader in both the development and the application of information technology. In the early days of computing, the National Security Agency played an instrumental role in the development of large-scale computers and networking environments. But with the coming millennium and the challenges that the Intelligence Community faces, it must now learn to *adapt* in order to successfully survive. Three general observations from this chapter underscore the need for change, and they apply to both the private sector as well as the U.S. Intelligence Community.

1) Connectivity is ubiquitous.

As Bran Ferren says, the Internet is like *fire*. He says that if you are not on the Internet and the Web now, you are growing illiterate, becoming "disconnected." He believes that there has never before been a new technology growth rate to match that of the Internet. Many enlightened leaders of the U.S. Intelligence Community believe that the Internet is the greatest enabling technology for them—and their adversaries. This new information paradigm now drives a new set of business decisions, all of which require connectivity and agility.

2)   Information should be considered a "capital resource."

The information business is *everybody's* business, whether or not the primary activity of the enterprise is a specific information product. And as Ron Elliott points out, that information should be considered a capital resource as much as the physical hardware or other tangible inventory of a business. Thus information needs to be invested in and managed just like any other critical resource of an enterprise. It is sometimes difficult to put an economic value on information (like charging "Dulles dollars" for intelligence information) and occasionally the information can be absolutely priceless (such as avoiding war, or saving lives). Finally, every organization must provide itself and its customers with the ability to access, reuse, and collaboratively share its information holdings—and in an "agile," adaptable environment.

3)   Technology requires accompanying cultural changes.

We *have* the technology. In the popular 1970's television series called the "Six Million Dollar Man," actor Lee Majors starred as an astronaut severely injured in a plane crash. The government then "rebuilds" him with futuristic technology blending cybernetics and biology that results in a "bionic" man with incredible, superhuman mental and physical powers. In the opening sequence, the narrator explains right after his crash, "We can rebuild him. We *have* the technology." Like the television government in the 1970's, the U.S. Intelligence Community of today *has* the technology. Indeed, as Paul Saffo and other futurists tell us, we have only begun to scratch the surface with information technology. But what really is needed in many organizations today, and certainly within the Intelligence Community, is the ability to change the cultural differences that separate and divide organizations. These cultural differences can be embedded deeply within organizations, lagging years behind technological change. Properly balancing these differences is an important component in effectively managing an organization, and is addressed in the next Chapter as we explain the concept of an "agile intelligence enterprise."

The Intelligence Systems Secretariat recently commissioned a special "white paper," written by members of the Intelligence Community and the MITRE Corporation, entitled "Managing Information as an Enterprise." The paper describes the need for the Intelligence Community to migrate towards an agile, collaborative environment, and issues a concluding challenge that is appropriate for many enterprises:

To achieve the agile collaborative enterprise that is our vision, we must become more agile as individuals, as agencies, and as a Community. We must establish and evolve a capacious and interoperable information infrastructure, within and among the intelligence agencies, one that supports collaboration and knowledge sharing among our members and our customers... We must acquire, install, and operate systems that are driven by changing intelligence needs, and we must account for our resource expenditures in ways that can identify the value received for the resources expended... We need systems that are able to adjust to rapidly changing world conditions... Finally, we need organizations that are able to evolve in response to a highly dynamic, constantly changing provider-consumer intelligence knowledge marketplace.

The final chapter of this book will explain how this is being done in the U.S. Intelligence Community.

Chapter **10**

Achieving a More Agile Intelligence Enterprise

Recall the following scenario introduced in Chapter 1:

The year is 2005. Tensions in the world have been steadily increasing for the past 16 months, as a former Soviet bloc country with significant nuclear weapons capabilities has entered into a defensive agreement with a coalition of several suspected Middle East-based terrorist organizations that combined forces shortly after the turn of the millennium.

For the past two weeks, the U.S. Intelligence Community has been operating under their highest state of alert. It is two and a half hours past midnight in Washington, D.C. National Imagery and Mapping Agency analysts have been monitoring troop movements from satellite imagery for the past two days. Major Jay Franklin, a U.S. Army intelligence analyst stationed at the Defense Intelligence Agency, receives an emergency call from the commander of an elite special forces unit in the Middle East.

At approximately the same time, the watch officer in the National Security Operations Center of the National Security Agency receives an automated, high priority signal from a special array of sensors. The signal comes from one of its computers at a remote classified location in Eastern Europe, alerting the U.S. Intelligence Community of possible impending troop movements. Meanwhile, analysts at the Central Intelligence Agency have been alerted to a possible attack scenario involving both chemical and nuclear weapons...

To continue:

Major Franklin contacts Colonel Robert Boldrey in his remote headquarters to start a chain of collaborative operations that will involve real-time sharing of information across all of the intelligence agencies as well as the involved members of the military services.

Using programmed software intelligence agents, Colonel Boldrey is able to immediately contact all appropriate collaborative participants tasked with analyzing the troop movements and other available data. The results of their efforts will then be used as the basis for recommendations to the Commander of a United Nations Peacekeeping Force, the Secretary of Defense, and the President.

Although geographically dispersed around the globe, the participants are simultaneously viewing the same information, as well as each other, on a large-screen 'whiteboard,' as though they were in the same room. With instantaneous access to databases containing all-source intelligence, Signals Intelligence, and imagery, over secure high-speed and high-transmission bandwidth Intelink facilities, they are in a much better position to address this latest crisis...

As we discussed in the beginning of this book, this is clearly a scenario with the potential for worldwide catastrophe. Although we added a possible response to the scenario, the important questions to ask for the future remain the same: Could the U.S. Intelligence Community:

1) *Respond* in the manner in which we described above, and
2) *Adjust* its collection, exploitation, and analysis capabilities.

(i.e., just how *agile* is the U.S. Intelligence Community?)

The answers are *yes*, if the Intelligence Community meets the goals laid out in its first effort to formulate a common strategy for the integration and interoperability of Intelligence Community-wide information systems. Known as the *Intelligence Community Information Systems Strategic Plan: Enabling a More Agile Intelligence Enterprise*, this plan provides overall guidance for managing information resources within the Intelligence Community. Published in November 1997 by the *Intelligence Systems Board*, this plan specifies five specific goals, providing a framework for the development and implementation of information systems and other resources from 1999 to 2003, and guiding the Intelligence Community towards its goal of cooperation and becoming a "more agile intelligence enterprise."

This concluding chapter will further define the concept of an "agile" intelligence enterprise, and explain how the Intelligence Community plans to achieve its goal. To accomplish this, Chapter 10 first will discuss the five strategic goals that promote this concept of Intelligence Community integration and interoperability of information systems. It will then define the concepts of "agility" and an "agile intelligence enterprise" and their roles in the world of "virtual intelligence." The book then concludes with a look at the *Joint Intelligence Virtual Architecture* (JIVA) program, explaining its vision and role in meeting the early 21st century objectives of the U.S. Intelligence Community.

10.1 INTELLIGENCE COMMUNITY INFORMATION SYSTEMS STRATEGIC PLAN

In Chapter 9, we discussed the tremendous changes that the Intelligence Community, with its diverse set of missions and organizations, has been undergoing since the fall of the Berlin Wall in 1989. To cope with these cultural and technical changes, and to bring focus to the management and operational needs of the Intelligence Community, the Strategic Plan includes five overall information technology goals. The five goals contain a number of supporting objectives and specific actions deemed necessary to meet each goal, enabling the Intelligence Community to become more "agile," while increasing its effectiveness and efficiency. An "implementation plan" is in the works to specify organizational responsibilities, methodologies, and an overall projected timeline for completion.

The Strategic Plan was requested by the *Intelligence Systems Board*, and prepared by the *Intelligence Systems Secretariat* and the Intelligence Community's Senior Information Managers Panel discussed in Chapter 9. In addition to the thirteen "official" members of the Intelligence Community, five other organizations participated substantially in creating the Strategic Plan, written by the ISS and a special team of Intelligence Community representatives under the leadership of Nancy Marsh-Ayers. These five organizations included elements of the Department of Defense, including the Office of the Assistant Secretary of Defense for Command, Control, Communications, and Intelligence (C3I) and the Office of the Joint Chiefs of Staff; the Defense Information Systems Agency; the National Drug Intelligence Center; and elements within the Department of Commerce.

The *Foreword* to the Strategic Plan is signed by the ISB co-chairs Richard J. Wilhelm (Executive Director for Intelligence Community Affairs) and Cheryl J. Roby (Acting Assistant Secretary of Defense for Intelligence and Security). The *Foreword* states:

> *...The rapid growth of technology and the increasing demands of our customers require formal Intelligence Community agreement on information technology. This plan represents a collaborative effort to develop inter-organizational opportunities for cooperation in information systems and technology... Implementing the goals, objectives, and actions in this plan will enable the Intelligence Community to better support the customers' mission needs, coordinate common direction, and manage information systems investments...*

The Strategic Plan's five goals and their primary objectives relate to the areas of cooperation and collaboration that are deemed to have the highest potential for benefit. Although they apply specifically to the U.S. Intelligence Community, they provide a framework to address information technology issues that are important for *any* enterprise, such as customer satisfaction, technology, security, management, and cost optimization. The five goals of the Strategic Plan are as follows. Please note: The bolded goals and italicized objectives are directly from the Strategic Plan. However, the explanatory dialogue under each objective is the view of the author.

1) Customer Satisfaction

Goal: Identify and provide information systems services based on customer needs.

Objectives:

A. Establish a process for recognizing and translating customer needs having Community-wide utility into information technology requirements.

There is no formal process within the Intelligence Community today to document and evaluate Community-wide customer requirements. In order to better serve its customers, the Intelligence Community must establish such a process in full partnership with its customers.

B. Use advanced information technology to enrich the knowledge environment of the customer and to meet evolving customer requirements.

There is a need to establish Intelligence Community partnerships and alliances with industry and academia that result in proof-of-concept prototypes of the more promising information technologies. These prototypes will allow the testing of new information technology approaches, helping to ensure that the final implementation is of high quality.

C. Monitor, measure, and evaluate mission benefits and customer satisfaction obtained from Community-level investments in information systems, services, and technology.

Quality control and performance measures as well as other metrics need to be established to assess overall customer satisfaction from investments in information technology.

2) Electronically connecting the Intelligence Community and its Customers

Goal: Evolve toward a fully integrated, distributed information space.

Objectives:

A. Develop an information model and technology architecture for the Intelligence Community leveraging existing models and architectures across the Intelligence Community and federal government.

This "information model" should describe the business and work processes of the Intelligence Community as a whole. It must be a cooperative effort across the Intelligence Community, building upon the modeling and architectural definition work that has already been accomplished at many of its individual intelligence agencies. In addition, an Intelligence Community-wide architecture must be developed, building upon the NSA *Unified Cryptologic Architecture 2010* effort and the DoD standards efforts discussed in Chapter 3.

B. Enable a robust and adaptable Community-wide and customer-wide telecommunications infrastructure.

The overall capacity of the existing telecommunications infrastructure must be expanded, leading to an eventual "INTELNET" consisting of worldwide networks, using asynchronous transfer mode (ATM) or similar high bandwidth switching technology, transmitted over optical fiber cable, for the seamless transfer of data among the classified networks of the Intelligence Community.

C. Develop a Community-wide, distributed "virtual" work environment.

This "virtual" work environment would be the future Intelligence Community information technology infrastructure, and would include the standards, policies, and procedures necessary to ensure effective intelligence dissemination and collaboration. A specific key action leading to this infrastructure would be the development of an architecture that would allow customer access to all components of this new infrastructure from a single workstation.

D. Migrate to a common data environment.

The concept of a *common* data environment across the entire Intelligence Community, including data sharing, metadata, and other mission enhancement tools, will significantly enhance interoperability. This, in turn, will improve timeliness and reduce costs associated with intelligence production.

E. Migrate to a community-wide information processing environment.

Similarly, implementation of the various standards activities addressed in Chapter 3 to an Intelligence Community-specific environment, as well as the use of commercial off-the-shelf products will also significantly improve interoperability. To accomplish this, a model is needed that can measure the levels of interoperability attained, and provide a metric of overall Intelligence Community-wide system performance.

F. Implement a Community-wide message handling system.

The *Defense Messaging System*, which will integrate messaging and electronic mail functions into a single system,[33] must be implemented within the Intelligence Community.

G. Facilitate the efficient production, dissemination, and use of electronic intelligence products.

The *information space* concept implemented by JICPAC and detailed in Chapter 8 must be expanded. The Intelink metadata initiative, and the use of SGML, document tagging and security-labeling schemes must be improved.

H. Enable the Intelligence Community with multilingual capabilities.

Information technology must be used to increase the foreign language capabilities of the Intelligence Community. This technology will assist language training as well as language analysis and processing.

3) Security and Protection

Goal: Protect the Intelligence Community's information resources and infrastructure.

---

[33] Discussed in more detail in Chapter 3.

Objectives:

A. Cooperate on policy formulation for information systems security in areas of common concern.

Information systems security is the number one concern in the implementation of the "agile," electronically connected Intelligence Community of the future. Security policy and goals must be jointly developed, as a single enterprise, and be responsive to the new Intelligence Community practice of *risk management* over the more restrictive *risk avoidance* policies of the past.

B. Enable adaptive security management.

Similarly, these security policies and goals must be supported by an overall Intelligence Community security management infrastructure that includes all aspects of security (see Chapter 4), including physical security.

C. Apply U.S. Government and commercial security technology to enable effective, appropriate use of global information networks and services.

The Intelligence Community must use both government security technologies, such as *Fortezza*,[34] as well as commercial security products to realize its security objectives.

D. Protect Community information resources and systems against information warfare and physical threats.

The use of security threat databases, vulnerability detection tools, and other information warfare and threat recognition mechanisms will facilitate this process.

4) **Management**

Goal: Establish a Community-wide information and technology management process.

---

[34] Described in more detail in Chapter 5.

Objectives:

A. Review, update, and continually improve Community management and governance processes oriented toward information technology programs of common concern.

The ITMRA legislation, discussed in Chapter 9, was only the beginning. In addition to the *Senior Information Managers Panel*, other mechanisms must be established to improve the overall management of information technology across the entire Intelligence Community.

B. Ensure that Intelligence Community organizations have a sufficient cadre of IT professionals.

The Intelligence Community must cooperate as a single enterprise to effectively recruit, train, educate, and retain the caliber of information technology professionals needed to sustain future operations. Mr. Bran Ferren, Vice-President of *Walt Disney Imagineering*, and a frequent advisor to the U.S. Intelligence Community, cites this need as absolutely critical as government salaries have continually failed to keep pace with the private sector.

C. Improve awareness and insertion of new information technology across the Community.

Develop mechanisms that are *dedicated to the Intelligence Community*, including business process reengineering, technology forums, and collaboration, to ensure awareness, support, and insertion of new information technology across the entire Intelligence Community.

D. Establish an Intelligence Community-wide information records management process.

This new process must address the legal requirements and business needs for a common approach to creating, using, classifying, and disposing of all Intelligence Community records.

E. Ensure continuity of information services.

In the event of a natural disaster or war causing a catastrophic disruption of network operations, the Intelligence Community must have an overall plan as well as various inter-agency support agreements in place to ensure uninterrupted service across the entire enterprise.

F. Sustain operations through the Year 2000.

Continuity of information services includes, of course, continuity into the next century, i.e., all systems modifications dealing with the "Year 2000" or Y2K problem must be resolved.

5) Cost-Effectiveness

Goal: Improve cost-effectiveness of Intelligence Community information systems.

Objectives:

A. Maximize the effectiveness of Community-wide information technology expenditures.

There are a number of ways in which the Intelligence Community can optimize funds expended on information technology. These include efforts to reduce duplication of efforts across the Intelligence Community, requirements to consolidate the Intelligence Community, to better exchange information. The development of "best practices," including joint projects, is also important.

B. Implement the Community's information system "migration" strategy.

The "migration" strategy refers to the process of identifying information systems that are common to all Intelligence Community members and then "migrating" to a single system that effectively addresses a particular area of concern. For example, efforts are underway to designate specific systems for payroll and personnel.

Since mission-critical systems are candidates for migration also, this effort will establish a baseline for such systems.

C. *Work with federal agencies and industry to leverage "off-the-shelf" solutions.*

In addition to reiterating the Intelligence Community commitment to commercial "off-the-shelf" solutions, this objective will require the establishment of a process to leverage work with industry by expressing Intelligence Community requirements with a single voice.

These five goals and their supporting objectives define what the Intelligence Community *wants* to accomplish in order to achieve the level of interoperability necessary to become more efficient and "agile." Next, we will look in greater detail at the concept of an "agile intelligence enterprise."

10.2 THE FUTURE WORLD OF INTELLIGENCE: "VIRTUAL INTELLIGENCE"

I believe that the Intelligence Community today is at a crossroads of progress: Our choices are evolution or revolution...
— Dr. Ruth A. David, October 1997

Intelink, with all of its advantages, is actually only the *beginning*. One of the primary goals of the U.S. Intelligence Community is an evolution towards what could be termed "Virtual Intelligence." *Virtual Intelligence* is the distributed "information space" that allows the creation of a tightly woven "Agile Intelligence Enterprise," based on the ability to collaborate, share data, and disseminate information electronically, across the globe, at any time. This concept of an *Agile Intelligence Enterprise*, which has been deemed as absolutely critical to the nation's security in the 21st century, is the vision of the current *Deputy Director of CIA for Science and Technology*, Dr. Ruth A. David. A Stanford University educated electrical engineer and information technology expert, Dr. David came to the CIA (Figure 10-1) from Sandia

National Laboratories in Albuquerque, New Mexico, where she most recently was *Director of Advanced Information Technologies.*

Like many businesses today, the Intelligence Community is at a crossroads of progress. The issue is how to tackle a long-range strategic problem: meeting the expectations and needs of intelligence customers that require greater speed, flexibility, and capacity. In addition, these expectations and needs must be met within an environment that is constantly changing in order to respond to rapid technology changes, an information explosion, an unstable global political environment, and certainly an era of declining resources. The answer: create a more "agile intelligence enterprise."

10.2.1 What Is Agility?

The concept of *agility* in an organization is not new. Manufacturing enterprises developed the concept of a leaner, flexible organization to meet changing market requirements in a global competitive environment. Early experts such as Rick Dove, Steven L. Goldman, Roger N. Nagel, and Kenneth Preiss at the Iacocca Institute of Lehigh University in Bethlehem, Pennsylvania authored a number of papers and books defining the concept. One notable paper was the *21st Century Manufacturing Enterprise Strategy*, written by Dove and Nagel in 1991 for an industry-led consortium partially funded by the Department of Defense, which examined U.S. manufacturing and its ability to be competitive in a global marketplace. According to Goldman, Nagel, and Preiss in their follow-on 1995 book entitled, *Agile Competitors and Virtual Organizations*:

> *For a company, to be agile is to be capable of operating profitably in a competitive environment of continually, and unpredictably, changing customer opportunities... For an individual, to be agile is to be capable of contributing to the bottom line of a company that is constantly reorganizing its human and technological resources in response to unpredictably changing customer opportunities.*

According to Steve Goldman, "Agility is a name. It's a name for the reorganization of production, adapted to distinctively new market forces that have undermined the mass production organization of business that previously

Figure 10-1 Central Intelligence Agency Headquarters, Langley, Virginia.

dominated the 20th century." Goldman says that these new forces include the following:

1) Intensifying global competition

2) Fragmentation of mass markets into niche markets

3) Cooperation among companies, even among companies that are direct competitors

4) Customer expectations that are evolving toward individualized, reliable products

5) Intensifying social pressures that make it impossible to do business in the way that companies were able to do prior to the 1980's

Goldman continues, "The organization of business in a way that is adapted to these new marketplace forces is what we call agile... The *agile enterprise* provides solutions to their customers, not just products. It works adaptively, responding to marketplace opportunities by reconfiguring its organization of work, its exploitation of technology, its use of alliances. It engages in intensive collaboration within the company, pulling together all of the resources that are necessary to produce profitable products and services regardless or where they may be distributed. And it forms alliances with suppliers, with customers, and with partnering companies. And finally, it is a knowledge-driven enterprise. The agile company is centered on people and information, not on technology alone, on people using technology in creative ways."

The *"Agility Forum"* is a leading provider of knowledge, products, and consulting services related to the concept of agility that are designed to strengthen the U.S. economy. The forum has assisted industry, government, education, and other services in the development of strategies to cope with dynamic, often unpredictable global markets. The *Agility Forum* has held a number of annual conferences to promote strategies for implementing this concept, and offers tools, consulting services, publications, and other education and training services.

10.2.2 Why Is Agility Necessary for the Intelligence Community?

To begin our discussion on applying the concept of agility to the U.S. Intelligence Community, we need to examine the composition of the various organizations that constitute the intelligence *producers*, as well as those that make up the community of intelligence *users*. Like many businesses, the Intelligence Community consists of a number of individual organizations that perform distinct missions, and yet support overlapping sets of customers. These separate organizations contain the discrete operations that collect, process, and exploit the various types of intelligence data. The autonomous nature of these organizations has led many people within the Intelligence Community to refer to them as "stovepipes" (Figure 10-2), which connotes the image of a large number of individual chimneys all heating the same building. Further exacer-

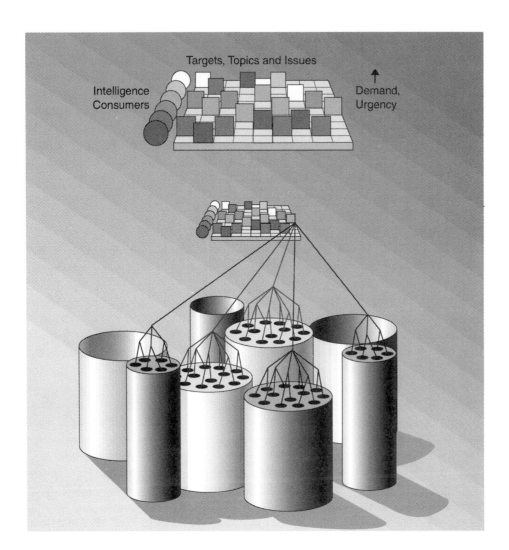

Figure 10-2 Stovepipe Orientation of Intelligence Community.

bating the problem, the very existence of some agencies is "classified information," i.e., a closely guarded state secret. For example, the predecessor organizations of the National Reconnaissance Office (NRO) date back to the Cuban Missile Crisis in the early 1960's, yet the existence of the NRO was classified information until only a couple of years ago. Other agencies, such as the Central Intelligence Agency and the National Security Agency, have existed openly for decades.

There are some benefits to having *stovepipes*: the ability to train and maintain individual specializations, better accountability, and improved security. In spite of these advantages, however, the Intelligence Community has developed separate cultures and artificial barriers that tend to separate the various agencies. For example, the long-time practice of reducing security risks by disseminating information on a "need-to-know" basis—that is, only to those who have been both approved and deemed to actually need the information to perform their job—further exacerbates the problems associated with the stovepipe concept. However, it is not the "need-to-know" principle itself that has caused problems, but the manner in which it is implemented. Previously based almost entirely upon the *originator* of the information, the approach no longer meets the demands of a dynamic, rapidly changing environment. What is required is an approach that is flexible and more responsive to these constantly changing needs.

Indeed, it is now recognized that these separate stovepipe cultures do *not* always serve the intelligence users well. For example, each individual customer is generally interested in a slightly different aspect of a particular intelligence topic. Thus a report that satisfies the needs of the State Department may very well miss the mark for the warfighter in Bosnia. Furthermore, at least one of the customers of the Intelligence Community—the U.S. Congress—as well as other "watchdog" organizations within the intelligence hierarchy, may view certain "stovepiped" activities as waste or redundancy. Studies of *finished intelligence* have shown that, in fact, little truly wasteful duplication exists. However, there appears to be an *enormous* amount of duplication on the input side, i.e., information gathering, modeling, and organization. Imagery analysts retain various files of information on their images, SIGINT analysts maintain files to help with SIGINT operations, and military analysts keep their own sets of information. Existing in all of the various stovepipes, this can be very wasteful. The Intelligence Community must make every effort to eliminate this duplication, particularly in the new era of fiscally restrained resources.

10.2.3 What Is an Agile Intelligence Enterprise?

One could view the Agile Intelligence Enterprise as a *conceptual business model* useful in formulating and communicating strategies for improving the internal processes that support the information management needs of the U.S. Government. As applied to the U.S. intelligence mission, there are three primary components in Dr. David's vision of managing information in an agile "Virtual Intelligence" enterprise: an electronic networking infrastructure; self-organizing, continuously forming and disbanding multidisciplinary teams; and shared data—linked, corporate-wide repositories of raw data, information, and finished intelligence.

1) Set of interoperable networks that electronically connect the Intelligence Community

The enabling technology for the Agile Intelligence Enterprise is the collection of global networks, protocols, hardware, and software that electronically connect the various components and customers of the U.S. Intelligence Community. As discussed throughout this book, Intelink serves as a prototype for this electronic infrastructure, allowing personnel in the White House, State Department analysts, generals in the Pentagon, even the warfighters, access to classified information on nearly any subject.

As the Intelligence Community increasingly connects its various intranets and other electronic messaging networks, it becomes more agile. Intelligence requirements can be electronically transmitted immediately across the entire Intelligence Community. Yet, instead of a broadcast call to every single user on the network, these needs can be narrowly disseminated to the specific people with the desired knowledge and expertise. While this takes place today within the various stovepipes, the ability to take advantage of needed expertise across the entire enterprise allows a concentrated, fuller examination of a particular intelligence issue.

Additionally, with properly configured networks, the Intelligence Community has more than just a capability to provide timely notification—it has a mechanism by which intelligence officers may indicate whether or not they can contribute to satisfying a new intelligence requirement. Imagery analysts, for example, could indicate whether or not relevant imagery existed. An NSA SIGINT analyst may be aware of information that may help. A military analyst at DIA might be in the position to coordinate the overall response. In the words of

Dr. David, "The notion here is that our geographically—and organizationally—scattered individual experts are in fact the very people best able to judge whether their expertise and responsibilities match the immediate problem that comes to their attention." The overall result is an enterprise-wide effort with a well-defined task and clear understanding of each contributor's responsibilities.

2) Self-organizing, multidisciplinary "virtual teams"

This component involves self-organizing teams of intelligence analysts from across the Intelligence Community, which are capable of dynamically forming whenever necessary in order to address the overlapping and ever-changing priorities, problems, and concerns of the various intelligence consumers. These "virtual teams" can take advantage of *intelligent software agents* and other tools on Intelink and other electronic networks to ensure that the right analysts are chosen for a particular problem. In this model, the experts continue to reside within their own stovepipe, with all of their normal resources at hand, but are able to collaborate with their counterparts in the other stovepipes. Upon completion of the given task, teams would then disband, ready to address the next crisis. Depending on their particular area of expertise, intelligence officers remaining at their own desks, within their own agency, might serve on a number of such "virtual teams" at the same time, providing enhanced capabilities to respond to changing requirements.

Andy Shepard, a senior intelligence officer assigned to the CIA's Directorate of Science and Technology, has stated that the benefit of self-organizing teams is easiest to illustrate when a high priority intelligence query requires a same-day response. In many of these cases, both the necessary data and the necessary expertise are dispersed over a number of different intelligence agencies. According to Shepard, "The distribution of talent is hard to exploit when deadlines are short." He adds, "It requires time to define the particular requirement, to communicate that need, to seek out the best people, and manage the overall response, including determining the best division of labor among the various team members that are selected." This time can often be measured in hours, or perhaps even days. Although not a problem for previous intelligence requirements that could wait for several days, the future environment will routinely require immediate, same-day responses. To be successful in that new environment, the Intelligence Community will need to form its teams and get them operational *immediately*, without any delay.

3) Shared intelligence data

In this third component, intelligence data that has been gathered using the resources of the individual stovepipes becomes a shared asset across the entire Intelligence Community. With these corporate holdings of data (raw and finished intelligence), linked electronically, the Intelligence Community is better postured to take advantage of the collaborative sum of these individual efforts. For example, when an intelligence analyst needs a particular piece of information that is located within his own agency, access to that information is relatively simple, assuming that he is "cleared," i.e., has the proper security clearance for that information. Unfortunately, an item of critical information that is absolutely necessary for that analyst to see in order to fully understand or respond to the requirement is very likely to have been gathered by, and therefore stored at, another intelligence stovepipe or agency. In order to become a true "agile intelligence enterprise," the intelligence users and producers must have access to all necessary information, regardless of where it resides.

Dr. David would be quick to point out that this sharing of data across the intelligence enterprise does not refer to a single unified database, i.e., one large monolithic database. Current databases are not designed to provide the necessary security protections, and the data that reside within these databases have not been placed there with the concept of sharing or distributed access in mind. Instead, she says, "Our future shared information repository will consist of distributed, but connected, archives of data existing at multiple security levels and in many different compartments. These individual compartments can be managed within a common system using advanced information security practices and tools."

The concept of shared data could result in a number of other benefits, as shown on the next page.

• Improved Exploitation of Fragmented Data

Supported by powerful search and collaboration tools, intelligence analysts frequently discover a variety of data related to the intelligence task at hand. Using the concept of "shared data," these related associations could be documented and become part of the "corporate-holdings," thereby providing a set of fragmentary data that is linked and correlated. This fragmentary data could be permanently stored in databases and later accessed by other analysts working similar or related intelligence problems in the future. These databases would become a true "information space," analogous to the JICPAC implementation in Chapter 8, allowing the Intelligence Community as a whole to benefit. This capability to define, build, and then access a robust repository of institutional knowledge, with different types of data applying to different audiences, would greatly increase the agility of the Intelligence Community.

• Collaborative "Just-in-time" Tip-Off

With the increase in shared fragmented data, the Intelligence Community can now develop an improved Collaborative Tip-Off process. The additional data provides an increased ability to recognize potentially important new intelligence. Each individual stovepipe cannot afford to store large volumes of seemingly unusable data. However, as an information space of databases, that data becomes available to the entire Community, which means data that seems unimportant to one component may be discovered to be very important when viewed in the Intelligence Community's all-source context. And, this information space can be manipulated by a common set of user tools, providing machine translation, or imagery manipulation, or other applicable collaboration or analyst tools. The result is "just-in-time" tip-off resulting from *inter-stovepipe* collaboration, and a more agile enterprise, better equipped to respond to changing requirements

• Consumer Access to Stovepipe Data

The Intelligence Community can become more agile if it allows its users—the intelligence consumers—direct access to a *view* of its "information space," the total holdings of the Intelligence Community. However, providing this capability is quite controversial, as it impacts upon the very core of intelligence production: the "sources and methods" that are used by the individual stovepipes to produce their specialty intelligence. Therefore, proper security is an essential enabler of the vision of an Agile Intelligence Enterprise. In the new "risk management" paradigm under which the U.S. Intelligence Community is operating, it is imperative to strike a balance between information sharing and information protection. For example, some concerns can be satisfied by allowing selected decision-makers to have special, tailored views of the database holdings. Using interest profiles and other techniques, this process could be automated.

10.2.3.1 Information Security Concerns

One of the most significant impediments to the success of this approach is *information security*. The use of Intelink-like networks, "virtual" teams, and shared data to enhance the speed, flexibility, and capacity of the intelligence production process requires Intelligence Community-wide agreement on a number of security issues. An approach is needed that will allow distributed data holdings that are satisfactorily protected from accidental or deliberate compromise. According to Dr. David, an acceptable level of protection could be accomplished by placing less emphasis on protecting data primarily at the system access point, and instead increasing the level of security of the individual data elements or other pieces of information contained within the data repository. She explains, "The concept is to retain some access control at the system entry points, but to prevent users from gaining *automatic* access to the contents." When a user discovers—for example, through the use of some sophisticated search tool—the existence of material that is more "sensitive," i.e., has a higher security classification, than their present information holdings (located, perhaps, at another agency), the network must be capable of determining whether or not that person can be granted access. In order to do this, the network needs to have enough information about the user to make its determination: security clearance level, agency affiliation, and other work-related security profiles. In addition, the automated search and collaboration tools need the ability to process data that is potentially classified at a level that is higher than the user may have. This, in turn, requires a set of guidelines, procedures, and policies—acceptable across the Intelligence enterprise—that determine what a user can see.

In order to manage risk properly, especially with the large spectrum of data within the Intelligence Community needing protection, a variety of options must be available in the system. That is, the network system would need to know enough about the data and the users to choose the appropriate rule for protecting more sensitive data. The figure below, provided by Dr. David, depicts different situations that might arise from diverse users scanning vast data repositories across the Intelligence Community.

10.2.3.2 Coordinating Intelligence Community Management

The concept of an "agile intelligence enterprise," supporting electronically networked operations, invoking virtual teams, and sharing corporate holdings across the enterprise is a fundamentally different way of doing business within the U.S. Intelligence Community. The success of this new approach will require innovative management techniques applied in a number of areas, including:

- Coordination of Intelligence Community-wide approaches to the re- solution of the information security concerns outlined in the previous section

- Management collaboration to produce the necessary mechanisms for network managed user profiles and security clearances

- Development of common approaches to data representation within their own data holdings

- Development of innovative approaches to cope with the *cultural issues* that derive from decades of separate agencies and stovepipe mindsets

10.2.4 Status: CODA—Implementing the Agile Concept

The Intelligence Community is currently defining and expanding Dr. David's vision of an Agile Intelligence Enterprise (AIE). Recently formed under the auspices of the Intelligence Community Management Staff, a special Intelligence Community-wide effort known as the "Community Operational Definition of the AIE" (CODA) has been launched. Indeed, CODA is one of several innovative efforts under the direction of Susan M. Gordon, Director of the CIA's new *Office of Advanced Analytical Tools* (AAT). Headed by Dr. Paul Shebalin, a senior intelligence analyst and information technology expert, the CODA effort will develop the implementation process for the Intelligence Community's transition to the electronically connected, agile enterprise of tomorrow.

In accordance with the Intelligence Community's *Information Systems Strategic Plan* outlined earlier in this chapter, Dr. Shebalin's activities are centered around the development of an information model and overarching Community-wide architectural "blueprint" for implementing the Agile Intelligence Enterprise. According to Shebalin, the CODA effort will serve as an *"executive agent"* for the entire Intelligence Community to:

- **Create an Information Model that will describe the Agile Intelligence Enterprise**

This *information model* should describe the set of interoperable networks that electronically connect the Intelligence Community, the self-organizing, multidisciplinary "virtual teams," and the enterprise-wide sharing of raw or fragmentary data and finished intelligence. In addition, the model should provide a framework for collaboration across the enterprise in a protected and secure environment.

The CODA effort is taking advantage of efforts already underway within the Intelligence Community. Building upon a series of working conferences with representatives from across the Intelligence Community held at a remote training facility, CODA is incorporating modeling efforts developed at the Operations Research staff of the

National Security Agency in support of the *Unified Cryptologic Architecture 2010* (UCA) efforts.[35]

• Develop an information technology architecture for the Intelligence Community

The architecture will specify how shared, Intelligence Community-wide information technology systems will be acquired and maintained in the future. As in the development of the information model, this effort will be coordinated with the Intelligence Community's UCA effort under the direction of Paul Newland, helping to ensure an effective integration of all applicable systems.

• Promote Intelligence Community prototyping of the Agile Intelligence Enterprise

CODA is promoting a series of operational, "proof-of-concept" prototypes that will enhance the definition of an Agile Intelligence Enterprise, and facilitate the implementation of this new concept. Clearly, Intelink has launched this effort, but these new prototypes would build upon the existing "virtual intelligence" environment established by Intelink, as well as the concept of an SGML-based "information space" implemented at JICPAC.[36] Early planned prototyping examples include projects oriented towards the policy-maker, the warfighter, and the intelligence analyst.

According to Avis Boutell, CIA information management expert and former chair of the Intelligence Community's *Electronic Publishing Board*, "The CODA efforts will be guided by an external Steering Group, and supported by various Intelligence Community Working Groups, representing all stakeholders." The CODA effort will leverage the efforts already underway at a number of individual intelligence agencies, enabling the Intelligence Community to fully exploit the tremendous potential of information technology, leading to a true "agile intelligence enterprise" for the future.

---

[35] Described in more detail in Chapter 3.
[36] Detailed in Chapter 8.

10.3 JOINT INTELLIGENCE VIRTUAL ARCHITECTURE

There are related efforts underway to ensure that the information management challenges of the U.S. Intelligence Community are met. One of the most significant efforts, in terms of scope, resources, and overall potential for change, is the Defense Intelligence Agency led effort known as the *Joint Intelligence Virtual Architecture* (JIVA). Specifically tasked with improving the Department of Defense intelligence agencies, JIVA's objective is to modernize defense-related intelligence analytical processes and methodologies, and so its focus is on delivery of information to the warfighter. Nevertheless, this effort is addressing the same set of issues, challenges, and even technologies that the Intelligence Community is confronted with as a whole as it moves towards the Agile Intelligence Enterprise of the future.

Specifically, the JIVA Program will provide the Intelligence Community's "all-source" intelligence workforce with the necessary set of tools, capabilities, and training to cope with the technology-driven, information-rich intelligence environment of the next millenium. According to the *JIVA Strategic Plan*, written by the *JIVA Integration Management Office* (JIMO):

> *The ability of the Defense Intelligence Community to satisfy consumer information requirements, particularly those of the warfighters, hinges on how well the Community manages knowledge bases, as well as develops and maintains robust and effective analytical capabilities. The Community must invest in key technologies and approaches that are critical to all-source intelligence production; employ technology to leverage the productivity of widely dispersed analysts; and enhance the speed and efficiency of processing and dissemination. Doing this requires planning, programming, and budgeting for new opportunities afforded by the emerging and evolving technologies.*

According to Chris Demme, Deputy Director of the JIMO, JIVA plans to accomplish this by, "integrating existing defense-related intelligence information systems, providing sophisticated tools and training for the analyst, enhance information sharing with state-of-the-art collaboration tools, and improving the quality of intelligence electronic distribution of finished intelligence that is specifically tailored to the requirements of the user" (see Figure 10-3).

10.3.1 JIVA Objectives

The concept of JIVA will provide the battlefield commander with what today's warfighter calls "dominant battlespace knowledge," or the concept of *information superiority* as we discussed earlier. The notion of "virtual teams," a major component of Dr. David's vision of an Agile Intelligence Enterprise, is also a key element of JIVA. The idea is to foster partnerships among intelligence agencies through the creation of these electronic teams, which can tackle analytical problems concurrently. With an overall goal of creating a "new intelligence environment for the 21st century," the specific goals of JIVA, as articulated in the *JIVA Strategic Plan*, include:

1) **Improving the quality of analysis, and utility of the substance of intelligence products**

This objective includes the selection of advanced analytical, collaborative, and decision support tools, cognitive aids, and tools to aid search and retrieval of data from shared heterogeneous databases. It involves the transition to a concept that JIMO calls "knowledge base" which includes: Intelligence Community-wide expertise and requirements registry systems, data warehouse capabilities, and storage for modeling and simulation results. To enhance this objective, JIVA plans to leverage expertise and key efforts at the CIA and NSA as well as other intelligence elements, including on-going initiatives at the Defense Advanced Research Projects Agency (DARPA).

2) **Providing specific and tailored intelligence to enhance the warfighter's ability to visualize the data and ensure total operational awareness**

JIVA plans to accomplish this objective by deploying advanced, DoD standards-compliant workstations powerful enough to handle the dissemination and collaboration tools suite—including modeling and

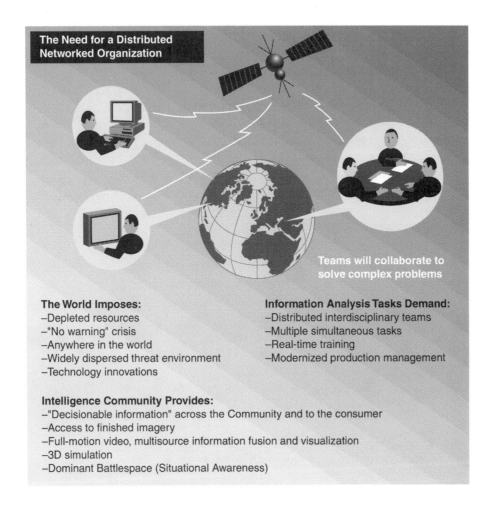

The Need for a Distributed Networked Organization

Teams will collaborate to solve complex problems

The World Imposes:
–Depleted resources
–"No warning" crisis
–Anywhere in the world
–Widely dispersed threat environment
–Technology innovations

Information Analysis Tasks Demand:
–Distributed interdisciplinary teams
–Multiple simultaneous tasks
–Real-time training
–Modernized production management

Intelligence Community Provides:
–"Decisionable information" across the Community and to the consumer
–Access to finished imagery
–Full-motion video, multisource information fusion and visualization
–3D simulation
–Dominant Battlespace (Situational Awareness)

Figure 10-3 The Need for a Distributed Networked Organization.

simulation tools—and other operational requirements of the future. This objective **includes** optimizing analytical training delivery, leading to the concept of a "virtual university."

3) Improving the throughput and speed of delivery of intelligence

JIVA will identify and evaluate customer information requirements and establish the resulting future communications needs of the Department of Defense intelligence agencies. This objective also includes identifying new techniques for the production and dissemination of finished intelligence in the new "virtual intelligence" environment.

4) Reducing or eliminating unnecessary redundancy

Using state-of-the-art mass storage devices, JIVA plans to use advanced data mining techniques and other tools to accomplish this objective. The objective also involves the creation of a networked organization capable of providing near real-time battlespace assessments, and exertion of influence over DoD intelligence budget deliberations.

5) Strengthening management and ensuring the existence of the necessary policies, procedures, and training to assist in operating the new information environment

This objective includes exploring and partnering with both private industry and academia to develop advanced virtual environment concepts. It also includes understanding the current *culture* of the Intelligence Community's intelligence production process. This is considered by many to be absolutely critical to success.

6) Establishing and integrating standards for commonality, interoperability, and modernization

Strategic alliances will be formed within the Intelligence Community and related standards bodies. JIVA standards will be developed, implemented, and consistently enforced through the budget, acquisition, and other decision processes.

7) Exploring leading-edge technology for future integration

To accomplish this objective, JIVA plans to leverage expertise across the Intelligence Community as well as academia and the private sector. JIVA will support and participate in the development of new "proof-of-concept" prototyping activities such as CODA, while identifying new technology with a high potential for use within the JIVA environment.

10.3.2 JIVA Focus Areas

JIVA is concentrating its efforts in three areas, providing the framework and resources to improve the analysis, production, training, automation, and other support infrastructures necessary to meet the overall JIVA goal of a new defense-related intelligence operating environment for the 21st century. The three focus areas the JIVA effort are to improve are show in Figure 10-4.

• **Analytical and Production Processes**

As we have discussed throughout this book, declining resources have resulted in fewer Intelligence Community analysts who must collect, process, and disseminate a tremendously increased volume of information. This focus area will address the development and implementation of cognitive, or "knowledge-based" tools, which are necessary to allow the analyst to sort, identify, and verify the validity of information. This area will also address the development and implementation of the necessary tools to support effective collaboration. The idea is to make the entire intelligence production cycle more meaningful and timely. Thus these tools will concentrate on information visualization tools, and other products that will assist in the presentation, analysis, fusion, and dissemination of finished intelligence. The collaboration enhancement process will involve the same types of high-bandwidth applications that were discussed in Chapter 6 such as "whiteboarding," advanced video teleconferencing, and image manipulation.

• **Defense Intelligence Training**

JIVA will use new and emerging training technologies to ensure that intelligence analysts have the necessary expertise to operate within the new "virtual intelligence" environment. They will include self-paced

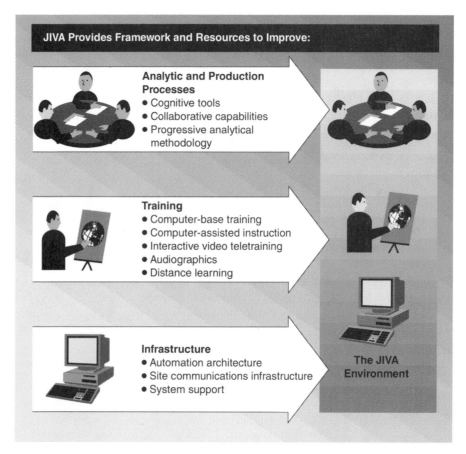

Figure 10-4 JIVA Focus Areas.

computer-based training (CBT) techniques, computer assisted instruction (CAI), the concept of "distance learning" or "virtual university," and, of course, conventional instructor-based training. JIVA will also examine "Audiographics," a learning technique that employs video-based graphics with an instructor's voice, delivered to remote sites electronically. All distributed training will focus on electronic delivery mechanisms such as Intelink and the global Internet.

• Defense Intelligence Infrastructure

The "Defense Intelligence Infrastructure" refers primarily to the eight intelligence agencies that fall directly under the jurisdiction of the

Secretary of Defense. This third focus area, in which much work has already been accomplished, involves the refurbishing of the hardware and other components necessary to accomplish the defense intelligence mission. Capital replacement programs, based on JIVA funding, have significantly enhanced defense intelligence capabilities. The next step—beyond the current capital replacement—will address communications and networking hardware that are necessary to operate in the future world of "virtual intelligence." JIVA must develop a responsive, "recapitalization" program, keyed to the rapid pace of the technology change cycle, in order to always stay ahead of technology obsolescence.

10.3.3 JIVA Implementation

It should be clear that the goals of JIVA—for the Defense Intelligence Community—are similar to the goals of CODA, an *Agile Intelligence Enterprise* for the entire Intelligence Community. In both programs, providing a new world of what could be called "virtual intelligence," for the production and dissemination of this nation's finished intelligence, requires a mechanism that will break down "stovepipe" barriers and associated cultures. This mechanism cuts across organizational boundaries with innovative technology in order to improve operations, increase efficiency and effectiveness, while reducing unneeded redundancy. For JIVA, this mechanism will be implemented in a two-phase approach (Figure 10-5).

• **Phase I: Near-Term Goals (1996–2001)**

This phase has begun, focusing on capital equipment replacement as mentioned above, as well as a number of parallel activities including prototyping of various collaboration capabilities, implementing new training strategies, and the initiation of improved management techniques. This phase also includes the actual fielding an initial set of specific JIVA collaboration capabilities and other mission-critical applications designed to support the new virtual production environment.

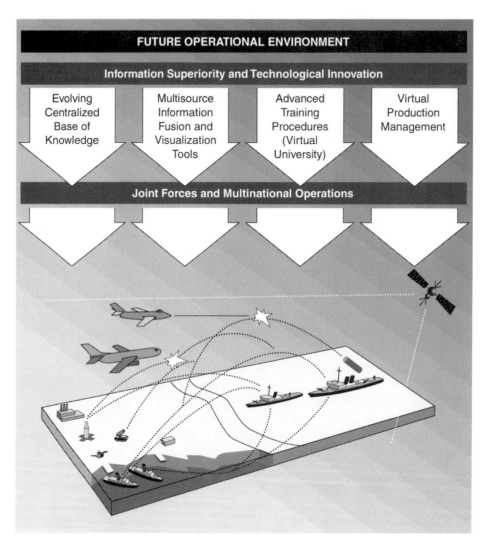

Figure 10-5 Future JIVA Operational Environment.

• Phase II: Long-Term Goals (2002–2007)

In this phase, JIVA plans to concentrate its efforts on the acquisition of new techniques, by leveraging technology to a number of mission-critical intelligence processes. In addition, JIVA plans to continue its "recapitalization" of information-related equipment—both hardware and software—throughout the Defense Intelligence Community. As in the CODA project, JIVA looks to a senior level Steering Group consisting of Intelligence Community leaders (as well as numerous working groups) for policy, guidance, and support.

10.4 CHALLENGE FOR THE INTELLIGENCE COMMUNITY

Many of the basic assumptions of intelligence have drastically changed since the fall of the Berlin Wall in November 1989. Prior to that time, the free world was faced with a Soviet nuclear threat masked behind the Iron Curtain of Warsaw Pact allies. The U.S. strategy was one of certainty—total and complete risk avoidance—with respect to Soviet capabilities and intentions. Today, rather than a single and primary intelligence goal (namely the Soviet Union—containment of Communism), there is a proliferation of potential intelligence areas of interest. The U.S. must deal with a diverse set of national security interests and focus on risk *management* over risk *avoidance.* In this post-Cold War era, the primary concerns are topics such as international terrorism, the proliferation of nuclear and other weapons of mass destruction, economic intelligence, and drug trafficking.

In addition to these new interests, the U.S. Intelligence Community finds a much more complex and ever-changing set of customers or authorized users of intelligence within the government. As the mission and functions of the various customer agencies expand, so does their need for intelligence to support those functions. The challenge, then, is to provide intelligence users the benefit of the *totality* of the distributed knowledge of the entire Intelligence Community, i.e., to leverage *all* of the information available when providing a response to a customer. That means they must take advantage of all of the information in all of the individual stovepipes; and they must do this cheaper, and faster. As shown in this book, an intranet—namely Intelink—that services the Intelligence Community and its customers is the first step towards providing this needed functionality. Yet, the Intelligence Community must not be content with their past successes such as those exemplified by ONI and JICPAC.[37] Rather, they

---

[37] Detailed in Chapter 8.

must continue to evolve into a fully "Agile Intelligence Enterprise," through implementation projects such as CODA and JIVA, if the United States is to be capable of dealing with the intelligence problems it will face in the next millenium.

10.5 HOW DOES THIS RELATE TO BUSINESS?

The primary example used in the book was Intelink, the classified, world-wide intranet for the U.S. Intelligence Community which addresses perhaps the world's largest data management problem, involving demanding requirements that are at the extreme of what normal enterprises require. Intelink, which is used for electronic publishing and distribution of intelligence reports, analytical research, collaboration facilities, and training, has become the *Information Management Improvement Model* of the Intelligence Community.

It can be very useful to assess what the Intelink experiences might mean to other government entities and to the private sector. Indeed, examining the approach taken by the U.S. Intelligence Community to help solve its own information management challenges can frequently be applied directly by the business leaders of today to their own enterprises. To facilitate this, we summarize a number of the overall lessons or conclusions relating to information management that a business enterprise might apply to its own environment. For example:

• Intranet Technology Is Profound

Not since the advent of the personal computer has a new business tool had such a profound effect on all facets of business. Business enterprises that effectively leverage the global Internet and its related technologies such as intranets and extranets will reap competitive benefits well into the next millennium. The Intelligence Community's information management model consisting of global Internet technologies, an "information space" of shared data that is managed across an "agile" enterprise, is directly applicable to business enterprises, large and small.

• Top Management Support Is Necessary

The Intelligence Community experiences clearly show that success is dependent upon senior management support, forward thinking involving careful planning, leadership throughout the implementation process, and sufficient resources. Proper attention and support by upper management early on will reduce the likelihood of unanticipated surprises in the future.

• Security Is Critical to the Business Enterprise

The culture of the global Internet is very open, and this frequently extends to intranet implementations. However, it is extremely important to balance the advantages of openness with the corporate needs of secure business information. Ranging from protection of basic customer information such as a credit card number to corporate liability to company trade secrets, security is as important to the business environment as it is to the Intelligence Community. Indeed, they both have the same fundamental reason for security: protect information from unintended access. The lessons learned from the security experiences of the U.S. Intelligence Community can be directly applied to the business enterprise.

• Standards Must Be Used

The individuals who are responsible for providing information technology and solutions within a company must recognize the critical nature of decisions involving the use of standards. They must prevent "locking" the company into a single vendor or proprietary standard without extensive discussions with the people affected by such a decision. The use of information technology standards, and commercial products that are compliant with these standards, provides a business enterprise with the most promise for eliminating system redundancies and incompatibilities, and reducing overall costs.

• Training Must Be a Major Focus

Whether you rely on business and community colleges, technical schools, and universities, or extensive in-house training programs, training must be a major focus in acquiring the necessary skills to optimize the use of intranet, web, and other related information technologies. The sheer number of applications and technologies has added another layer of complexity to the diverse set of challenges facing most business enterprises. The experiences of the case studies cited earlier in this book, as well as the emphasis that has been placed on training by the Intelink Management Office and the new JIVA program demonstrate the commitment that the Intelligence Community has placed on training—a commitment that is directly applicable to the business enterprise.

The global Internet, intranets, extranets, and Web technologies are now at the forefront of the information technology industry, and have had a profound impact on the cultural and economic institutions of the world. Their impact on the business enterprise cannot be stressed enough. Over the next decade, this technology will continue to change the very core and structure of entire industries including the manner in which companies compete. Responding to these profound changes, business enterprises must adapt—or risk losing competitiveness and perhaps even cease to exist.

Appendix

Intelligence Community Overview

*T*he *United States Intelligence Community* refers to those agencies and organizations within the Executive Branch of the United States Government that are responsible for carrying out the nation's various intelligence activities. The Intelligence Community is led by the Director of Central Intelligence (DCI), who provides oversight to the thirteen national agencies described in this Appendix. The DCI is also the Director of one of the thirteen agencies, the Central Intelligence Agency.

According to the *Community Overview* published by the Intelligence Community, the goal of U.S. Intelligence is to "support decision-makers with the best possible information, no matter what the source. The Intelligence Community employs cutting-edge technology, innovation, and quality management to connect with its customers, stakeholders, employees and the public, and to ensure the nation's security."

The following descriptions have been extracted from the *Community Overview* document.

A.1 THE CENTRAL INTELLIGENCE AGENCY

Our vision is to be the keystone of a U.S. Intelligence Community that is pre-eminent in the world, known for both the high quality of our work and the excellence of our people.

The CIA was established by the National Security Act of 1947. The mission of the CIA is to support the President, the National Security Council, and all officials who make and execute U.S. national security policy by providing accurate, evidence-based, comprehensive, and timely foreign intelligence related to national security; and conducting counterintelligence activities, special activities, and other functions related to foreign intelligence and national security as directed by the President.

INTERNET: http://www.cia.gov

CIA Office of Public Affairs: (703) 482-7588

A.2 THE DEFENSE INTELLIGENCE AGENCY

Military Intelligence—Shaping the Future; Quality People, Trained, Equipped, and Ready for Joint Operations, Anywhere, Anytime.

The DIA, a Department of Defense "combat support agency," is the major producer and manager of intelligence for the Department of Defense. Established in 1961, DIA provides timely, objective, and cogent military intelligence to warfighters, force planners, and policy makers to meet a variety of challenges across the spectrum of conflict.

INTERNET: http://www.dia.mil

DIA Public Affairs Office (703) 695-0071

A.3 THE NATIONAL SECURITY AGENCY

Information Superiority for America. One Team, One Mission.

The NSA is the nation's cryptologic organization and employs this country's premier codemakers and codebreakers. Founded in 1952, NSA is a separately organized agency within the Department of Defense and a designated "combat support agency." NSA protects the security of U.S. signals and information systems and provides intelligence information derived from those of the nation's adversaries.

INTERNET: http://www.nsa.gov

NSA Public Affairs Office: 301-688-6524

A.4 ARMY INTELLIGENCE

An integral part of the Nation's Full-Spectrum Force for the 21st Century—One Vision ... One Voice ... One Vector.

Army Intelligence, in conjunction with other military services and national agencies, provides timely, focused, seamless, and synchronized Joint and Service intelligence and electronic warfare support to tactical, operational, and strategic commanders and users worldwide—from "boots on the ground" to the Commander-in-Chief-across the full range of military operations. In war, electronic warfare operations support the winning of engagements, battles, and campaigns. Army intelligence seeks to advance *information superiority* on a global basis.

INTERNET: http://www.134.11.36.7

Army Intelligence Public Affairs Office: (202) 761-1803

A.5 NAVAL INTELLIGENCE

Naval intelligence products and services support the operating forces, the Department of the Navy, and the maritime intelligence requirements of national-level agencies. The Office of Naval Intelligence (ONI) is the national production center for global maritime intelligence and is the center of expertise for every major maritime issue—from the analysis of the design and construction of foreign surface ships to the collection and analysis of acoustic information on foreign sensor systems, ocean surveillance systems, submarine platforms, and undersea weapons systems.

INTERNET: http://www.ncts.navy.mil

Naval Intelligence Public Affairs Office: (703) 697-9020

A.6 AIR FORCE INTELLIGENCE

Air Force "Information Operators" enable our forces to know, enter, and dominate the air, space, and information domains.

The mission of Air Force Intelligence is to deliver on-time, tailored intelligence and information to joint and allied users worldwide... operations forces, acquisition community, and policymakers alike. Air Force Intelligence, Surveillance and Reconnaissance assets further the Air Force's core competencies of precision engagement and *information superiority.*

INTERNET: http://www.hq.af.mil/xo

Air Force Intelligence Public Affairs Office: (703) 697-4100

A.7 MARINE CORPS INTELLIGENCE

Under Marine Corps doctrine, intelligence is considered the foundation on which the operational effort is built and the premise on which all training, doctrine, and equipment are developed. It encompasses the policy, planning, direction, collection, processing, dissemination, and use of intelligence to meet Marine Corps Service and operational missions in maritime, expeditionary, land, and air warfare. The Marine Corps Intelligence mission is to provide commanders at every level with seamless, tailored, timely, and mission-essential intelligence and to ensure this intelligence is integrated into the operational planning process.

INTERNET: http://www.usmc.mil

A.8 NATIONAL IMAGERY AND MAPPING AGENCY

NIMA guarantees the information edge—instant access to the world's imagery, imagery intelligence, and geospatial information.

The National Imagery and Mapping Agency is a designated Department of Defense "combat support agency." Established on 1 October 1996, NIMA is chartered to provide timely, relevant, and accurate imagery, imagery intelligence, imagery-derived products, and geospatial information in support of national security to a wide variety of customers from the national level to the tactical and civilian user.

INTERNET: http://www.nima.mil

NIMA Customer Help Desk (800) 455-0899

A.9 NATIONAL RECONNAISSANCE OFFICE

Freedom's Sentinel in Space: One Team, Revolutionizing Global Reconnaissance.

The National Reconnaissance Office (NRO) is the single, national program to meet U.S. Government spaceborne reconnaissance needs. It was created in 1961 from the combined U.S. Air Force–CIA team that built the U-2 reconnaissance plane. The mission of the NRO in the 21st century is to enable U.S. global *information superiority* during peace and through war. The NRO is responsible for unique and innovative technology, large-scale systems engineering, development and acquisition, and operation of space reconnaissance systems and related intelligence activities needed to support global *information superiority.*

> INTERNET: http://www.nro.odci.gov
>
> NRO Office of Corporate Communications: (703) 808-1198

A.10 FEDERAL BUREAU OF INVESTIGATION

The Federal Bureau of Investigation was founded in 1908. Its overall mission is to uphold the law through the investigation of violations of Federal criminal statutes; to protect the United States from hostile intelligence efforts; to provide assistance to foreign and other U.S. Federal, state, and local law enforcement agencies; and to perform these responsibilities in a manner that is faithful to the Constitution and laws of the United States. The FBI is the principal investigative arm of the U.S. Department of Justice.

> INTERNET: http://www.fbi.gov
>
> FBI Public Affairs Office: (202) 324-3000

A.11 DEPARTMENT OF TREASURY

The *Office of Intelligence Support* (OIS) within the US Department of Treasury was established in 1977. Executive Order 12333 lists the Special Assistant to the Secretary (National Security) as a senior intelligence officer of the Intelligence Community. Under the Special Assistant's direction, the OIS is responsible for providing timely, relevant intelligence to the Secretary and other Treasury Department officials.

> INTERNET: http://www.ustres.gov
>
> Department of Treasury Public Affairs Office: (202) 622-2970

A.12 DEPARTMENT OF ENERGY

The *Office of Energy Intelligence* (OEI) within the Department of Energy is the Intelligence Community's premier technical intelligence resource in the following four core areas: 1) Nuclear weapons and nonproliferation; 2) nuclear energy, safety, and waste; 3) science and technology; and 4) energy security. The OEI provides timely, accurate, high-impact foreign intelligence analysis to the Department of Energy, policy-makers and the Intelligence Community. It also provides quick-turnaround, specialized technology, operational support to the intelligence, law enforcement, and special operations communities.

INTERNET: http://www.doe.gov

Department of Energy Public Affairs Office: (202) 586-4670

A.13 DEPARTMENT OF STATE

The *Bureau of Intelligence and Research* (known as the INR) within the Department of State is the primary source for interpretive analysis of global developments. The INR was established in 1946 to provide insights from intelligence on a real-time basis. The INR is the focal point within the Department of State for all policy issues and activities involving the Intelligence Community. It coordinates the State Department's activities on issues concerning intelligence, intelligence policy and coordination, security, and counterintelligence.

Glossary

AAT (Advanced Analytical Tools)   CIA Office-level organization tasked with bringing new tools and technologies into the analytical environment and forging new partnerships with analysts, technologists, information service providers, industry and academic leaders, and Intelligence Community management.

ADNET (Anti-Drug Network)   An Intelink *Community of Interest* network operating at the SECRET collateral level that supports U.S. national detection and monitoring of drug trafficking.

Agile Intelligence Enterprise (AIE)   A conceptual model for improving the internal processes that support the US Intelligence mission that includes three primary components: 1) an electronic networking infrastructure; 2) self-organizing, continuously forming and disbanding multidisciplinary teams; and 3) shared data-linked, corporate-wide repositories of raw data, information, and finished intelligence.

Advanced Information Processing and Analysis Steering Group (AIPASG)   Chartered by the *DCI Advanced Research and Development Committee*, the AIPASG is tasked with defining and improving the information environment of the intelligence analyst. Its primary responsibility is to articulate key analytical processes in order to facilitate the development and proliferation of critical emerging technologies that enable analysts to capture, reveal, represent, create, and share knowledge.

CIA   Central Intelligence Agency

CMS   [Intelligence] Community Management Staff

CODA (Community Operational Definition of an Agile Intelligence Enterprise) An Intelligence Community initiative to develop the implementation process for the Intelligence Community's transition to an electronically-connected "agile" intelligence enterprise.

COSPO (Community Open Source Program Office) An office within the CIA that develops, coordinates, and oversees implementation of the Community Open Source Program that was established by DCI Directive 2/12. Responsibilities include all aspects of the open source program, including strategic planning, program formulation and representation, sponsorship of new initiatives, operational services, systems architecture, and open source advocacy across the Intelligence Community.

COTS Commercial off-the-shelf

DIA Defense Intelligence Agency

DCI Director of Central Intelligence

DCI Advanced Research and Development Committee (AR&DC) An Intelligence Community committee that advises the DCI on the overall National Intelligence Advanced R&D Program and on technologies that will best contribute to the attainment of national intelligence objectives.

DII (Defense Information Infrastructure) The set of communications networks, computers, software, databases, applications, and other capabilities that meets the information processing and transport needs of DoD users, both in peace as well as all crises, conflict, humanitarian support, and wartime roles.

DII COE (Defense Information Infrastructure Common Operating Environment) Provides an integrated infrastructure that includes a standard environment, off-the-shelf software, and a set of programming standards that describe in detail how mission applications will operate within the DII environment.

DISA Defense Information Systems Agency

DISN Defense Information System Network

DMS (Defense Message System) Incorporates all the hardware, software, procedures, personnel, and facilities required for electronic exchange of messages among organizations and individuals within the U.S. Department of Defense. Thus, DMS provides secure, reliable messaging for strategic, and tactical national intelligence, as well as various business applications, across multiple commercial vendor platforms.

DoD Department of Defense

DODIIS Department of Defense Intelligence Information Systems

DODIIS Functional Reference Model-Intelligence Framework and methodology for documenting the relationships among the missions and tasks, intelligence functions, generic activities and their supporting means, and the tools used to create a future intelligence operational architecture, similar to the *Technical Reference Model* concept in Volume 2 of the TAFIM.

Electronic Publishing Group (EPG) An Intelligence Community group chartered in 1993 to ensure cooperative interoperability among the various intelligence agencies on all matters pertaining to electronic publishing media and facilities. The EPG promotes the achievement of efficiencies through the broader application of electronic publishing as well as the adoption of document standards such as SGML and XML for the preparation of documents across the Intelligence Community. (Formerly the *Electronic Publishing Board*)

Extranet Term used to describe a special type of intranet. While *intranets* are internal systems designed to connect users within a specific "community of interest," *extranets* are extended intranets that connect to outside customers and other more strategic partners. There must be some sort of security associated with this connection, of course, and frequently this is accomplished through the use of passwords or other application level mechanisms. Therefore, a typical extranet strategy might be two discrete intranets with a secure link between them.

Firewall System or combination of systems that enforce a boundary between two or more networks; a gateway that limits access between networks in accordance with a local security policy.

Global Internet   A global network of individual networks interconnected through a specific set of conventions that allow communication to take place between two or more separate machines. It is characterized by ubiquitous access by the public with variable forms of security. Thus, the Internet has evolved into a massive global infrastructure with a universally accessible collection of networks supporting culture, diversity, academia, and business, and now has over 40 million users. Many experts believe that it will grow to over 200 million users by the turn of the century.

IMD   Intelink Management Directorate

IMO   Intelink Management Office

Information Space   The totality of data, information, and knowledge available to the members of a particular group or enterprise, regardless of format or media, where it is located, or who is responsible for it.

Information Superiority   The unimpeded capability to collect, process, and distribute information while exploiting or preventing an adversary from doing the same.

Intelink   Intelink is a secure, private collection of networks implemented on existing government and commercial communications networks. These networks employ web-based technology, use well-established networking protocols, and are protected by firewalls to prevent external use. Within the Intelligence Community, Intelink is commonly perceived as the intranet/extranet that interconnects various intelligence organizations and operations, i.e., connects the various providers and users of intelligence information.

Intranet   A private network that uses the methodology, tools, and protocols of the global Internet, i.e., a private, unique network implementation based on the technology, services, protocols (such as TCP/IP), and applications (such as the Web) of the Internet. Its purpose is to support an internal information system, and it is either physically separate, or protects itself from the outside world through the use of some security system, e.g., a "firewall," a hardware device or software that restricts the types of traffic or access to a network.

Intelligence Community The Executive Branch agencies and organizations that work in concert to carry out the intelligence activities of the United States enumerated in Executive Order 12333, "U.S. Intelligence Activities," including all echelons, national level agencies through tactical organizations.

Intelligence Systems Board (ISB) Advises the Director of Central Intelligence (DCI) and the Deputy Secretary of Defense on policy and requirements pertaining to the design of inter-organizational information architectures, as well as the design, development, and operation of automated intelligence information systems implementing those architectures, used by the DoD and organizations comprising the *National Foreign Intelligence Program* (NFIP). Its principal focus is on means of enhancing the interoperability of existing and planned systems and on improving support to operational military components.

Intelligence Systems Secretariat (ISS) A permanent staff element responsible for the day-to-day activities necessary to fulfill the mission and functions of the Intelligence Systems Board. Serves as the Intelligence Community coordinator for interagency matters pertaining to automated information handling and security policy under the purview of the Director of Central Intelligence. Staffed jointly by member organizations across the Intelligence Community and organizationally integrated within the Intelligence Community Management Staff.

Joint Intelligence Virtual Architecture (JIVA) Department of Defense program designed to modernize defense-related intelligence analytical processes and methodologies, with a focus on delivery of information to the warfighter. Specifically, the JIVA Program will provide the Intelligence Community's "all-source" intelligence workforce with the necessary set of tools, capabilities, and training to cope with the technology-driven, information-rich intelligence environment of the next millenium. Thus, JIVA is addressing the same set of issues, challenges, and even technologies that the Intelligence Community is confronted with as a whole as it moves towards the *Agile Intelligence Enterprise* of the future.

Joint Technical Architecture (JTA) The JTA mandates the minimum set of standards and guidelines for the acquisition of all DoD systems that produce, use, or exchange information. It specifies a set of performance-based, primarily commercial, information processing, transfer, content, format and security standards. These standards specify the logical interfaces in command, control and intelligence systems and the communications and computers that directly support them. One of the primary objectives of the JTA is to facilitate and improve the ability of systems to support joint or combined military operations.

Joint Worldwide Intelligence Communications System (JWICS) Top Secret SCI (Sensitive Compartmented Information) portion of the *Defense Information System Network*. The host network for Intelink-SCI, it incorporates advanced networking technologies that permit point-to-point or multi-point information exchange involving voice, text, graphics, data, and video teleconferencing.

Multilevel Information Systems Security Initiative (MISSI) A network security effort being developed by the National Security Agency. Refers to a broad set of products that are intended to become the basis for the U.S. Government standard for network security. For example, MISSI specifies a particular *Security Management Infrastructure* (SMI) that involves commercial "Certificate Authority" workstations running trusted, government-certified operating system software. The core component of this SMI is reliance on the use of user-specific hardware *tokens* to contain user certificate information. The cards are also programmed with a set of approved cryptographic algorithms, which in turn are the mechanism by which they can provide such critical security services as authentication and end-to-end confidentiality of data. The two primary versions of these hardware tokens are known as *Fortezza*, and more recently *Rosetta*, cryptographic cards.

National Foreign Intelligence Program (NFIP) A U.S. Intelligence Community funding program that encompasses most of the activities of the primary national intelligence agencies (CIA, NSA, NRO, DIA, and NIMA) as well as other designated programs. The NFIP programs are not specific organizations, but rather, the financial accounts that provide the funding for intelligence operations and activities.

"Need-to-know" Principle Security practice of the U.S. Intelligence Community of reducing security risks by disseminating information only to those who have been both approved and deemed to actually require the information in order to perform their job.

NIMA   National Imagery and Mapping Agency

Non-Proliferation Center (NPC)   Organizationally contained within the Central Intelligence Agency, the NPC is concerned with analyzing the global proliferation of nuclear and other weapons of mass-destruction such as the chemical weapons used by Saddam Hussein against the Kurdish people earlier this decade.

NRO   National Reconnaissance Office

NSA   National Security Agency

Open Source Information System (OSIS)   Electronic network that provides both access to and sharing of unclassified U.S. Government and other open source information among Intelligence Community agencies and selected other organizations with similar information requirements.

Standard Generalized Markup Language (SGML)   International standard (ISO 8879) for document and data interchange used to facilitate interoperability across hardware platforms and software applications. The eXtensible Markup Language (XML) is a subset of SGML, and the Hypertext Markup Language (HTML) is a specific instantiation of SGML.

Unified Cryptologic Architecture 2010 (UCA 2010)   An Intelligence Community framework for a coherent, integrated cryptologic architecture for all cryptologic assets. Patterned after the same three basic architectures (operational, systems, and technical) of the Joint Technical Architecture, the UCA addresses the total cryptologic process, from requirements to the delivery of products and services. It includes specific common technical standards, security mechanisms for the protection of Signals Intelligence, and metrics for evaluating cost/benefit studies

Index

S

LICENSE AGREEMENT AND LIMITED WARRANTY

READ THE FOLLOWING TERMS AND CONDITIONS CAREFULLY BEFORE OPENING THIS CD PACKAGE. THIS LEGAL DOCUMENT IS AN AGREEMENT BETWEEN YOU AND PRENTICE-HALL, INC. (THE "COMPANY"). BY OPENING THIS SEALED CD PACKAGE, YOU ARE AGREEING TO BE BOUND BY THESE TERMS AND CONDITIONS. IF YOU DO NOT AGREE WITH THESE TERMS AND CONDITIONS, DO NOT OPEN THE CD PACKAGE. PROMPTLY RETURN THE UNOPENED CD PACKAGE AND ALL ACCOMPANYING ITEMS TO THE PLACE YOU OBTAINED THEM FOR A FULL REFUND OF ANY SUMS YOU HAVE PAID.

1. **GRANT OF LICENSE:** In consideration of your purchase of this book, and your agreement to abide by the terms and conditions of this Agreement, the Company grants to you a nonexclusive right to use and display the copy of the enclosed software program (hereinafter the "SOFTWARE") on a single computer (i.e., with a single CPU) at a single location so long as you comply with the terms of this Agreement. The Company reserves all rights not expressly granted to you under this Agreement.

2. **OWNERSHIP OF SOFTWARE:** You own only the magnetic or physical media (the enclosed CD) on which the SOFTWARE is recorded or fixed, but the Company and the software developers retain all the rights, title, and ownership to the SOFTWARE recorded on the original CD copy(ies) and all subsequent copies of the SOFTWARE, regardless of the form or media on which the original or other copies may exist. This license is not a sale of the original SOFTWARE or any copy to you.

3. **COPY RESTRICTIONS:** This SOFTWARE and the accompanying printed materials and user manual (the "Documentation") are the subject of copyright. The individual programs on the CD are copyrighted by the authors of each program. Some of the programs on the CD include separate licensing agreements. If you intend to use one of these programs, you must read and follow its accompanying license agreement. If you intend to use the trial version of Internet Chameleon, you must read and agree to the terms of the notice regarding fees on the back cover of this book. You may not copy the Documentation or the SOFTWARE, except that you may make a single copy of the SOFTWARE for backup or archival purposes only. You may be held legally responsible for any copying or copyright infringement which is caused or encouraged by your failure to abide by the terms of this restriction.

4. **USE RESTRICTIONS:** You may not network the SOFTWARE or otherwise use it on more than one computer or computer terminal at the same time. You may physically transfer the SOFTWARE from one computer to another provided that the SOFTWARE is used on only one computer at a time. You may not distribute copies of the SOFTWARE or Documentation to others. You may not reverse engineer, disassemble, decompile, modify, adapt, translate, or create derivative works based on the SOFTWARE or the Documentation without the prior written consent of the Company.

5. **TRANSFER RESTRICTIONS:** The enclosed SOFTWARE is licensed only to you and may <u>not</u> be transferred to any one else without the prior written consent of the Company. Any unauthorized transfer of the SOFTWARE shall result in the immediate termination of this Agreement.

6. **TERMINATION:** This license is effective until terminated. This license will terminate automatically without notice from the Company and become null and void if you fail to comply with any provisions or limitations of this license. Upon termination, you shall destroy the Documentation and all copies of the SOFTWARE. All provisions of this Agreement as to warranties, limitation of liability, remedies or damages, and our ownership rights shall survive termination.

7. **MISCELLANEOUS:** This Agreement shall be construed in accordance with the laws of the United States of America and the State of New York and shall benefit the Company, its affiliates, and assignees.

8. **LIMITED WARRANTY AND DISCLAIMER OF WARRANTY:** The Company warrants that the SOFTWARE, when properly used in accordance with the Documentation, will operate in substantial conformity with the description of the SOFTWARE set forth in the Documentation. The Company does not warrant that the SOFTWARE will meet your requirements or that the operation of the SOFTWARE will be uninterrupted or error-free. The Company warrants that the media on which the SOFTWARE is delivered shall be free from defects in materials and workmanship under normal use for a period of thirty (30) days from the date of your purchase. Your only remedy and the Company's only obligation under these limited warranties is, at the Company's option, return of the warranted item for a refund of any amounts paid by you or replacement of the item. Any replacement of SOFTWARE or media under the warranties shall not extend the original warranty period. The limited warranty set forth above shall not apply to any SOFTWARE which the Company determines in good faith has been subject to misuse, neglect, improper installation, repair, alteration, or damage by you. EXCEPT FOR THE EXPRESSED WARRANTIES SET FORTH ABOVE, THE COMPANY DISCLAIMS ALL WARRANTIES, EXPRESS OR IMPLIED, INCLUDING WITHOUT LIMITATION, THE IMPLIED WARRANTIES OF MERCHANTABILITY AND FITNESS FOR A PARTICULAR PURPOSE. EXCEPT FOR THE EXPRESS WARRANTY SET FORTH ABOVE, THE COMPANY DOES NOT WARRANT, GUARANTEE, OR MAKE ANY REPRESENTATION REGARDING THE USE OR THE RESULTS OF THE USE OF THE SOFTWARE IN TERMS OF ITS CORRECTNESS, ACCURACY, RELIABILITY, CURRENTNESS, OR OTHERWISE.

IN NO EVENT, SHALL THE COMPANY OR ITS EMPLOYEES, AGENTS, SUPPLIERS, OR CONTRACTORS BE LIABLE FOR ANY INCIDENTAL, INDIRECT, SPECIAL, OR CONSEQUENTIAL DAMAGES ARISING OUT OF OR IN CONNECTION WITH THE LICENSE GRANTED UNDER THIS AGREEMENT, OR FOR LOSS OF USE, LOSS OF DATA, LOSS OF INCOME OR PROFIT, OR OTHER LOSSES,

SUSTAINED AS A RESULT OF INJURY TO ANY PERSON, OR LOSS OF OR DAM-AGE TO PROPERTY, OR CLAIMS OF THIRD PARTIES, EVEN IF THE COMPANY OR AN AUTHORIZED REPRESENTATIVE OF THE COMPANY HAS BEEN ADVISED OF THE POSSIBILITY OF SUCH DAMAGES. IN NO EVENT SHALL LIABILITY OF THE COMPANY FOR DAMAGES WITH RESPECT TO THE SOFT-WARE EXCEED THE AMOUNTS ACTUALLY PAID BY YOU, IF ANY, FOR THE SOFTWARE.

SOME JURISDICTIONS DO NOT ALLOW THE LIMITATION OF IMPLIED WARRANTIES OR LIABILITY FOR INCIDENTAL, INDIRECT, SPECIAL, OR CON-SEQUENTIAL DAMAGES, SO THE ABOVE LIMITATIONS MAY NOT ALWAYS APPLY. THE WARRANTIES IN THIS AGREEMENT GIVE YOU SPECIFIC LEGAL RIGHTS AND YOU MAY ALSO HAVE OTHER RIGHTS WHICH VARY IN ACCOR-DANCE WITH LOCAL LAW.

ACKNOWLEDGMENT

YOU ACKNOWLEDGE THAT YOU HAVE READ THIS AGREEMENT, UNDERSTAND IT, AND AGREE TO BE BOUND BY ITS TERMS AND CONDI-TIONS. YOU ALSO AGREE THAT THIS AGREEMENT IS THE COMPLETE AND EXCLUSIVE STATEMENT OF THE AGREEMENT BETWEEN YOU AND THE COMPANY AND SUPERSEDES ALL PROPOSALS OR PRIOR AGREEMENTS, ORAL, OR WRITTEN, AND ANY OTHER COMMUNICATIONS BETWEEN YOU AND THE COMPANY OR ANY REPRESENTATIVE OF THE COMPANY RELAT-ING TO THE SUBJECT MATTER OF THIS AGREEMENT.

Should you have any questions concerning this Agreement or if you wish to contact the Company for any reason, please contact in writing at the address below.

Robin Short
Prentice Hall PTR
One Lake Street
Upper Saddle River, New Jersey 07458

About the CD

The CD-ROM contains actual Intelink pages, tools, and software. To view it, use any Web browser to open the file "index.htm" in the root directory. The CD is usable on any computer running Windows 95/98/NT or on a Macintosh using System 7 or later.

NOTE: The contents of the CD are an extract from a much larger intranet. Because of this, there are a number of links that will not work.

Please note: Prentice Hall does not offer technical support for this software. However, if there is a problem with the media, you may obtain a replacement copy by emailing us with the problem at disc_exchange@prenhall.com